Lockdown

Lockdown

Inside Brazil's Most Dangerous Prison

Drauzio Varella

SIMON & SCHUSTER

London · New York · Sydney · Toronto · New Delhi

A CBS COMPANY

Originally published in Brazil in 1999 as Estação Carandiru by
Companhia das Letras
First published in Great Britain in 2012 by Simon & Schuster UK Ltd
A CBS COMPANY

English language translation © Alison Entrekin, 2012
Obra publicada com apoio do Ministério da Cultura do Brasil /
Fundação Biblioteca Nacional.
Work published with the support of Brazil's Ministry of Culture / National Library.

MINISTÉRIO DA CULTURA
Fundação BIBLIOTECA NACIONAL

Picture permissions: Drauzio Varella 1, 2, 3, 4, 5, 6, 7, 8, 9, 11, 12, 13;
Rachel Guedes 10; João Wainer 14; Folha Imagem 15 (Lalo de Almeida),
16 (Jorge Araújo), 17 (Luiz Carlos Murauskas)

1 3 5 7 9 10 8 6 4 2

Simon & Schuster UK Ltd
1st Floor
222 Gray's Inn Road
London
WC1X 8HB

www.simonandschuster.co.uk

Simon & Schuster Australia
Sydney

Simon & Schuster India
New Delhi

A CIP catalogue copy for this book is available
from the British Library.

ISBN: 978-1-84983-865-8 (B format paperback)
ISBN: 978-1-47110-106-9 (Export trade paperback)

Typeset by Hewer Text UK Ltd, Edinburgh
Printed and bound in Great Britain by CPI Group (UK) Ltd,
Croydon, CR0 4YY

CASA DE DETENÇÃO

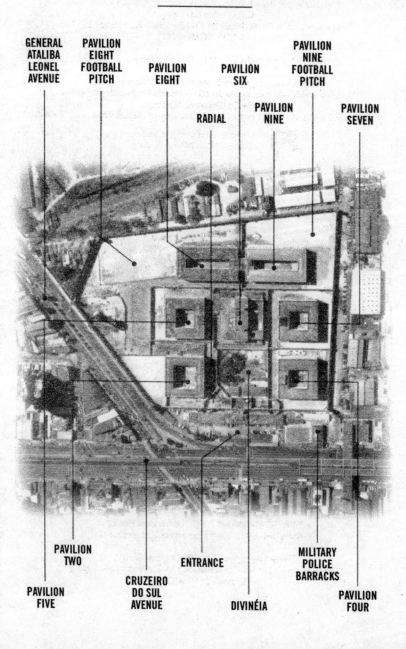

GENERAL ATALIBA LEONEL AVENUE

PAVILION EIGHT FOOTBALL PITCH

PAVILION EIGHT

RADIAL

PAVILION SIX

PAVILION NINE

PAVILION NINE FOOTBALL PITCH

PAVILION SEVEN

PAVILION TWO

PAVILION FIVE

CRUZEIRO DO SUL AVENUE

ENTRANCE

DIVINÉIA

MILITARY POLICE BARRACKS

PAVILION FOUR

Introduction

When I was young, I would watch black-and-white prison films – in which the inmates wore uniforms and planned breathtaking escapes – while riveted to my chair.

In 1989, when I had already graduated and had been working as an oncologist for twenty years, I filmed a video about AIDS in the infirmary of the São Paulo State Penitentiary, a building designed by Brazilian architect Ramos de Azevedo in the 1920s, in the Carandiru prison complex in the city of São Paulo. When I walked in and the heavy door slammed behind me, I felt the same tightening in my throat that I had as a boy at matinées in Cine Rialto, in the São Paulo neighbourhood of Brás.

In the following weeks, I couldn't get the images of the prison out of my mind. The prisoners at the doors of their cells, the unshaven warder, a distracted military police officer on the rampart, holding a machine gun, echoes in the gloomy corridor, the smell, the

1

swagger of hardened criminals, tuberculosis, cachexia, loneliness and the silent figure of Dr Getúlio, my former student, who cared for the prisoners with AIDS.

Two weeks later, I went to see Dr Manoel Schechtman, in charge of the prison system's medical department, and offered to implant a voluntary AIDS-prevention programme at the prison. Dr Schechtman told me that the epidemic wasn't as bad at that penitentiary as at the Casa de Detenção, Brazil's largest prison, with 7200 inmates, located in the same complex, just ten minutes from the bustling heart of downtown São Paulo.

The programme was implemented in 1989. With the support of the private Paulista University, we conducted epidemiological research into the prevalence of HIV, organised talks, recorded videos, published the comic book *O Vira Lata* ['The Stray'], written by Paulo Garfunkel and illustrated by Líbero Malavoglia, and I treated the sick. As the years went past, I gained confidence and was able to pass freely through the prison. I heard stories, struck up true friendships, and furthered my knowledge of medicine and many other things. The experience gave me an insider's understanding of certain mysteries of prison life to which I wouldn't have had access if I hadn't been a doctor.

In this book, I try to show that the loss of freedom and restriction of one's physical space do not lead to barbaric behaviour, contrary to what many people think. In captivity, men, like all other large primates (orang-utans, gorillas, chimpanzees and bonobos), create new rules of conduct in order to preserve the integrity of the group. In the case of the Casa de Detenção, this adaptive process was governed by an unwritten penal code, as in Anglo-Saxon law, which was applied with extreme rigour: 'Among us, there's no statute of limitations, Doctor.'

Paying one's debts, not informing on fellow inmates, respecting other people's visitors, not coveting the neighbour's wife, and exercising solidarity and altruism gave prisoners dignity. Failure to observe the above was punished with social ostracism, physical punishment and even the death penalty. 'In the world of crime, a man's word is stronger than an army.'

The objective of this book is not to speak out against an antiquated penal system, to offer solutions for crime in Brazil or to defend human rights. As in the films of old, I seek to walk among the characters who inhabited the prison: thieves, swindlers, smugglers, rapists, murderers and the handful of unarmed warders who watched over them.

The narrative is interrupted by the characters themselves so that readers may appreciate their stories first-hand. For ethical reasons, the incidents described didn't always happen to the characters to whom they have been attributed. As the criminals themselves used to say: 'In a prison, no one knows where the truth resides.'

Carandiru Station

'Prison is a place inhabited by evil.'

I took the metro to Carandiru Station, where I got off and turned right, in front of the military police barracks. In the background, as far as the eye could see, stretched a grey wall with guard towers. Next door to the barracks was a majestic entrance with CASA DE DETENÇÃO written above it in black letters.

The gate from the street led into a full parking lot. Through it circulated lawyers, women carrying plastic bags and corpulent warders in jeans who talked about work, laughed at one another and changed the subject whenever someone they didn't know approached. They had to be greeted decisively; otherwise, your hand would be crushed by their handshake.

Thirty paces into the complex was a small administration building, behind a green gate in which a smaller gate for pedestrians was set. You didn't need to knock to enter; all you had to do was put your head near the window in the gate and the guard's poorly lit face would appear, telepathically, on the other side.

The opening of the gate obeyed the old prison routine, according to which a door could only be opened when the ones before and after it had been closed. It was good manners to wait without useless demonstrations of impatience.

I heard the clink of the gate unlocking and found myself in the 'Rat-trap', a barred atrium with two booths on the left, where visitors had to identify themselves. Behind the booths was a corridor leading to the director general's office, which was large and full of light. The table was old. On the wall behind it was a photograph of the governor and a copper plate, hung there by one of the directors, an experienced jailer, that said: 'It is easier for a camel to pass through the eye of a needle than for a rich man to enter the Casa de Detenção.'

I returned to the Rat-trap, waited for the inner gate to open and found myself facing the wall that surrounded the prison, guarded by military police officers armed with submachine guns.

I stepped into Divinéia, a large funnel-shaped courtyard. At the narrow end was the body search room, a compulsory stopover for those entering the prison, except for doctors, directors and lawyers. Before gaining access to the pavilions, it was necessary to enter this room and lift your arms up in front of the friskers, who would merely pat your waist and the sides of your thighs.

Frisking was another prison ritual.

Those who thought such a mechanical search was just for show, however, were mistaken: people were frequently caught with drugs, arrested and ended up doing time in the Criminal Observation Centre.

Once, five inmates from Pavilion Five armed with knives took some warders hostage in the laundry and demanded to be transferred to another prison. Police officers and reporters with cameras swarmed to the prison door. A warder took advantage of the confusion to enter carrying 1.5 kilos of cocaine. He was caught in the body search room. Jesus, director of security, a former professional wrestler turned Protestant pastor, did everything in his power to identify who the cocaine was for.

'You're better off talking. Look at your situation: in the morning, you come to work as the head of a family, respected; in the afternoon, you leave here under arrest. You're going to get five or six years over in the Criminal Observation Centre. Your boys are now a con's sons. Your wife is no longer married to a public servant, but a criminal.'

The emotional appeal was useless. Contact with the inmates had taught the drug-dealing employee the supreme commandment among criminals: 'Crime is silence.'

Another time, a thickset, moustached Pavilion Eight warder tried to smuggle in a package of crack strapped to his inner thigh. The frisker, who was somewhat suspicious, found it. Caught out, the warder sprinted off into the prison hoping to make it to Pavilion Eight, at the back of the complex, where he could count on the help of the drug owners to have him let off. He was unsuccessful; he was knocked down in the chase by his colleagues.

Next to the body search room was the director's kitchen, a more recent construction built by the inmates themselves. When it was almost done, one of them had made a point of showing me his work. Eyes shining with pride, he had pointed at the beams in the ceiling painstakingly aligned by himself and a companion with a squint who was standing beside him, vigorously shaking his head in complete agreement with the chief-carpenter's explanations. Finally, I shook their hands and said goodbye. Only then did I hear the helper's voice: 'Reform Xavier at your service, Doctor.'

Divinéia was bustling during the day. Everything entering or leaving the prison had to pass through it. Without crossing it, the only other way in or out was to jump the wall or dig a tunnel. Trucks would offload food, bricks, wood and material for the work in the labour departments, in addition to removing tons of rubbish. It was humanly impossible to inspect everything that entered. It would have paralysed the prison.

Divinéia was the last stop for the police vans that would bring prisoners in or take them away: to give testimony in court, to identify suspects in police line-ups or to be transferred to other prisons.

Newcomers would climb out of the backs of the

police vans in handcuffs, blinded by the sudden light. At night, when it was dark in Divinéia, the scene of people arriving in the prison was melancholic. The Casa de Detenção had a bigger population than many towns. There were more than seven thousand men, double or triple the projected number in the 1950s, when the first pavilions were built. In its worst phases, it housed as many as nine thousand.

Because the work of loading and offloading was done by the prisoners, it was in Divinéia that I had my first contact with them. They were easy to recognise by their beige trousers, the compulsory uniform. Jackets were prohibited and their hair had to be worn short. They were not allowed to go barefoot, shirtless or unshaven. Shirts, jumpers and sweatshirts were allowed; T-shirts were sovereign. The black and white kit of the Corinthians, one of the country's most popular football teams, was by far the most popular, outnumbering Palmeiras, São Paulo and Santos colours combined. In FIFA World Cup periods, Brazilian *seleção* shirts would tinge the corridors canary-yellow, then fall into disuse and disappear. No one wore T-shirts with political propaganda; it was frowned upon.

A toothless inmate came strutting towards me, in a pair of flip-flops and an impeccable New York University T-shirt.

'Just got here, Doctor?'

'Yes. How was your weekend?'

'OK.'

At the wide end of the Divinéia funnel, the court-yard was closed off by a big wall decorated with Christmas figures painted years earlier: a pastor against a starry sky, snow-tipped mountains and three kindly sheep. Behind them rose the upper floors of the central pavilion, Six.

To the left of Divinéia, there was a wood with monkeys in the trees and a rickety bandstand. A paved path through the trees led to the gate to pavilions Two, Five and Eight.

On the other side, next to the director's kitchen, were a flowerbed and a little fountain in a pond lined with fragments of ceramic, where ornamental fish once swam.

The fountain was simple: three concentric discs lined with blue tiles, increasing in diameter from top to bottom, sat on a concrete axis. From the top disc, a trickle of water drizzled onto the others, too exhausted to spout up into the air and, when it fell, oxygenate the water where the fish once lived, according to the original design. It did no justice to the Brazilian tradition of fountains.

On this side, opposite the entrance to Two, between the country-style garden and the fountain, was the gate to the pavilions on the right side of the prison: Four, Seven and Nine. On the top floor of Four was the infirmary, the setting for many of the stories in this book.

The Big House

The Casa de Detenção was an old, poorly conserved prison. The pavilions were grey, square, five-storey buildings (counting the ground floor) with central courtyards, outdoor games courts and football pitches.

There were cells on both sides of a corridor – universally referred to as the 'gallery' – that followed the four walls of the building. As such, the inside cells had windows facing onto the inner courtyard, while the others had windows looking out of the building.

There were high walls separating the pavilions, and a wide paved path, nicknamed 'Radial' after a busy São Paulo avenue, connected them to one another.

The gate to the pavilions was guarded by an unarmed warder in plain clothes. Staff were differentiated from inmates by the dark trousers or jeans that they wore. No one was allowed to enter the prison armed, except for the feared military police riot squad on search days.

The cells were opened in the morning and locked in the late afternoon. During the day, the prisoners were allowed to move freely through the courtyard and the corridors. Approximately one thousand inmates had transit cards which enabled them to circulate between pavilions. They were cleaners, loaders, postmen, messengers, bureaucrats, people who were trusted by administration, in addition to those who got hold of such cards by illicit means. For the warders, this coming and going made the prison uncontrollable, and, if each pavilion could have been isolated as an autonomous unit, guarding them would have been easier.

For security purposes, the entrance to each pavilion was a barred cage with outer and inner doors that restricted access to the stairs and the ground-floor galleries. The same cage system was repeated at the entrance to each floor. When the cages were locked, anyone coming through the gallery had to open two doors to get access to the stairs and another two when they reached the ground floor in order to get out of the pavilion.

There were no electric doors like in films: they were opened and closed manually.

Casa folklore contains many references to Rua Dez, or 'Street Ten', where many violent disputes took place. Rua Dez was in fact nothing more than the section of gallery opposite the entrance to each floor, on the other side of the building, out of the sight of the guards who to get there had to move through the side galleries, where they could be seen by spotters, strategically located at the two ends of Rua Dez at critical moments.

There were no fistfights on Rua Dez; differences were

settled with pieces of wood and knives under the excited gaze of onlookers. The loser, when he came out alive, would head down to Incarceration and ask to be transferred to a different pavilion, generally Five. His adversary would move up in the ranking. At other times, a condemned man would be lured there and stabbed to death by a varying group of men. In these situations, some would take the opportunity to deliver a few extra blows, even to people who hadn't done them any harm.

Old Jeremias, with his head of white tightly curled hair, survivor of fifteen rebellions and father of eighteen children by the same wife, didn't consider bravery the forte of such attackers. 'I've been inside for many years, Doctor,' he once told me, 'and I've never seen anyone kill a man on his own. Some twenty or thirty'll mill about and take a swipe at the one who's gonna die. It doesn't matter how strong he is, he can't defend himself. Prison warps men's minds so much that the guy'll be getting a workin' over and people who've got nothin' to do with the story'll jump on the bandwagon and take a stab at him too, out of sheer cruelty. It's the height of cowardice!'

The support sectors were located on the ground floor of the pavilions: electricity, hydraulics, a medical room, Incarceration (where the prisoners' files were kept), a school and chapels. There were no computers on desks, just typewriters. Employees would sit at them, assisted by teams of inmates who worked in admin. There was invariably a blackboard on the wall showing the pavilion's numerical data. The pace of transfers and releases was intense.

The population of the Casa de Detenção fluctuated: approximately three thousand men were released or transferred annually. Originally built to house only remand prisoners awaiting trial, it had become a general prison. Criminals sentenced to over a hundred years did time alongside petty thieves who were in for a few months.

The Pavilions

Although the external architecture of the pavilions was similar, their internal divisions and human geography were very different. Those arriving in Divinéia from the street found themselves facing Pavilion Six, in the middle. On the left were pavilions Two, Five and Eight, while opposite them, on the right, were Four, Seven and Nine.

Pavilion Two

This was where prisoners had their induction to prison life. It housed 800 prisoners, who worked in administration: general administration, Incarceration, the loudspeaker service and the staff cafeteria. In addition to the support sectors, operating on the ground floor of Two were a tailor's, a barber's, a photographer's, a clothes deposit and 'labour therapy', which dealt with sentence reductions for the inmates who worked (for every three days of work, sentences were reduced by one).

15

When prisoners arrived at the Casa de Detenção, they would climb out of the police van in Divinéia and be sent straight to General Control in Pavilion Two, where they were registered, photographed and distributed among the pavilions.

It was in the inner courtyard of Two that the arrival ritual took place: after registering, prisoners were made to strip down to their underwear in front of everyone and leave their clothes in the deposit. They were given a pair of beige trousers and a bowl cut, their first and last free haircut in prison. It really did look like someone had placed a bowl on their heads and shaved everything from there down. It gave them a rough look, especially in the case of older prisoners.

Thus depersonalised, newcomers were taken to Distribution Cell One, on the ground floor, a four-by-eight-metre cell, which was often overflowing depending on the intake of prisoners on any given day. The next day they were taken to Distribution Cell Two, on the third floor, where they waited to be allocated to a pavilion, which had to be done by one of the three directors: the director general, the director of correctional services or the director of security. Kept closed twenty-four hours a day, Distribution Cell Two could hold sixty, seventy or even eighty men at a time, depending on the number of new entries.

When there were rebellions at local police lock-ups, fifty or more prisoners could be brought in at once. In one such incident, 200 prisoners were transferred to the Casa. The staff used to say: 'It's worse in here than a mother's heart – there's always room for more.'

Or, in a more prosaic vision: 'The city sewer dumps its contents here.'

During distribution, the director would address groups of ten to fifteen men who, hands held respectfully behind their backs, would listen to the rules of the house:

> You have come to the São Paulo Casa de Detenção to pay a debt to society. This is not your grandma's or auntie's place; it's the biggest prison in Latin America. Those who are humble and disciplined can count on the staff to help them leave here the way we like them to: through the front door, with their families waiting. However, the man who comes here insisting he belongs to the world of crime, with blood in his eyes, if he doesn't leave in the Institute of Forensic Medicine morgue car, he can be sure that we're going to do everything in our power to make his life difficult. We're in the habit of forgetting people like that in here.

Special attention was paid to the safety of newcomers. Security director Jesus had a particular way of dealing with the problem: 'If, perhaps, one of you gentlemen finds himself with social difficulties in one of the pavilions, don't be shy; you can pour your heart out to me. Let us help you now, before your enemies do.'

Then, one by one, to be sure of the nature of the crime for which each prisoner was convicted, and anticipating the invariable denial of guilt, he would ask seriously, 'What is the crime they say you committed?'

The distribution criteria weren't rigid, but they did obey some basic rules. For example, rapists were normally sent to Pavilion Five; repeat offenders to Eight; first-timers to Nine; and the extremely rare prisoners with university degrees got private cells in Pavilion Four.

In distribution, many would ask to remain in Two itself. Due to the availability of work and perhaps because it was located at the front of the prison, closer to administration, the pavilion was renowned for being calm: 'It's easier to focus on getting out.'

Pavilion Four

Pavilion Four was located on the other side, opposite Two. It held less than four hundred inmates, housed in individual cells, the only place in the prison where this occurred. During distribution, when newcomers asked to be sent to Four, the director would reply, 'You don't say! Even I'd like to live in Four, my boy.'

It was originally designed for the exclusive use of the health department. The ground floor did, in fact, house the inmates with tuberculosis and the general infirmary operated on the fifth floor. However, due to the need to protect prisoners with a death warrant on their heads, administration had to create a special maximum-security sector on the ground floor, known as the 'Dungeon' – the worst place in the prison.

The Dungeon faced the entrance to the pavilion. It was guarded by a heavy door, next to which was a sign warning that the entry of unauthorised persons was strictly prohibited. There were eight cells on one side of a dark gallery and six on the other, all stuffy and over-crowded. The number of inhabitants in the sector never dipped below fifty, with four or five in each cell, deprived of sunlight, locked up the entire time to escape the war cry of crime: 'You're going to die!'

It was a lugubrious environment, infested with scabies, lice and cockroaches that climbed up through the drainpipes. During the night, grey rats scampered through the deserted gallery.

The cell windows were sealed with a sheet of iron with tiny holes in it, stopping light from coming in. Due to the lack of ventilation, there was a strong stench of people crowded together and a phantasma-gorical fog of cigarette smoke hung in the cell. Bathing required an act of contortionism under a pipe jutting out of the wall or with mugs of water from the tap over the sink.

The Dungeon was inhabited by those who had lost all hope of living among their peers. There was no other place in the prison left for them; not even in the high security wings, such as 'Yellow' in Five, for example. They stayed locked away until the prison system bureaucrats decided to transfer them to another prison.

Periodically, the name 'Dungeon' would attract the attention of the press and prisoners' rights organisations and the Inspector General's office would be obliged to carry out an inspection. On one such visit the director general, irritated by an inspector who was blaming him for the inhumane conditions in which the inhabitants of the wing were living, said, 'Sir, I'm going to open each cell, one by one, and you can ask if anyone is willing to be moved from here to any other pavilion. If they agree, I'll move everyone and close the sector in your presence.'

After opening the second cell, the inspector understood that all of the men wanted to be sent to another prison, not another pavilion, but as long as that didn't happen they refused to leave the Dungeon, as they felt safe there.

On sunny days, in the courtyard of Four, visitors would see many inmates in rickety wheelchairs. They were almost always burglars who had been left paraplegic from shoot-outs, and they served their sentences in Four, where their urinary catheters and bedsores that wouldn't heal were tended to. In addition, they could use the pavilion's lift, the only one still working in the prison. The paraplegics were treated with respect by companions who helped them with day-to-day tasks.

On the second floor, there was a section of the gallery whose cells bore a card that read: 'MP', to identify the 'mental patients'. The criteria for assigning such a label were uncertain, since there wasn't a specialised psychiatry service in the prison. Some of the MPs arrived with serious behavioural disorders, while others began to display psychotic symptoms while in prison, trying to strangle a fellow prisoner without provocation, attempting suicide, falling into deep depression or destroying their brains by smoking crack.

Genival, one of the inhabitants of this sector, said he had lost his mind because of the vision of a man he had killed in a robbery: 'When night fell, his lost soul would come to haunt me, on the stairs, in the gallery and even in the locked cell. I tried to commit suicide twice to escape the persecution.'

Like in nineteenth-century insane asylums, the inmates spent their time isolated in their cells. They all received practically the same psychiatric medication.

The lives of these prisoners would have been worse if it weren't for the touching dedication of a converted Salvation Army pastor with wavy hair, serving a twelve-year sentence for crimes he said he had tried everything to forget, who for a long time headed up a group of helpers in charge of hygiene, medication and spoon-feeding those who couldn't feed themselves.

The lack of doctors specialised in psychiatric

disorders left the door open for unprincipled inmates to fake psychiatric problems in order to take refuge among the MPs to avoid the retaliation of their enemies.

According to Moustache, a man of character who lived in this pavilion for a long time, former leader of a gang of pirates in the port of Santos who was serving a 213-year sentence, 'To get out of his own vile mess, he pretends he's lost his mind and ends up in the middle of the MPs, in Four. Tomorrow he gets out and brags that he did time in the Casa, because he's a villain through and through.'

Some such individuals may have found punishment in the psychiatric medication they were prescribed, which impeded motor coordination and caused various neurological alterations, leading among other things to impregnation of the central nervous system, tremors and loss of sphincter control.

For security reasons, the directors discreetly made Four the destination of certain rapists as well as contract killers who were generally hired by shop owners in lower-class neighbourhoods to kill local thieves. Because the pavilion was less populous and calmer, these inmates had a better chance of escaping the collective wrath. Their hidden presence, however, meant that the inmates in Four were regarded with mistrust: 'Nobody knows who's who in there.'

Pavilion Five

This was the pavilion in the worst state of repair. It had stairs with crumbling steps, electrical wires dangling from walls that were damp from leaks, puddles of water and burnt light bulbs in the galleries. The inmates wedged poles through the windows to dry clothes on. It looked like a slum.

Five was the most densely crowded pavilion in the prison. Its corridors were intensely busy. At times, there wasn't room for a single prisoner more. One thousand six hundred men lived there, triple the sensible number for an entire prison. The Casa had eight to ten warders watching over them during the day and five or six at night, sometimes less.

On the ground floor, in addition to Incarceration, the medical room and a classroom with an impoverished library, was Solitary Confinement, a group of twenty cells that held four to ten men squeezed into each one. They were inmates who had been caught committing offences within the prison itself, such as carrying weapons, possession of alcohol, trafficking, disrespecting a staff member or planning to escape. They would do thirty days in these dark, humid cells, whose windows were covered with perforated metal sheets like those in the Dungeon. The bar on the door was hard and enduring and the thirty days were without sunlight.

Lupércio, who was over eighty years old and had

been in and out of the Casa for smoking and selling marijuana, said it was nothing:

> In the old days, they used to lock so many in a cell that the men had to take turns to sleep. Half of 'em would stay standin' – quietly so they wouldn't wake up the others. They'd urinate when changin' shifts. You couldn't eat much, because you couldn't have a bowel movement in the cell. Only on Wednesdays and Saturdays, when it was unlocked for an hour so you could shower and use the toilet. The punishment was ninety days, not the no-sweat thirty days they get now.

On the second floor lived the cleaners, who took care of general cleaning and the distribution of meals, in addition to those who worked in the labour and legal departments, and delivering bags of food brought in during the week to those who were fortunate enough to be able to count on their families.

The third floor was known as the floor of rapists and contract killers, although not all of its occupants belonged to these categories. Experience had taught that it was best to put the two groups together so they could protect one another in the event that the other prisoners, who abominated rapists and those who hunted thieves down, decided to take revenge.

The fourth floor was the destination of those who were unable to get a better placement, who had been kicked out of other pavilions due to their failure to abide by the rules, or who had lost personal disputes, in addition to more rapists and contract killers. Most strikingly, however, this floor was where the transvestites lived, with their silicone-inflated cheekbones, tight trousers and mincing walks. During the day, some would solicit at their cell doors.

On the top floor, on the right, was the wing of the Assembly of God, the evangelical group with the strongest presence in the prison. You couldn't miss them: they always wore proper shoes, never trainers; their long-sleeved shirts were buttoned up to the collar; and they all carried faded black bibles. They prayed day and night under the supervision of an energetic chief pastor and his helpers. It was a church and a rehabilitation centre at the same time. On the left, adjacent to the born-again Christians, was Yellow, a high-security sector that was kept closed twenty-four hours a day. Those who had received death threats were sent there, along with a few unfortunate souls who simply didn't have anywhere else to live. Yellow housed five to six hundred inmates, almost 10 per cent of the prison population, with at least six or seven men in each two-by-three-metre cell.

Five was the pavilion of inmates with no family, the homeless and the destitute. Although men who were respected did time there, it was considered the pavilion of the rabble. I saw grown men cry like babies when they were transferred there.

Because contract killers, rapists, informers and inmates who were in debt to others all rubbed shoulders in the local population, the residents of Five, aware of the danger they were in, needed to be ready to defend themselves. They could live in peace for years, but one day the prison might get turned upside-down and they could wind up on the tip of a knife. As the inmates used to say: 'Here, anyone who's made a cock-up in the world of crime lives on tenterhooks.'

As a result, in addition to being the traditional producer of *maria-louca*, the clandestinely distilled firewater, Five was also considered the most heavily armed pavilion, and was often referred to as the prison's 'knife factory'.

Pavilion Six

Pavilion Six was located between Two and Four, in the centre of the complex. It held approximately three hundred prisoners.

The general kitchen operated there until 1995, when it was deactivated and the Casa began to order in food for the prisoners. At night, the abandoned kitchen looked like the set of an expressionist film: enormous pressure cookers covered with dents, a potholed floor, loose wall tiles and leaks in the ceiling.

On the second floor was a large auditorium, where we gave talks on AIDS prevention, sometimes to more than a thousand inmates at a time. A cinema used to function there until it was destroyed in a rebellion. Only the big hall itself remained, with a raised wooden stage at the front.

On the second and third floor of Six were the rooms used by administration: security, correctional services, and the sports and legal departments.

The cells began on the fourth floor. Two, three, five – as many as fifteen prisoners in each.

On the fifth floor, a sector called PSM (Preventive Security Measure) was created as an alternative to the overcrowding in Yellow; however, due to the disruptive impact of crack on the prison's internal order, once inaugurated the PSM filled up immediately.

Visitors to Six would see groups of black men speaking a strange language. They were Nigerians speaking in their native dialect (although almost all of them spoke English and sometimes Portuguese, with strong accents). They were part of the Nigerian connection in cocaine trafficking, detained in Brazil and obliged to do time here.

Ball-Sinker – a thief doing five years in Six, who had got $20,000 in a bank robbery, bought a grocery shop and given up crime as his wife had asked him to, and who six months later was forced to follow and kill two adolescents who had held up his shop so as not to lose face – shared the opinion of the majority about the Nigerians: 'If you ask 'em a question, they answer and keep it short; if you don't ask, they keep to themselves. They aren't villains, that lot. They're adventurers – their business is trafficking. They don't help or hinder thieves. They're down-to-earth, good guys. We respect 'em.'

Pavilion Seven

The cells of Seven held three to six men at most, and most of the inmates worked.

Like in the other pavilions, the ground floor housed the bureaucratic departments, maintenance and labour, which organised work commissioned from outside the prison: inserting spirals in notebooks or elastic in box files, building miniature sailboats (an old tradition in Brazilian prisons), sewing footballs and other manual jobs.

A group of twenty to thirty men employed in cleaning lived on the second floor and the other inhabitants were distributed throughout the other floors without any apparent order. On the fifth floor were the Solitary Confinement cells reserved for punishing those who had broken prison rules.

The courtyard had a games court and two small, dusty football pitches, the setting for sporting battles in which the athletes weren't exactly famed for their technique, much less the elegance of their attire.

Seven was built to be a working pavilion. Work, sports and its relative lack of overcrowding were responsible for its reputation as a calm pavilion. Indeed, two or three years often passed without a single death in Seven.

Because it was the pavilion closest to the external wall, however, Seven was the preferred site for underground escapes. It was known as the 'tunnel factory'.

Pavilion Eight

Eight was situated at the back of the prison on the left, opposite Nine, and together they were known as the problematic rear of the prison.

The pavilion was square-shaped like the others, but enormous, with galleries that were almost a hundred metres long. In total, some 1700 men lived in Eight, more than six times the population of Alcatraz in the United States, which was closed in the 1960s.

The cleaners' cells, housing 150 to 200 men, were located on the second floor.

On the upper floors, in each of the cells facing onto the inner courtyard, lived an average of six men. Those on the outside wall of the pavilion were semi-communal, with two or three men, or communal, with ten or twelve. On the fifth floor there were eight Solitary Confinement cells, similar to the ones in the other pavilions.

On the ground floor, in addition to the bureaucratic sectors, there was a Catholic chapel; an Umbanda centre; an Assembly of God, Universal Church, and God is Love Pentecostal Church temples.

The courtyard of Eight had the prison's largest football pitch. Internal football tournaments were held on its beaten earth surface, in addition to friendly games against district teams who were invited to take on the prison squad. Any inmate who treated a visitor disrespectfully on these occasions would live to regret it.

Eight's cells, like those in Seven, Five and Nine, had owners, a tradition in the Casa de Detenção which I will explain later. As such, those who didn't have three or four hundred *reais* to purchase a cell had to live in the 'showers'. Originally communal bathrooms, the showers housed six to ten men in a two-by-three-metre space. There were showers on the third, fourth and fifth floors.

The main characteristic of Eight, however, wasn't its physical layout or overcrowding, but its human landscape. This was the destination of repeat offenders; first-timers were rare. The concentration of inmates who knew the laws of the prison established well-defined behavioural codes.

Rolney – who spent ten years in this pavilion and was released, only to return because when he found his wife shacked up with his best friend in his own house, he invited him for a beer at the local watering hole and when the friend tried to console him by saying that 'that was life', he put two bullets in him to prove that it wasn't – described Eight in the following manner: 'The men who live here have already been through the prison's playgroup. With us there's no dithering about. Things are black and white. Something is or it isn't. If it isn't, you're dead.'

Nineteen-year-old, HIV-positive Gersinho – a first-time offender who was accepted in the pavilion because a thief who had known him since he was a baby, and who may have been his mother's boyfriend, had invited him to live in his cell – said he learned a lot from his contact with the inhabitants of Eight: 'In Eight, each man bears his cross in silence. Sufferin' for years inside teaches cons to lock themselves away in their own solitude. It's a school of wise men.'

It was the pavilion of those who had made their names in crime. The inhabitants of Eight tended to be older and stayed out of disputes. They would watch, listen and stay quiet. Their motto was not to act; but *re*act: 'They're like rattlesnakes: they only strike when stepped on.'

Pavilion Nine

Nine could house over two thousand convicts, most serving their first term in jail. It had the same dimensions, organisation of service sectors and distribution of cells as Eight. That was where the similarities ended, however.

In Nine, there were two distribution cells in which up to thirty prisoners slept head-to-toe on the ground, taking care not to let their feet touch their cellmates' faces.

The distribution cells were kept locked at all times. The prisoners were only allowed downstairs to greet visitors on Sundays or Wednesdays between eight and three, when they were let out to look for a cell to live in (to be explained further in the next chapter), a difficult task for unknown newcomers, because the inmates had owned their own living quarters for quite some time.

When the pavilion was renovated after fighting broke out and led to a massacre in 1992, the wooden bunk beds riddled with bullets were replaced with concrete slabs. For this reason, in Nine, those who couldn't afford an entire cell could only acquire the exclusive right to a 'slab', or bed.

As soon as newcomers arrived, the other inmates would head up to see if there were any friends or enemies among them. In the case of the latter, the rival was threatened with death and had two alternatives: to ask for refuge, disgraced, in the Yellow wing of Five, or face the knives of his enemy and companions. 'Nine is a pavilion of confrontations,' the warders used to say.

Although the prison directors deliberately kept some more experienced prisoners in Nine, the high concentration of impetuous young men was responsible for the frequent fighting in the pavilion.

After the 1992 massacre, a cleaner in Eight said of his companions in Nine: 'They're a bunch of idiots, Doctor. In the middle of that kind of mess, lettin' the warders go and leavin' the cons alone in the pavilion is just askin' for the riot squad to step in. Somethin' like that would never have happened in Eight.'

Majesty, a robber from the 1970s who had been in

Nine for twenty years, explained the difference between Eight and Nine: 'You can slip up in either one, except that in Eight, if you do, it's your own fault. In Nine, it's other people's, and they'll even spread soap on the floor for you to slip on.'

The Cells

The cell was the functional unit of the prison. Their dimensions varied without any apparent logic: some, even quite spacious ones, were individual, while ten, twenty, or even sixty men – which was the case in the distribution cells – were packed into others.

The prison administration had lost cell ownership in the bigger pavilions – Five, Seven, Eight and Nine – many years earlier. In these pavilions, each cell had an owner and a market value. In Pavilion Five, they were cheaper: 150 to 200 *reais*; in Eight, there was a luxury cell worth 2000, with top-quality tiles, double bed and mirrors.

The origin of this ownership is lost in the past, when the prison's resources began to dry up and cell maintenance was left to the prisoners themselves, explained Juscelino, an inmate with a winning smile who used to buy marijuana in the backlands of Pernambuco and return to São Paulo in a sleeper coach with the drugs in his backpack: 'A guy spent his money on the upkeep of his cell. Then the screws'd try to stick someone else in there to live for free. Where was the justice in that?'

According to Dr Walter Hoffgen – who started out as a prison warder when he was still young, got a law degree and worked his way up to director general – the only way to solve the problem would have been to transfer all of the inmates, close the prison and start again: 'In the middle of the night, you send a prisoner to a cell. The next morning, he comes out and says there's no way he's staying there, and he won't explain why. You can insist, make threats, do whatever you want, but he won't go back; he's afraid of dying. There are cells where the owner is released and leaves a tenant paying rent or a friend living in it for free. If the owner comes back to the Casa, the occupant has to return the property. Look at the state we've got ourselves into!'

In the beginning, administration went as far as to expel all of the occupants from a cell and lock it up for fifteen days. When they reopened it, it was useless: not a single prisoner was willing to live there.

The situation was especially adverse for those who arrived in the prison without friends or money. Valtércio – a thief who stole eight television sets from cars on a World Cup day and later lost everything in a confrontation with the police – said bitterly: 'Look where this country's at, Doctor, having to pay to live in jail.'

Light entered the cells through the barred windows. Opposite the windows were heavy metal doors with a sliding bar on the outside, which was locked with a robust padlock. The padlock, however, didn't ensure the safety of those who were locked in, because the prison housed practitioners extraordinary in the art of picking any kind of lock. For this reason, some prisoners would weld a metal ring to the inside of their door, another to the doorjamb and padlock them together to lock themselves in. It was against prison rules and could cost a man thirty days in Solitary.

One night, in Pavilion Five, during the distribution of the second edition of the comic book *Vira Lata* we published, I asked through the little window of a darkened cell how many men lived there, to know how many comics to give them. A big black man woke up, jumped out of bed and came to the door brandishing a knife (he took it out so quickly that it could only have been hidden under his pillow). Until he had grasped what was going on, he just stood there, utterly still, with terror in his eyes and the knife pointing at the door. He probably didn't trust that the door bar was firm enough.

In the middle of the door was a small window, covered inside with a curtain, through which deliveries were made and the daily head counts – a strict prison ritual – were conducted. The window was wide enough to allow a man's head through it, which was how the inmates saw what was happening in the gallery at lockup time.

To ensure the privacy of the space inside, a sheet was hung from the ceiling, almost to the ground, a little behind the door.

Unlike prisons in the cinema, in which the doors are barred so the prisoners can be seen at all times, in the Casa de Detenção, the men locked in their cells couldn't be seen by anyone walking through the galleries. If the warders wanted to know what was going on, they had to be satisfied with what could be seen from the window or open the cell. When the situation was serious and they opted for the latter, the best technique was to have the inmates come out naked and place their hands on the gallery wall opposite the cell.

Every cell had an old, but generally clean toilet, of differing varieties. Some were French-style, with a hole and two foot-supports; others were the classic ceramic bowls set in an upside-down concrete cone. The toilets ended in a dry hole, where the waste went when it was flushed. To sterilise it, the inmates would pour boiling water down it at night after the last man had used it. The more careful ones would cover the hole with a plastic bag filled with sand, to stop odours, cockroaches and rats coming in from the plumbing. So they didn't have to touch the bag directly, they would hang it from a rope that passed through a pulley on the wall.

All of the cells had a sink and a shower, or at least a water pipe jutting out of the wall. Many enjoyed the comfort of electric showers, which could be sold at a time of financial hardship or a deep craving for cocaine.

In Pavilion Eight, at the back of a communal cell of twenty-seven men was a bathroom with a pipe so close to the wall that one could barely get under it, through which ran a trickle of water. Despite the gymnastics involved, having a daily shower was mandatory, even in the cold of June. The older ones made it their business to impose this obligation on the newcomers.

The prison's hydraulics were in a serious state of disrepair. Leaks were routine; they would infiltrate walls and flood galleries, the inner courtyard and the insides of cells. Some pipes had been patched so many times that they were hard to keep fixing.

The bunk beds were made of bricks and mortar or wood, sometimes ingeniously placed over doors, next to the barred windows or so close to the ceiling that their occupants had to slither like snakes into the meagre space.

Privacy in bed was obtained with colourful curtains that slid along wires attached to the bunk above them or the ceiling itself. 'The curtain's a must, otherwise there's always someone lookin' at me. Have you got any idea what it's like, Doctor; year after year and not a minute to yourself? That's where a lot of weaker men lose it and take their own lives.'

In the big communal cells, like the distribution cells with sixty or seventy people in them, beds were replaced with small latex-foam mattresses laid side by side on the ground. Space could be so scarce that the men slept feet-to-face: 'Cause it ain't right for villains to be rubbin' noses.'

The less fortunate didn't even have the small comfort of the foam, as there either weren't enough mattresses to go around or they had been sold to pay off debts, as was routine among the crack-heads. In these cases they would lie on blankets or pieces of cardboard, with flip-flops for pillows.

In the distribution cells, with men arriving and leaving all the time, priority in the choice of space was given to those who had been there the longest: 'The last one in gets the short end of the stick. There's nothin' to ask; he goes and snuggles up next to the crapper. He only leaves there the day a newer recruit comes in.'

The furniture was rustic: small cupboards for crockery, a few hangers for clothes and shelves for personal belongings; benches were roughly thrown together with wood that came from no-one-knows-where.

At the end of one year, the São Paulo City Council set up a stage next to the football pitch in Pavilion Eight for a show in which a number of bands performed, including Reunidos por Acaso, the prison's traditional *pagode* musical group. A few days later, when the organisers went to take the stage down, they discovered that it had disappeared. 'So many planks just sittin' there, Doctor, and there we were in such dire need; it was a godsend . . .'

A fundamental item in every cell was the cooker: a brick with a groove in it through which snaked an electric heating element connected to the wiring that ran along the outside of the wall. When they received their meals many inmates would wash the food, add other seasonings and re-cook everything, which meant they often didn't eat at the official mealtimes.

Demonstrating cooking skills could be decisive when vying for a place in a decent cell. In exchange for a dwelling the cell cook would be responsible for everyone's meals.

The food that the prison served was a sorry affair. There wasn't a man in the prison who could stomach it for more than a few days; the complaint was universal. Those who didn't have work in the prison itself (and could thus buy themselves food) or a family to help, suffered. Saturated with starch and fat, the diet made the inmates put on weight. Obesity, together with the lack of physical exercise, was one of many health problems in the Casa.

The galleries were washed late every afternoon by the cleaners, a group of men who comprised the spinal cord of the institution, as we shall see further along. Everything was clean; no one dared litter inside the prison. One rarely saw a dirty cell, but when it happened, its occupants were sworn at and treated with contempt.

In the 1994 World Cup I watched Brazil play the United States in a cell with twenty-five inmates in Pavilion Two. There wasn't a speck of dust on the furniture and the floor was spotless. The occupants took turns doing the daily cleaning: after breakfast, they would scrub the floor, pour a pan of boiling water into the two toilets, dust the furniture and beat the rugs; when lunch was over, a good sweep and boiling water in the toilets; after dinner, another scrub and the pans would be put on the cookers again to boil up water to pour down the toilets one last time.

Songbird – a former São Paulo City Hall driver who used the official car to deliver cocaine in the city centre, until he fell in love with a City Hall employee and was reported to the police by his jilted wife – explained the system: 'We spend years in this place, so we have to look after it as if it was our home. I clean today and then I'm only up again twenty-six days from now. There's no excuse for not givin' it your best. Besides, it wouldn't work. Tryin' to pull a fast one among the likes of us never has a happy ending.'

Wet clothes were hung to dry in the cells themselves, in a corner of the aisle between beds or pegged to a pole wedged through the window. Many made a living offering washing services.

I once saw an argument in the gallery of Pavilion Five because Jaquelina – a transvestite doing time for a scam in which her customers were surprised having sex with her by her lover armed with a revolver – had been caught soaping up her clientele's clothes in the toilet. Outraged, they were calling her names, while a haughty Jaquelina, hands on her waist, swore up and down that the can in her cell was cleaner than the beds that those classless no-goods slept on.

Naked women decorated walls, cupboards and, typically, the backs of doors. These pictures were racy, clipped out of men's magazines, which were exchanged or sold on small news stands set up in the galleries, displayed next to packets of pasta, ground coffee, tins of peas and old trainers. The most popular ones were the blondes on all fours photographed from behind, gazing provocatively over their shoulders at the lens. The inmates had no qualms about hanging them alongside images of saints, the goddess Iemanjá, Our Lady of Aparecida or the Sacred Heart, in colourful ecumenical panels.

Never pictures of men; only if they were of a father, a brother or an actor in a transvestite's cell. Those with jealous or religious wives would carefully remove their muses the day before visits, leaving solitary saints on the walls.

In particularly well cared for cells, the little curtains, embroidered rugs, patchwork quilts and saints gave them the feel of a house in the country.

The cell was a sacred place. It took a lot of pluck to enter another man's uninvited. Even so, according to old Jeremias – the one with eighteen children by the same wife, doing seven years this time: 'Without the owner there, you don't go in. No matter how well you know the guy. It's really overseppin' the mark! I've seen a man die 'cause of a bread roll. He was good friends with the other guy, smoked some weed, got the munchies and went into his cell while he was in court. There were two bread rolls; he ate one. The other guy came back and said he'd been saving the roll so he wouldn't have to eat his cold dinner. That night, he killed him in his sleep.'

When caught stealing, 'cell rats', as they were known, were attacked with pieces of wood and knives. They would show up in the infirmary invariably claiming that they had fallen down the stairs, covered in blood, with head wounds, their bodies marked with welts and superficial stab-wounds, especially around the buttocks, the punishment dealt out when an inmate wanted to disgrace the offender. The thieves made it explicit that their penal code was unrelenting when they were the victims. 'There's that old saying: "A thief who steals from another thief has a hundred years of pardon," except that when we catch 'em they're in trouble.'

Day and Night

The day started at five for the inmates who served breakfast. They all lived together, generally on the second floors of their pavilions, and were part of the brotherhood of cleaners which was the spinal cord of the prison, as I have said before.

They pushed bread rolls and large urns of coffee around on iron trolleys. As the group passed, mugs and dented coffee pots would appear through the windows in the doors of the locked cells. Late risers would leave their mugs on the window ledge and hang a plastic bag on it so they could still get their buttered roll and avoid the torture of getting out of bed.

When it was still dark, the cell lights were turned on in silence, out of respect for anyone who was asleep, explained Not-a-Hope, a skinny mulatto who had earned his nickname for the way he ended sentences: 'You've got to be quiet. If you wake up early, when everyone's asleep, and go relieve yourself and flush the

44

toilet or make any other noise you'll have to change cells. Wake up criminals? Not a hope!"

At around five o'clock in the morning, the warders on the night shift would take a head count. They'd have the inmates get out of bed and stand before the cell window, to be sure that everyone was present and alive before turning over their shift. According to one warder who had been doing it for years, 'At that hour, all you see is scowls.'

At eight, the unlocking of the cells began. From the entry cage on each floor, one pair of warders would head down the gallery to the right, while another would head left. Holding a set of keys, the one in front would open the padlocks, while the man behind him would remove them and slide back the bar. Metallic sounds would echo down the halls. The men would come out of their cells in silence, like ants.

In the work pavilions, they would quickly take up their posts. Others, such as the football sewers, for example, did their work in their own cells. I watched them on many an occasion, admiring the elegance with which they sewed. They would work sitting down, the sections of the ball between their knees, and, with the palms of their hands protected with strips of leather, they would pass the needle back and forth in precise, rhythmic movements until they reached the spot where they'd tie it off. It was a manual ballet.

Although the really lazy inmates were still in bed, the traffic in the gallery and on the worn stairs was infernal. The prisoners invariably walked fast, climbed the steps two at a time; and no sooner had they gone downstairs to the field, then they'd nip back to their cells and come back down again. They looked like businessmen who had places to be.

The hustle and bustle would die down at around nine, the strange hour at which lunch was served. Because the pavilions didn't have general mess halls, the cleaners were back at work again. With the doors open, the ritual was somewhat different to breakfast: each man had to be in his cell, leaving the gallery free for the food trolleys laden with piles of takeaway containers or, when the general kitchen was still in operation, with big pans of rice, beans and a mixture of meat with potatoes and carrots. A man's presence in the gallery at this delicate moment was interpreted as disrespect for food hygiene and punished severely.

I once tended a large man with a squint and a crew cut who was covered in abrasions. He claimed to have fallen out of bed, which I could see from the characteristics of his wounds was obviously a lie. I heard the real story a short time later from Shorty, a 1.5-metre-tall fellow with a lisp who had killed four military police officers whom he claimed had murdered his parents: while the cleaners were serving lunch, the big fellow had absent-mindedly strolled out into the gallery with his shirt unbuttoned and a towel around his neck. One of the cleaners immediately turned to him and said, 'You've got some cheek, sonny boy.'

That was the cue for the other cleaners to push him down to Rua Dez, beat him up and return to work as if nothing had happened.

Old Lupércio, a dyed-in-the-wool pothead, said that back in the days when people were more respectful, a blanket was spread out on the floor of the cell and the plates were placed on it. The man who had been in jail the longest would choose his; the newest was the last to serve himself. The rules of conduct at mealtimes were rigid: 'You couldn't use the can, hawk up or cough, much less clean your teeth with your tongue, or you'd cop it on the spot.'

Most of the sporting and leisure activities took place in the morning: football, boxing, *capoeira*, weight-lifting, music and adult education classes. The most popular by far was football. In games, if a patrolling military police officer happened to pass a stray ball that had ended up on top of the wall, he would rarely return it to the field. The explanation for this disregard – given by an officer who was transferred to this duty after the death of a colleague, and the retaliatory gunning-down of four members of the gang who had killed him – was vocational: 'I didn't join the force to be a ball boy for criminals.'

Tournaments were organised with regulations that were committed to paper, after endless discussion, by the members of FIFA (the Internal Federation of Amateur Football, in Portuguese), a close-knit group of experienced, well-respected inmates, chosen by direct election among the football squads of each pavilion, led by the head of the sports department, Waldemar Gonçalves, who was in the habit of chewing on cloves which he kept in a little pastille tin.

With so many players it was possible to put together a general squad with a good technical level, which nonetheless didn't stop them from obtaining disastrous results against the excellent district teams that were invited to play them. Although they disappointed the inmates, these occasional defeats never provoked disrespectful retaliations against the visiting team.

Reinaldo Drumond, one of the warders who worked at the prison door, black and strong as an ox, once proposed bringing a district team in to take on the prison's squad. 'I know they're gonna lose, 'cause the boys are good,' he told Waldemar. 'But my intention is to get the local guys who're going astray, who are thinking about getting involved in crime, to see where that life'll take you.'

Years ago, in a tournament for seniors (players over the age of thirty), I was invited to give the kick-off. Honoured by the invitation, which came directly from the older members of the prison, not only did I give the kick-off but I also sought to watch all of the games. In the deciding match the squad from Pavilion Eight beat the one from Two, 3–1.

At the end, the athletes gathered around the FIFA representative's table at the side of the field for the awards. There was a special award for the most outstanding players in the squads who had won first and second places. Waldemar handed me a medal hanging from a blue and white ribbon and announced the name of the best player on the squad from Pavilion Two, the vice-captain.

It was Gaúcho, a fullback with the typical features of an Amazonian, who had arrived in São Paulo twenty years earlier, as a tiler. He had been doing well at work until he became friends with a thief who lived in the district and got involved in a fight in which two contenders lost their lives. As a result, he fled his home, lost his job and everything he had, and ended up partnering with his thief friend, who stood by him in his time of need. After hanging the medal around his neck, I held out my hand to shake his. He was shaking with excitement, averting his moist eyes, which were glistening like those of a primary-schooler who had just won a prize, so as not to betray his emotions.

At around two or three in the afternoon, dinner was served, with the same ritual of cleaners, trolleys, empty galleries and the obsessive respect for hygiene. From this hour on, anyone who was hungry had to make do on their own.

The odd mealtime was again justified by the head count, which had to take place at five o'clock in the afternoon, and made re-cooking meals and the need for 'jumbos' important: 'Jumbos are the bags our families bring us when they visit, or leave with the doormen on weekdays. They help a lot, though there are some idiots that sell their jumbos to pay off drug debts.'

At five o'clock, everyone would return to their floors and the cages were locked, except those of the men whose activities justified their being out of them, such as cleaners and nurses, for example.

Lock-up time was another of the prison's rituals: the gallery would be busy, full of light, beans on the boil, the doors open with the naked women visible, voices, music from radios, people coming and going with pans and clothes. Suddenly, a warder would appear in the cage and beat a padlock against the bars or a pipe on the ground: clang, clang, clang, rhythmically, without stopping. The inmates would hurry to their cells, because lock-up was no time for messing around. The warders would lock up in pairs: the first one would put the padlock through the loop, while the one behind him would slide the bar into place and snap the padlock shut. It all happened very quickly and no man could be left outside of his cell. Offenders' names were taken down the first time; if it happened again, they got thirty unforgettable days in Solitary Confinement. 'If we're not strict, mayhem breaks out, Doctor,' the warders told me. 'Everyone here's a criminal, most with nothing to do but sit around looking for something to take advantage of. If you slack off one night, the next night you won't lock anyone up.'

Once the cells were closed, the sound of plates, talking, laughter and nightly news programmes could be heard in the galleries. Later, gradually, lights would go out and a heavy silence would fall. Even the night-owls who watched TV until the last film had ended took care with the volume, because a jailbird's sleep was sacred.

Without the bustle of the day, with men heading up and down the stairs, coming and going from the different floors, the prison lost its human face and became a deserted building with dark galleries and little altars of Our Lady Aparecida surrounded by flickering candles and plastic flowers.

Late at night, walking through these haunted corridors, with the silence broken by an anonymous cough, a cat's meow, or a door banging in the distance, I understood why men commit suicide in the morning, after nights of depression or claustrophobic panic, elbow-to-elbow with other men, unable to cry: 'Men who cry in jail don't deserve respect.'

Lupércio – who had grown up in an orphanage and, as a young man, had been a masseur with the famous São Paulo Futebol Clube before becoming a wholesale marijuana dealer – told me he'd lost count of how many had hung themselves from the bars on the windows, and thought that nights became calmer after intimate visits were allowed. 'It used to be worse. In the middle of the night you'd hear shoutin' that echoed through the whole prison. Then the men'd start beatin' their mugs on the bars. You could bet on it: someone had been raped.'

Weekends

By noon on Friday, there would be water in the cells, flooding the galleries and tumbling down the stairs. A strong smell of soap would fill the air and *pagode* and *sertanejo* music would mix in the corridor with the knocking of mops and brooms. The inmates would hang their clothes in the window, drag furniture about and hide the naked women.

Cleaners in rubber boots, under the watchful eye of that floor's head cleaner, would push the water down the stairs, while those following up the rear would dry the gallery. The cleaner in charge would move about among them, quickly and courteously, to ensure that not a single wet patch was left. On the stairs, the bubbling cascade would fall to the ground floor cage and flow into the black waters that another column of cleaners would push with mops along the path connecting the pavilions. In the words of the head cleaner of Pavilion Seven: 'It's all so visitors'll find us in a more appropriate environment in terms of hygiene and civilisation.'

Family members would start gathering at the prison doors in the small hours, the vast majority of them women. They were girlfriends, wives, sisters, aunts and the mothers who were inseparable from their sons, rarely abandoning them behind bars no matter how low they had sunk. Over the course of ten years, I saw so many demonstrations of motherly love that, I confess, I found wisdom in the saying 'the only true love is a mother's'.

An old lady with a bun in her hair and legs covered in varicose veins travelled 600 kilometres from the state of Paraná by bus every fifteen days, religiously, to visit her son, who had been sentenced to 120 years. Four years earlier, the fellow, at the invitation of a dealer friend of his, had gone into a house whose residents he didn't even know and murdered six people who had supposedly asked the police to shut down the drug den owned by his friend, across the street from their home. One Sunday, his mother begged a prison guard to look after her boy: 'I know my son did something wrong because of the company he kept, but when I look at him, I can't believe he took the lives of those people as they say he did. In my mind's eye I can still see him as a little boy in my arms, laughing.'

One Saturday, on the football pitch of Pavilion Eight, I saw Pirate's mother, a short, stout woman, on tiptoes waggling her index finger in his face. The chief of a gang that had raided ships at the entrance to the port of Santos, where they would attach a rope with a hook to the railing and use it to climb onto the ship carrying machine guns, Pirate listened to her scolding with his head down and hands clasped behind his back, as humble as a fullback before a yellow card.

Visitors to the prison came carrying plastic bags stuffed to the brim; plastic containers full of deep-fried pastries, potato salad, pasta, fried sausages and roast chicken. There wasn't the slightest concern with cholesterol: they only brought what the prisoners liked.

Visitors included many babies who were wrapped up warm, most conceived in the prison itself, in addition to older children bored by the waiting around with nothing to do.

It was an incredibly diverse population of poor people, who spent hours queuing: long-suffering elderly women, born-again Christians with braided hair, mothers, brunettes in tight jeans and platinum blondes who talked and strutted like the criminals themselves. Some arrived looking sad, with their children in tow. Others brought folding chairs and greeted the entire queue.

Because women will always find something in common to talk about, as the hours passed the queue would thicken into circles of women while the platoon of little devils would scamper among them, trip over, spill ice cream down their clothes and get reprimanding pinches from their mothers.

The sacrifice these people made was no small thing. Once, Mavi, the chief warder of Pavilion Nine, asked a group of prisoners who were complaining about the food: 'What are you complaining about? You don't have to work to eat; you get free medical treatment and medicine, which whether good or bad is a right that people who work don't have; when you mess up and a fellow prisoner decides to kill you, we transfer you to the security wing. The ones who do time are your families, who leave home before dawn with plastic bags, catch three different buses and, to top it off, scrape together the money they've earned with the sweat off their own backs for you lot to spend on crack.'

When the sun was high in the sky, a horde of itinerant street vendors would swoop in and portable barbecues would fill the air with smoke. They sold canned goods, biscuits, coconut sweets, snow cones, hot dogs and two-litre bottles of soft drinks. Stalls displayed T-shirts and used trainers, and would rent blazers to men (a requirement that was no longer enforced) or respectable dresses for the more scantily clothed women, because the atmosphere was one of decency.

Everywhere you looked there was someone selling packets of cigarettes, the official currency behind bars. The basic unit was a ten-pack of Commander, sold for seven *reais*. On the inside, each packet was worth fifty *centavos*; Hollywood and Marlboro cost double that. The value of a packet obeyed the law of supply and demand: when there were a lot of cigarettes in circulation, the price would fall; when they were scarce, it would go up. Because supply fluctuated according to the financial situation of families, who, in turn, reflected the country's economic situation, in periods of national crisis, visitors would bring in fewer cigarettes and the price would rise.

During the Collor Plan, when Brazilians' bank accounts were temporarily frozen, Xanto – an inmate who, when visiting his aunt, had shot not only his drunken uncle who'd had the unfortunate idea to beat her up in his presence, but also his two cousins who had gone to their father's aid; he had shot them all in the chest because, he recognised, not knowing how to shoot a man in the legs was one of his flaws – provided the following analysis: 'That'd never have happened among us. Just think, a young lady shows up and announces that our money, earned with the sweat off our backs, is frozen? She'd be a goner, Doctor, not even the thoughts in her mind'd be left when we were done with her.'

Pavilions Two, Five and Eight, on the left for those entering from the street, received visits on Sundays; the others, on Saturdays. On the last weekend of each month visits were allowed on both days.

The gates opened at seven, when the queue was already huge. Everyone had to pass through the body search room. The men's search was more superficial; the women were frisked by female employees who even looked inside their underwear and, when they were suspicious, would ask the woman to remove it and squat down to see if she had a foreign object in her vagina. No matter how tactful the friskers were, the search was always uncomfortable, especially for modest elderly women.

Until eleven o'clock, the queue would move quickly, so everyone could be out again before four o'clock, when the head count was conducted. On an average weekend, two to three thousand people would visit. When it was cold the numbers would drop, and rain would bring them down even further. At Easter, Mother's Day and Christmas, the crowd that gathered was enormous.

On the Monday afternoon just before Christmas of 1997, I arrived at the prison to tend to the sick and there was already a small queue with blankets, folding chairs and camp beds. They were women and children who, after the previous day's visit, hadn't returned home: they had set up camp there, to wait until the following weekend.

Over the next few days, the queue grew; they took turns eating takeaway food, using the bathrooms in local bars and changing babies' nappies right there, protected only by a makeshift asbestos roof that the prison administration had built over the pavement in more recent years.

That Friday after work, the prison employees went out for some beers. After midnight, as we left the bar, the queue had grown long, well past the shelter, passing the military police barracks and all the way down to the metro station.

A mulatta with a frank smile, Zilá, one of the first in line, was happy because her husband had had a take-away container of pasta that he had cooked in his cell sent to her, much to the envy of her friends in the queue. Zilá had four children, of whom only the oldest had been conceived with their father out of prison, six years earlier. That day, in order to keep Zilá company and to be introduced to a friend of her husband's, Fran – her thin, shy neighbour, who couldn't have been more than twenty years old – had arrived. Although she was going along with Fran's intentions, Zilá had warned her friend against it: 'What I tell Fran is if you want to meet Roberval I'll take you, but I don't wish this life for anyone – the weariness of queuin', the humiliation in the body search room, always being alone, missin' your man so badly, the children askin' when daddy's comin' home. A woman can only bear this life with a lot of love in her heart.'

Next to her, Fran, her face picked out of the penumbra by light from the lamp post, nodded her head, but she intended to spend the night there determined to meet Roberval, a moustached skirt-chaser who had been Zilá's husband's partner in his cargo-theft business.

Visitors entered the prison through small doors that opened straight onto the outside pavement, deposited their bags in front of the guard, who inspected them, and were then given a body search. It was an absurdly difficult task to search so many people; it would have taken days to do it thoroughly.

This strategic difficulty created opportunities for employees to come to an understanding with visitors and turn a blind eye to the entry of prohibited items, a risky procedure for those bringing them in and for those allowing them to pass. They were watched by their own co-workers, as one of them explained: 'Over two hundred people were hired at the same time as me. Ten years later, there are only five or six left. With this low salary, some are contaminated by crime and led astray. Except we never know who they are. You have to be suspicious of everyone, unfortunately.'

Later, I heard that the suspicious author of the words above, in turn, also aroused suspicion among his co-workers. According to Dr Walter Hoffgen, the director general, 'The hardest thing in a prison is identifying those who are involved with the inmates.'

Visitors who smuggled drugs into the prison ran great risks. When caught, they were taken to the closest police station, where they were charged with trafficking, for which there was no bail. One Sunday, I saw a young lady of nineteen being escorted out of the facility in tears; she had been caught smuggling in twenty grams of cocaine for her boyfriend. On another occasion, prison administration unexpectedly replaced a guard on the door and surprised a visitor bringing in thirty-two kilos of marijuana in two plastic bags. The seizure caused internal problems: 'It left us doing cold turkey. As a result, the price of crack went up.'

The women who brought in drugs did it to get their

partners or sons out of trouble or so they could support their families from behind bars.

The warders who worked on the doors were like sniffer dogs with extra-sensory perception. One of them, a large mulatto with a gentle gaze, used the following technique: 'I search the bags, but I don't neglect the queue. When I notice someone acting unnatural, I give them a quick look in the eye, then again. As she (I say she because it's almost always women who bring stuff in) gets closer, my stare grows longer. By the time she puts the bags on the table, I don't even look at them. My eyes are boring into hers. The ones who've got something to hide can't hack it. They give themselves away.'

Others would hold out their hand to greet the visitor with a handshake and feel if it was cold, shaky or sweaty. Looking out of the corners of their eyes, not a single detail of the person would go unnoticed: their clothes, their hard-to-hide swagger, a tattoo, their demeanour and the slang they used: 'If the girl walks up and says, "Hey, big boy," I know she's dodgy!'

A keen sense of smell was a powerful ally of those who guarded the exit: the smell of prison seeped into the inmates. It was an odour that was hard to define. It seemed to be a mixture of several: fried garlic, musty cleaning rags, sweat and a dash of disinfectant. Although it couldn't be classified as horrible, it was unpleasant. Hot and heavy. It was so relentless that whenever the warders opened the crowded Solitary

Confinement cells, they would never stand right at the entrance: 'Don't stand in front of the door, Doctor. The stench sticks to your clothes and doesn't come out in the wash.'

Visit days required that the guards pay extra attention. Leaving disguised as a visitor is a traditional escape strategy. Once, an inmate changed out of his beige trousers and into a pair of jeans and left with a group of employees. The guard on the door got a little confused, as so many people worked in the Casa de Detenção.

'What group are you from?'

'I'm from such-and-such a group, I'm here as back-up.'

'Did Raimundo authorise it?'

'Of course he did!'

'Well, con, you're in a fix now, 'cause there's no one here by the name of Raimundo!'

Another prisoner, small in stature and using the same disguise, came face to face with an enormous guard, whom I once heard answer the phone identifying himself modestly as the 'Black Prince of the Door'. His Highness thought the short inmate looked a little pale.

'What group are you in?'

'Group one.'

'And your number?'

'Number one.'

'All number ones! What's going on?'

These cases, which later become a part of the prison folklore, were punished with thirty days in Solitary, but no one got mad about them. 'If he comes in peace, fine, it's his right. If he hasn't jeopardised anyone, he's treated with respect. It's his job to escape, and ours to not let him. He goes to Solitary for the standard time. But if he tries to use force, like one who stuck me up at the gate with a cocked revolver pointed at my head, but was caught before he could get to the corner, well, that's another kettle of fish. Unfortunately, he was asking for it.'

Dealing with the queue required social tact. The guards had to be patient with people who were upset, help elderly and pregnant women, and be firm with the rude ones. Many knew the natural ringleaders and, through them, were able to tranquillise the others in moments of tension. It was a task for skilled professionals, who suffered from the psychological impact of their work, as the guard with the gentle gaze once told me: 'My co-workers think I'm tolerant. To them I might be, but my family complains that I've changed. I used to be a homebody, calm, I visited my godmother every day, chatted. But after twelve hours on this job, I get home with a hot head, eat quietly and go to bed. I don't even remember my godmother exists.'

Intimate Visits

The origins of intimate visits were nebulous. They were said to have started in the early 1980s, surreptitiously, with inmates who would improvise tents in the pavilion courtyards on visiting days. Others – mercenary types – would push two long benches together, cover them with blankets and rent the space under them to couples so they could get intimate.

At the time, the authorities turned a blind eye, convinced that those moments of privacy would appease that week's violence. When the first complaints about minors who had become pregnant in these furtive encounters began to arise, it became evident that the situation had got out of control. Unable to put an end to the privilege already acquired, they decided to make intimate visits official: women of age were allowed in their partners' cells, as long as they had been previously registered with ID and photographs. In this manner, in the best style of Vargas Llosa's Pantaleón and his lady visitors, sex was bureaucratised in São

Paulo's Casa de Detenção and the system spread throughout the country.

Each inmate had the right to register one woman. Wife, mistress or girlfriend – legal ties were not required. In the case of a break-up, another one could only be enrolled after six months. With a little diplomacy, however, this period was sometimes substantially reduced. There were over two thousand women in the programme at any given time.

The routine was thorough: after being frisked, they headed for the pavilion, where the men were waiting in freshly pressed clothes, combed hair and scent. On the ground floor, at a table by the door to the stairs, was a warder with a box of registration cards. The couples would line up in front of the table, the woman would hand over her ID card and the warder would check the photo, attach the ID to the woman's registration card with a paper clip and keep it until she left. From that door in, there were no warders; the inmates managed their own visits.

In the more populous pavilions, such as Five, Eight and Nine, the inner courtyards would become so crowded that inmates without visitors avoided going there to make more room, and because they couldn't stay in the cells occupied by couples, they would wait standing in the corridor. The galleries were full of men.

People unfamiliar with the prison probably imagine that the stronger men would take the weaker men's women in these corridors, full of criminals leaning against the walls. Nothing could have been further from the truth: the place was more respectful than a nunnery. When a couple walked past, everyone would look down. It was not enough to look away; the men had to bow their heads. No one dared disobey this procedural rule, no matter whether a woman was a man's wife, fiancée or a prostitute.

On one occasion, Genésio, a Northeasterner with a lisp who had blown the proceeds of over one hundred robberies in nightclubs, recognised a prostitute he had been with: 'A mate was walking along with his arm around her shoulders. I turned to face the wall so she wouldn't see me and show any sign of recognition. See what a gentleman I was, Doctor!'

If only one resident of a cell had a visitor, all of the time available was his; if there were several, the time was divided equally. There was no need to knock on the door; the men were highly punctual. In larger cells, with twenty or thirty men, where they had no choice but to use the cells at the same time, they would improvise private spaces by hanging blankets. To drown out the more enthusiastic demonstrations of female pleasure, they would turn up the volume on their radios.

Those without visitors could rent out their cells to more fortunate inmates: 'Nothing's free in a prison.'

If an inmate could afford it and knew a few people in the right places, it was even possible to receive a visitor in another pavilion, a stratagem used to receive the wife in the original cell, on the Saturday, and the girlfriend in another pavilion with Sunday visits. There were not enough warders to deter infidelity.

Due to an unfathomable mystery of the female psyche, many men found girlfriends while doing time. Once, an inspector general, after examining so many requests involving inmates and their women, complained to the director general, 'What do they have that we don't?'

Many women would come to visit a relative and were introduced to a friend of his. Others would answer letters in women's magazines and would be invited to meet the author, invariably a fellow with good principles who had made an error of judgement and hoped to find the strength to turn over a new leaf with a woman's love.

Visitors felt protected there. By removing the warders from inside the pavilions, administration had wisely handed over the management of visits to the only ones capable of ensuring total security. Men behind bars are terrified of losing their lady loves.

Not-a-Hope, an experienced thief, spoke of the cunning of a 'Ricardão', a generic name for a woman's lover: 'If visits aren't respectful, Doctor,' he told me, 'they'll be afraid to come back, and then one girl'll tell the next one about somethin' unfortunate that happened to her and before you know it: "I'm not goin' there no more!" "If you're not, I'm not, it's dangerous!" And there you go. Here we'll be, frothin' at the mouth, and they'll be havin' a good time on the outside, 'cause there's a Ricardão on every corner, ready to exploit the fragility of a lonely woman. Not a hope.'

An inmate had to know how to proceed: he could never covet another man's woman and order had to be kept at all times. No offence was considered small; the slightest slip was very serious.

A moustached con artist once struck his wife during a visit and her cries were heard in the neighbouring cells. The wife-beater was lucky that a warder, minutes later, heard three men in the courtyard plotting to kill him as soon as visiting hours were over, and immediately had him transferred to Yellow, where those sworn to death are sent.

This strategy was only partially successful: in the early hours of the following morning, right there in the high security wing, the man was stabbed twice. He was taken to the Mandaqui Hospital in a critical condition, underwent surgery, spent four days in intensive care, lost eighty centimetres of intestine and was given a colostomy, but came out alive. 'He got lucky!' said the inmates.

Although women of all ages participated in the programme, the majority were young. At the exit, one couldn't help but notice the number of young women with babies. Many left with their hair wet, from the shower they had taken in the cell.

Slamming

My work at the Casa de Detenção started with the diagnosis of an epidemic. From May to August of 1990, we took blood samples from 2492 inmates and conducted an epidemiological survey about sexual practices and drug use, among other things.

In the morning, when they opened the cells, the warders would call seventy to eighty men, who were escorted to Pavilion Four and made to wait in the locked ground-floor cage, so they wouldn't come into contact with their enemies in that pavilion. In groups of ten, they were taken from the cage to the laboratory to have their blood taken and to answer our survey.

The study was carried out with the decisive assistance of six prisoners from Pavilion Four. Among them were those in charge of taking blood, former users of injectable cocaine for whom it was never impossible to find a vein; when there were no other options, they could access invisible ones in elbows. The most skilful of them all – a guy with curly hair and darting eyes who laughed at the wrong times, doing time for conducting robberies with the wife of his best friend, who wanted to kill him when he found out – modestly justified my praise of his technique: 'Doctor, for someone who's shot up coke in the dark with a blunt needle washed in rainwater drippin' from a roof, takin' blood with this disposable material that you bring could even be considered cowardice on our part.'

The results showed that 17.3 per cent of the inmates of the Casa de Detenção were HIV-positive. Among them we identified two significant risk factors: the injecting of cocaine and the number of sexual partners in the year before the survey. In addition to these inmates, we studied a group of eighty-two transvestites doing time at the prison, of whom 78 per cent tested positive. Of those who had been in the prison for more than six years, 100 per cent were positive.

While working with the transvestites, we came across Sheila, sentenced to three years and two months for having bought electrical appliances as wedding presents for an ex-boyfriend – with whom she was still in love – with a cheque book stolen from a Protestant pastor who had picked her up. With her enormous breasts and blouse knotted above her navel, Sheila confessed, in the presence of witnesses, to having had more than a thousand sexual partners in the Casa de Detenção in the year prior to our study. With them she had had unprotected passive anal sex, the sexual practice associated with the highest risk of AIDS transmission. She was HIV-negative. Her test was repeated and confirmed at the Laboratório Bioquímico in São Paulo and the retrovirology department of the Cleveland Clinic in the United States, showing that some people do not become infected even after extensive exposure to the virus.

Almost simultaneously, a group from the University of São Paulo conducted a similar study with prisoners the day they arrived in Pavilion Two for distribution. The results obtained were very similar to ours, suggesting that the vast majority had become infected on the outside, before they were incarcerated. At the time, shooting up cocaine was the latest trend. Warders would find syringes around the prison and punish the owners. After riot squad searches, there were always piles of used syringes alongside the knives seized.

Chocolate – an unlucky thief who had unwittingly burgled his drug-dealing uncle's girlfriend's house and been beaten with a chain for his mistake, and then burgled another, not knowing that it belonged to the son of a district chief of police – once told me about a riot squad visit: 'They came with dogs and tommies. They opened our cell and told us to walk out naked, place our hands on the gallery wall and not look 'em in the face. They found a spike with blood still in it under Scratchy's bed. They didn't even ask whose it was – they just started layin' into us with their batons, with the German shepherds going wild.'

Repression, contradictorily, favoured the spread of hepatitis and AIDS, since it encouraged the communal use of syringes and needles, which were rented or sold already full of the drug to users who injected it in fractions proportional to how much they had paid, without any precautions whatsoever, with the needle passing directly from one arm to the next.

With a used Bic pen and an old flip-flop, Chico Ladeira – a softly spoken burglar married to a beautiful woman of whom he was extremely jealous, who had been caught by armed security guards while robbing a Universal Church temple – made good money manufacturing syringes. 'I get the Bic and take out the inside tube. I heat up a hypodermic needle, which I get by my own personal means, and slot it into the tip of the pen. Then I heat it to melt the plastic around it. I make the plunger with a little piece of round rubber that I cut out of a flip-flop strap, attached to a section of hard wire. I guarantee its sturdiness. If it leaks you can bring it back and I'll give you a new one.'

Many bore on their arms the stigma of addiction: hardened veins and scars from abscesses. In addition to casual users, there were the IVers, enslaved to their addiction, looking forever startled in the galleries, glancing over their shoulders, from side to side and even at the ceiling, as if something was about to fall on their heads, victims of the persecution complex that dogs chronic cocaine users.

Scratchy – who earned his nickname because a friend

had seen him in the red light district asking a prostitute to scratch his back – described this delirium:

> I used to slam coke at a friend's place. He was shacked up with a woman who was ugly as sin. When we was both straight, everything was cool. But the minute we shot up he'd get all paranoid that we had to get out of there, or I'd fuck his girl. We'd run 'til we was out of breath, then we'd come down and think straight: what's all this about, man? Then we'd head back to his place, normal, best of friends, and shoot up again. The paranoia would all come back and we'd have to run again. When the snow was really good, we'd get back so tired that we'd drop to the ground like idiots, knackered.

The situation was serious. There was an epidemic of cocaine slamming in the prison, a reflection of the epidemic spreading through the poorer districts of São Paulo and other Brazilian cities.

Once, while filming an educational video, I watched a group slamming cocaine, sitting around a table in an abandoned warehouse. There were four participants: a black Jamaican, recently released from prison, who said he had been unfairly arrested when visiting some Columbian friends from Medellin in a small hotel on Rua Aurora; a second-generation Arab who looked older than his years; a thin Brazilian with rotting teeth, father of two, who used to hold up metro ticket booths; and a Japanese-Brazilian who was a member of the mafia involved in white slavery in the nightclubs of Liberdade, São Paulo's Asian neighbourhood.

Each one arrived holding a little package of cocaine rolled up in wax paper and a small syringe with a fine needle, the ones diabetics use to inject insulin, essential to avoid leaving marks on one's arms. They placed three glasses in the centre of the table: one empty, another full of tap water and a third with boiled water; in the middle of these was a thoroughly washed soup spoon.

The Jamaican filled a third of the syringe from the glass of boiled water, while the sex-slave trader poured a dose of cocaine onto the dry spoon. The Jamaican emptied the syringe into the spoon and used the syringe cap to mix the powder and liquid, praising the quality of the cocaine, which was dissolving easily. On his right, the sex-slave trader silently squeezed the muscles of his arm, staring at the veins that were beginning to pop out.

The Jamaican used the syringe to draw up the cocaine diluted on the spoon and slowly pressed the needle into the sex-slave trader's arm, until his blood flowed back red. In a part of the ritual with which I was un-familiar, he injected only a quarter of the contents of the syringe and used the plunger to draw back an amount of blood equal to that of the liquid injected. He repeated this operation of injecting and drawing back several times. The sex-slave trader kept his bulging eyes trained on the syringe, fascinated by the blood flowing into and out of his arm. The whole episode lasted two or three minutes, after which the sex-slave trader got up and started talking non-stop, while the second-generation Arab made the veins of his forearm pop out.

The procedure was repeated in silence with the other two participants: the dilution of the powder on the spoon, the slow introduction of the needle, the blood flowing in and out, eyes staring at the syringe, and the concomitant agitation and monologues.

To my surprise, however, the effect of the injection was ephemeral. The Jamaican was still holding the needle in the vein of the father of two, the third in the circle, and the anxious sex-slave trader was already tapping his arm again. While he was taking his second dose, it was the second-generation Arab's turn to get agitated, after the father of two and so on, in a growing frenzy that only ended when the last speck of powder had been consumed.

After the first round, before starting the second, the Jamaican washed the bloody syringe in the glass with tap water and squirted it into the empty glass. After repeating this cleaning operation twice, he filled the syringe again from the glass of boiled water to dilute the new dose of powder on the spoon. In the end, the glass of tap water was almost dry and the one that had been empty contained a solution tinged with blood.

It was a field day for the HIV virus. Although each

one had brought his own syringe, all it would take was for someone in the group to be infected with the virus for it to spread through the water used to wash the syringes and also contaminate the spoon that everyone was using. This may explain why I later found so many former users with AIDS who swore they'd never shared needles.

When it was over, the group continued talking without stopping or listening, their mouths dry from the effect of the alkaloid injected so many times. In the end, as we packed up the equipment, I saw the father of two pick up the glass with the bloody solution and raise it to his lips, without anyone around him paying the slightest attention.

'Don't drink that!' I shouted.

He didn't understand and started drinking the liquid thick with blood. He drank at least half the glass before I could grab his arm.

'Look what you're drinking! That's pure blood!'

'Ah! I didn't notice, I thought it was water.'

In the Cinema

Then came the talks in the cinema. The Casa de Detenção had an enormous hall with a cement floor on the second floor of Pavilion Six, with a seating capacity of over a thousand, where a cinema had operated before it was destroyed in a rebellion. We took three or four hundred men there, set up a screen with sound equipment, showed educational videos about AIDS and I answered questions from the audience.

Moving so many men from their pavilion to the cinema and getting them back unscathed wasn't simple. The operation, led by Waldemar Gonçalves, the head of the sports department, started at eight o'clock in the morning. The cells on the floors whose occupants were going to hear the talk were unlocked before the others and the inmates headed for Pavilion Six. Afterwards, at about eleven, they walked back in an orderly fashion.

Week after week, for years, hundreds of prisoners came and went, often crossing paths with mortal enemies, and there wasn't a single incident. Among the inmates, there was a pact of respect for the Friday cinema.

Hernani – a forger, or '171'[1], as the inmates liked to call him, who bragged that he was more dangerous with a pen than his mates with a revolver – explained this calm: 'You, Luís and Ricardo come to do somethin' good for us. If some fool causes trouble, tries to settle a score with someone, or does somethin' silly, he'll be affectin' the general wellbein'. And that'll be a problem! He'd have to really hate being alive.'

The men came in groups. Most, as a matter of principle, would go straight to the back and sit on the floor, even if there was plenty of space on the benches up front. On the screen, as they were entering, we showed videos of popular singers. They listened attentively, keeping time by discreetly swinging their feet. They would never dance or move their bodies: 'When have you ever seen convicts dancin' in front of each other?'

At around nine, we'd stop the music, turn on the lights and I would get up on the stage to say: 'Attention, inmates, there's an AIDS epidemic in the house. Your mates grow thin and weak, then they go to the infirmary in Four and never return. We're going to show a video and then answer questions about the disease. Save any comments for later. Nothing is sadder in a man's life than ending his days in jail.'

---

[1] The number of the article of the Brazilian penal code that deals with fraud.

During the first few talks, Florisval, the director of correctional services, would stand on the stage, with his back to me, and glare at the audience. One day, I told him not to worry and I was left alone with the inmates. It worked; I began to relate to them better.

While the AIDS video was showing, chatting could sometimes be heard from the back of the room. One morning, during the screening, in the dark, I decided to cross the cinema and sit among them at the back, just to see if the talking would stop.

I went, driven by a rational feeling of confidence, but I was afraid. I slowly walked across the cinema. When I got to the back rows, the talking stopped. I sat on the ground, in the middle of the inmates, and watched the video. My hands were cold and my heart was beating fast. I felt as if someone might jump at me from behind and strangle me. I controlled my fear and stuck it out to the end. Then I got up and returned to the stage with no hurry. On my way there, I noticed that the walk wasn't exactly mine: it had a touch of swagger from the streets of Brás, where I had grown up. The following week, I repeated the experiment. The fear came back much less intense. The third time, it was gone.

Once the video was over, I would answer the questions asked on a microphone taken to the inmates by Santista – a thief who claimed to have enjoyed life: he'd be the last one to leave a nightclub, he'd buy drinks for everyone, then he'd go snort cocaine in a motel with the strippers and, being the generous sort, would cover their bodies with stolen money.

The questions the inmates raised were concrete. AIDS for them wasn't a theoretical concern, it was a practical problem. They wanted to know what to do if they came into contact with the bodily secretions of someone who was sick, the risk of transmission to family members, the first symptoms and the time the disease took to develop.

After answering the last question, I would summarise three essential ideas in two minutes at the most. First: solidarity with a sick cellmate didn't present a risk because AIDS wasn't transmitted through casual contact. Second: without a condom, the virus could pass from a man to a woman and from a woman to a man, and in homosexual relations the active partner was also at risk. Third: everyone who shot up cocaine was going to catch the virus; it was just a matter of time.

At the end, I would add in an evangelical tone of voice: if you can't escape the hell of cocaine addiction, swallow it, use it in a suppository form, smoke it, but don't shoot it up, for God's sake!

My recommendation that they substitute injectable cocaine was left until last because, at the end, when I insisted that they smoke it rather than inject it, they would break into a round of applause permeated by long whistles, which created a dramatic atmosphere for my exit from the hall.

At the time, this last message about injectable cocaine

was given like that because I felt it was ridiculous, in that place, to repeat naïve slogans such as 'say no to drugs'. The reason for so much applause, however, I would only fully understand much later, when it became clear that crack was going to sweep cocaine out of the prison.

The task of getting hundreds of prisoners out of bed by eight o'clock in the morning to watch an educational video followed by medical recommendations, considered unrealistic by more experienced staff members, was decisively facilitated by Hernani – a grey-haired gentleman who had specialised in a scam in which he would open bogus firms to then bankrupt them and skip out on debts: 'Doctor, waking up these louts is a problematic problem. Why don't you show an erotic video at the end of the programme? In their current state of deprivation, they'll pack out the cinema.'

We did a test. At the end, after I left the hall, an explicit sex video was shown. The strategy of combining music, preventive medicine and sex was a box office success. It could work in other prisons, as long as certain precautions are taken: no one should be allowed to only watch the last video, because the programme is an indivisible package, and, most importantly, the erotic film should only start when the doctor has left the room.

As early as the first few talks, I was surprised by the respect that the men showed me. In their questions they used terms and expressions such as 'anal sex', 'penetration', 'prostitution', 'homosexuals' and 'prison wives' – never slang, much less four-letter words. On one occasion, when I interrupted a video of the singer Daniela Mercury to put on the AIDS video, three or four men at the back of the hall whistled like high-school students messing around. It took Waldemar Gonçalves a great deal of work to convince the men who helped set up the equipment not to stab the whistlers for their antics. Santão, a muscular mulatto doing eighteen years for bank robbery, who helped set up the sound equipment, was one of the angriest: 'What's with those guys? Do they want to make fun of the doctor who comes to raise awareness about the dangers of this evil and give us all a bit of recreation? They're not disrespecting the doctor, they're disrespecting us!'

The following week, before the talk started, Benê – the son of an alcoholic who hated drunks and had shot two of them in a bakery because they were bothering a young lady he didn't even know; respected enough among the inmates to referee the last game of the internal football tournament that year – approached me accompanied by three young men:

'Doctor, the boys here want to have a chat with you.'

The oldest of the three, who had lost his left eye as the result of a stray bullet when he was a teenager, spoke with his head down and his hands clasped behind his back:

'Speaking on behalf of myself and my mates here, we came to say we're very sorry for the whistling. We didn't mean no harm, but if it upset our comrades, we're not gonna cause trouble.'

This atmosphere of sincere respect towards the doctor who had brought them a little help heightened my sense of responsibility towards them. After over twenty years of clinical experience, it was among those considered the dregs of society that I fully realised the importance of the figure of the doctor in the collective consciousness, one of the mysteries of my profession.

Rita Cadillac

We held an AIDS-prevention poster contest sponsored by the Paulista University, with a prize of $1000-worth of cigarette packets, the local currency, shared among the five winners. Sports department head Waldemar Gonçalves and a group of inmates from the pavilions' cultural centres handed out white poster paper and black marker pens. Copies of the best posters were later displayed throughout the prison.

The winning artist drew a condom with a syringe dripping with blood inside it. At the bottom, it said: 'You can avoid AIDS.'

I had seen numerous AIDS posters before, but never had I seen anyone so skilfully bring together the idea of condoms and syringes in a single message. Our winner was a thin fellow with awful teeth who had stopped studying in primary school and was doing five years for small robberies, which he had committed with an older cousin.

The prizes were presented on a hot afternoon in the

cinema in Six. Over one thousand inmates were present. To brighten up the ceremony, Waldemar had invited Rita Cadillac, the former singer-dancer who had mesmerised the men on TV on Saturday nights. The inmates' band Reunidos por Acaso played.

After the fifth song, the master of ceremonies, Demétrio – an elderly man with a bald head and a ring on his pinky, addicted to the horse races – announced:

'Dear inmates of this penal establishment, your humble presenter here is honoured to introduce a great television artist, unparalleled in the art of dance, who danced and sang on the programme of the great Chacrinha, may he rest in peace. On this festive occasion, I would like to invite up to the stage the muse of the Casa de Detenção: Rita Cadillac!'

He drew out the last syllables of the artist's first and last names interminably.

In a short skirt, Rita climbed the stairs to the stage, breasts swaying in her half-open blouse. There was howling and whistling in the audience. She looked at them with a naughty smile, signalled to the musicians and began to dance samba with incredible sensuality and rhythm.

The excited crowd shouted. 'Turn around! Turn around, Rita, for the love of God!' She pretended not to understand and continued her provocative dance facing the begging men, at the most turning slightly to the side. 'Turn around, the way we like it! Turn around, Rita, just once!' When the shouting reached a crescendo,

Rita, with her black skirt and schoolgirl way, pressed her index finger to her lips and with the other made an imaginary circle in the air, as if confirming the inmates' request. 'That's it, turn around! C'mon, Rita, kill us!' Perspiring, with two buttons undone, she finally did her fans' bidding.

The clamouring stopped immediately. There was total silence.

With her back to the enraptured audience, to the rhythm of the song by the Reunidos por Acaso, she began sinuously moving her hips in growing circles. When the movement couldn't get any bigger, Rita Cadillac, with one hand behind her head and the other beneath her navel, gradually bent her knees without letting up the movement, until her thighs were parallel to the stage. She stayed swaying in this position for a long time, in high heels and with a straight back. Then she began her ascent. Halfway up, when her thighs were at a forty-five-degree angle to the stage, her backside suddenly stopped mid-air for a few seconds. With her face in profile, chin on her shoulder, left hand lifting her hair off her moist neck, she finally jerked her hips backwards and upwards and, with great poise, danced off towards the *pandeiro* player, to the delirium of the inmates, who almost brought the old cinema down. With all due respect.

Tumult in Divinéia

Often, after talks, inmates would stop me in the halls to tell me about their health problems. They complained of night sweats, feeling weak, swollen lymph nodes, coughs, skin lesions and venereal diseases. They were thin, short of breath and had symptoms characteristic of the advanced stages of AIDS.

It was impossible to resolve their cases in those on-the-spot consultations, palpate necks, or examine inflamed throats or genital sores amid a throng of curious onlookers. There was no way I could avoid those consultations or not be drawn into their individual dramas. Sometimes, something as banal as oral thrush, common in babies' mouths and easily cured with a few pills, was stopping the man from swallowing his own saliva. People with symptoms suggestive of tuberculosis self-medicated themselves with useless vitamins and wormseed, a plant said to have medicinal properties.

The medical assistance in the prison was unprepared to deal with an epidemic of that scale. There were ten

doctors, if that, to care for 7000 prisoners. The low salaries and lack of decent working conditions had corroded
the spirits of most to such an extent that few of this
already small group carried out their work honourably.

In those days, I would leave the prison feeling a
mixture of impotence and guilt. On the one hand, I was
unable to forget the sunken eyes of the sick; on the
other, what did I have to do with it all? Wasn't it enough
that I already volunteered my time to give talks and
risked circulating in that environment? Additionally,
many of the men whose facial expressions moved me
as a doctor had quite possibly never shown mercy to
their defenceless victims.

There were two solutions to my impasse: to stop
going to the prison or to find time to treat the sick, in an
organised fashion.

The second alternative won. That world had worked
its way under my skin and it was too late to try and
escape it. As a doctor, it wasn't my place to judge my
patients' crimes; society had judges trained for that.
Besides, practising medicine in that place with only a
stethoscope, like the physicians of old, after so many
years of clinical practice supported by laboratorial
exams and X-ray images, was a challenge.

One winter morning, I made my way up to the fifth
floor of Pavilion Four to work out the details with Dr
Mário Mustaro, head of the prison's medical service,
who, coincidentally, had been my biochemistry teacher
at university. We talked about the internal bureaucracy,

the most prevalent pathologies, and I met my first nurse, Edelso, a guy with a middle-class demeanour, doing time for automobile theft and practising medicine without a licence. We were in the middle of this conversation when a staff member came in.

'Doctors,' he said, 'you need to get out quick. Three inmates have taken a hostage over in Five and are coming towards Divinéia.'

On the stairs, the head doctor, who had been in the public service for over thirty years, said to me, 'See what it's like? The facilities are primitive, we're lacking in supplies, medicine, personnel, everything, and when someone wants to extend a helping hand, they run into the problem of discipline. Want my advice? Don't waste your time here.'

When we got downstairs, he headed for the exit while I, curious to see the tumult, found a pretext to stay behind with a guard, who explained what was happening.

Three prisoners from Yellow, each with his own knife, had taken a warder hostage, telling him, 'This is how it works, boss: if you try anything, you're dead!'

With the warder at knifepoint, they had made their way to the ground floor and left the pavilion. The other prisoners stood back to allow them passage through the courtyard. At the door between pavilions Five and Two, the guard realised the situation his colleague was in and said, 'The three of you can go through and I'll lock up again. The rest are staying!'

It took a while to unlock. Meanwhile, there was enough time to bring in the inmates who had been in the Pavilion Two courtyard and close the internal cage.

A short, stocky mulatto with his shirt unbuttoned was holding the hostage's left arm behind his back with one hand and pressing a thirty-centimetre blade against his thorax with the other. A white inmate with unkempt hair and no teeth was doing the same thing on the right side, so that the ashen-faced warder had his arms crossed behind his body and a knife at either side of his chest. The third man, muscular from weight-lifting, was pulling the hostage along by his shirt collar while pressing a knife to the underside of his chin.

They walked along the path connecting the pavilions, and stopped in front of the gate to Two, which led into Divinéia. At this point, on top of the wall, three military police officers were closing in nervously, ready to fire. Inside Divinéia, a group of older warders took up position.

Negotiations to open the door to Divinéia were tense; by this time blood was streaming from the underside of the hostage's chin. The inmates were demanding to be transferred to another prison, while the police officers were waiting for an opportunity to open fire, and the warders, to jump on them. There were death threats on both sides, a locked door, shouting and indecision.

When the order was finally given, only the small pedestrian door was opened – a passage that was narrow for two, impossible for four. The warders forming a circle around the gate stepped back to allow them through.

The muscular inmate went first with his knife under the hostage's chin; the two on either side hung back. Big mistake. A police officer on the wall cocked his gun. At the sound, the mulatto ducked in reflex. The toothless one, behind him, was forced to stop. As if rehearsed, two gun barrels sang in the air. Startled, the muscular inmate turned around, relaxing the arm holding the bloody knife. It was a fatal error. The hostage grabbed his kidnapper's arm and immobilised the weapon.

A crowd of men in jeans formed around the three prisoners. It was impossible to see details.

When everything had calmed down, the hostage, as white as wax, his face contorted with pain, was carried away by his colleagues, with his right foot having been fractured in revenge. The mulatto and the muscular inmate, bruised and battered, were carted off in a trolley used to transport pans of food. The toothless one, his shirt in tatters, blood running down his front, right eye swollen closed, incapable of taking two steps in a straight line, accompanied the trolley. Seeing him stumbling towards the infirmary, a warder who had just arrived from Divinéia shouted:

'Still walking, scumbag? My colleagues went easy on you!'

Welcome

The week after the attempted transfer, I returned to Pavilion Four.

The lift was broken, so I took the stairs to the fifth floor, followed the corridor and came out in the infirmary. It was a gallery with twelve cells on one side and ten on the other, a kitchen at the end of the corridor on the left, a large bathroom with more tiles missing than still on the walls and three electric showers, of which only one actually heated the water.

Under this one, with the water falling in thick drops, a shirtless prisoner who looked like a boxer was rubbing a soapy rag on the skeletal back of a patient while holding him by the armpit with his other hand to keep him standing. The patient had an extensive, red sore on his face that covered the whole right side of his forehead, eyelids and cheeks, caused by shingles, an opportunistic virus frequent in AIDS patients. The boxer-nurse holding up the sick man with the disfigured face was like a scene from a horror film.

The rooms were, in fact, ordinary cells painted baby blue on the bottom half and white on the top half, high-ceilinged, well lit during the day and dimly lit by night. Inside each was a metal trundle bed with a foam mattress cut with a knife, a toilet, a sink and nothing else. On the wall opposite the heavy door, there was a barred window with a broken pane.

In the scant space between the bed and the wall, the patients would pile up a few items of clothes, a pair of trainers, flip-flops, plastic bags of food, bananas, stale bread and coffee mugs.

Some looked in good health; they were recovering from surgery after shoot-outs, knifings, orthopaedic problems, burns from having boiling water poured over them by their enemies, crises of bronchitis and dermatitis. Others, thin from the tuberculosis that was epidemic in the prison, wandered about in Bermuda shorts and flip-flops, filling the gallery with coughing fits and Koch's bacillus. On the beds, rolled up in blankets, lay men with fevers, breathing difficulties, the insides of their mouths covered in thrush, bodies wasting away and wet with their own urine. They were in the terminal stages of AIDS and had the resigned gaze that death imposes when it comes slowly.

With Edelso and two other inmates, I did my first round. At the end, I entered a room where a young car thief, who was just skin and bones, was coughing uncontrollably and spitting out a bloody secretion. The floor was covered with bright red phlegm; there was nowhere to walk.

'You can't spit like that!' I said. 'You've got tuberculosis. Anyone who comes in here will step in it and spread the illness through the whole infirmary.'

'Doctor, if I was coughin' less and felt stronger, I'd be able to spit into the sink, but like this, barely breathin', I just can't.'

The nurses and I stopped outside the infirmary, along with other curious passers-by. I explained to them that the tuberculosis bacillus was present in phlegm and that the invisible droplets were released into the air by coughing, and that the risk of it being transmitted in that environment was real, including to ourselves.

I finished writing out prescriptions, gave a few instructions and said goodbye. One of the nurses, Juliano – a big, moustached man with a limp, who had been shot in an ambush in which his brother and another partner had lost their lives – walked me to the lift and said, 'Goodnight, Doctor. Will you be coming back?'

I went home afraid of catching tuberculosis.

Making a Difference

In those days, I had twenty years of clinical experience with critical and terminal patients, and I felt familiar with the prison environment. Even so, I was shocked. I spent the week introspective and uninterested in social events, with memories of the infirmary popping into my mind from time to time. My wife said she'd never seen me so quiet.

My introspection, however, didn't reflect the sadness that perhaps I should have felt, as a doctor, faced with that human misery. The perspective of delving deeply into the criminal world, although frightening, fascinated me so much that, to be honest, I was happy, excited about my work and in love with medicine, a profession as demanding as a jealous lover, capable of provoking unexpected crises of passion in me my whole life.

I began to study tuberculosis, which I hadn't treated since the 1970s when we thought it would be completely eradicated in Brazil in the near future. For many years, whenever I remembered the prison, I recognised inner sensations that reminded me of my childhood chasing balloons in the district of Brás. Life pulsed stronger there.

I returned the following week and called together my trio of helpers: Edelso, the fake doctor; Juliano, with the limp, specialised in banks and armoured cars; and Pedrinho, with a thick beard, mysterious past and three bullets lodged in his thorax, who was sentenced to twenty-two years. Before going to the infirmary, I taught them how to administer the medication for tuberculosis and look after the patients. They listened with interest, asked questions and made suggestions on ways to improve the care given.

The atmosphere was very different to that of the previous week. Several patients said their coughing and night sweats were improving and they were feeling better overall. When we visited the guy who had been spitting blood, he was sitting up in bed, dunking a bread roll in a cup of white coffee. Another, with AIDS-associated pneumonia, in agony from shortness of breath the previous week, was slowly walking around the gallery.

From cell to cell, from late morning until mid-afternoon, I examined the patients. The three nurses accompanied me and went without lunch, entirely focused. As we left, there was a feeling of professional respect between us. I left thirsty, as I hadn't had the courage to drink the tap water.

The next week, on my way to the infirmary, sitting on the bench by the door to the consulting room, half a dozen inmates were waiting. One of them, who had been bodyguard to a drug baron in the Rio de Janeiro *favela* of Rocinha, whose arms were covered with sores that he scratched incessantly, approached me:

'With your permission, Doctor, we know you come here to treat the guys in the infirmary with HIV, but me and my friends from Eight here are in a bad way. Some of us have fevers and feel weak, others have body itches that won't let us sleep. So we've come to appeal to your goodwill to help us out.'

They were visibly in need of help. Of the six, four were in advanced stages of tuberculosis, one had a set of peculiar neurological symptoms and the bodyguard with the itch had dermatological lesions all over his body and I had no idea what they represented.

I finished examining them and went to the infirmary with my trio of helpers. With the exception of one or two AIDS patients who were progressively deteriorating, the others continued improving. We even discharged some.

Several hours later, as I was leaving, there was a new surprise at the door of the consulting room, this time more numerous: fifteen patients all claiming that they needed help.

Night had fallen when I finished. Juliano came downstairs with me and called the warder to unlock the cage. He came over with a set of keys.

'Still here, Doctor? I didn't know you were still up there. And that's it for you, Juliano. Off you go, 'cause I'm locking up.'

Juliano gave him a strange smile and went back upstairs. I left the pavilion, crossed Divinéia and knocked at the gate that leads to the main entrance. Through the little window, the night guard looked me up and down.

'Who are you?'

'I'm a doctor, I was seeing patients over in Four.'

He stared at me again, slowly, then lowered his eyes to look at my trousers.

'Look, I'm going to talk to the guys on the night shift, and if no one knows you, you stay.'

'I'm a doctor, you can ask the warder who opened the cage in Four for me.'

'You're not going to tell me who to ask. Wait there.'

He stared suspiciously into my eyes again and hurried off towards the Rat-trap.

Although I knew everything would end up being clarified, the fact that I was on the inside and feeling the gruffness of the contact with he who held the key gave me a feeling of discomfort, perhaps similar to what I had noticed in Juliano's smile when he went back upstairs to be locked in his cell.

I was lucky; the guard returned with a warder who knew me and apologised.

'Don't take it the wrong way, Doctor. There're 7000 men in there. It's my job to be suspicious!'

Biotônico Fontoura

In the following weeks, reality proved to be more complex than I had anticipated. The number of patients who came from the pavilions to the consulting room steadily rose. They didn't just have AIDS and tuberculosis. The complaints were varied: knifings, asthma attacks, diabetes, hypertension, abscesses, epileptic fits and all sorts of dermatitis. There were crack-heads with laboured breathing, paraplegics with bedsores and even healthy inmates looking to take advantage of the naïve doctor. It was like a crowd flocking to a miracle healer.

I had to be quick: listen to their complaints, palpate them, examine them with a stethoscope, look them over generally, make a diagnosis and prescribe medication in five minutes at the most. Accurately, if possible. It was old-school medicine: listen, examine and medicate.

Laboratory exams were pointless because the results, when they came, didn't arrive on time to be of any use.

An old X-ray machine would stay broken for weeks or waiting for radiographic film to be purchased.

There was no shortage of difficulties. All medications prescribed were subject to complicated bureaucratic processes and when inmates were transferred from one pavilion to another, which was not infrequent, prescriptions got lost along the way. The bureaucracy was so great that six copies had to be made of admissions and discharges in the infirmary, then brought for signing without carbon paper. Often, as is characteristic of the public service, there was an abundance of expensive antibiotics and antiviral medicines, while there was a shortage of aspirin and medicine for scabies.

In addition to these operational problems, there was also the ignorance of the patients themselves. Traditionally, in the treatment of tuberculosis the symptoms tend to disappear after four to eight weeks, but the medication should be taken for six months at least. Otherwise, there is a risk of a relapse and, worse, the appearance of highly lethal resistant bacilli that can infect others who come into contact with the patient. Adhering to the treatment programme was an insurmountable difficulty for most of these patients, many of whom were addicted to drugs that were used compulsively, such as crack.

To make matters worse, I wasn't fully prepared for that antiquated kind of medicine, without X-rays or laboratorial confirmation. The spectrum of pathologies was too far-ranging for someone like me, trained in an era of medical specialisation.

Skin complaints, for example, which were epidemic in the crowded cells, encompassed the entire field of dermatology: eczema, allergies, infections, bedbug bites, scabies and body lice – a bold variety that hides in folds in clothes and can jump long distances from one person to the next.

I once treated an inmate by the name of Thousand and One – a reference to his four missing top incisors – who was doing thirty days in Solitary because he had been caught with two hundred grams of crack and eight television sets, supposedly taken from people who owed him money, in his cell. He was HIV-positive and had small sores on his legs and lower abdomen, which were leaking a clear liquid and had miniscule white larvae crawling out of them. He didn't stop scratching for a second as he spoke to me. I treated the associated infection, but frustratingly I never did find out what was causing it, because Thousand and One was transferred to the State Penitentiary as a result of the television-set issue.

Of all the problems, however, the worst was lying. In that prison, everything was complicated. Alongside patients with serious problems, others would fake illnesses, and distinguishing one from the other wasn't always easy. An inmate would come in looking pale, with dishevelled hair, claiming weakness, diarrhoea, vomiting, dizziness and malaise. His appearance was that of a sick person, but how to be sure? He may have been pale because he had intentionally gone without eating, had been up all night, had been doing crack or was a good actor; how to prove subjective complaints? The objective of these inmates was to get transferred to the infirmary or to avoid being discharged from there. Despite the poor state of the facilities, that place was luxurious, as Juliano explained: 'They show up here covered in lice, 'cause this here is a three-star hotel compared to where they've come from.'

Almost all of them asked to be prescribed vitamins, with a strange predilection for B12 injections. At first I thought it was because they felt weak and believed that the food served at the Casa de Detenção was of poor quality. I even went so far as to give them some of these useless prescriptions, thinking of the possible placebo effect that might give them psychological comfort. I soon realised that many of the inmates believed in the miraculous powers of vitamins and mineral salts, creating a busy parallel market for these products, in which the painful B12 injection, for example, was worth five crack rocks.

I discovered this thanks to the honesty of Shorty – the little fellow with the lisp who had confessed to killing the four military police officers who he believed had murdered his parents, and who got a serious working over every time the military police riot squad searched the prison:

'Doctor, I need some vitamins, but I'm not gonna lie to you. It isn't me who's gonna take 'em. I'm gonna sell 'em to buy soap and toilet paper. I'm on my own, I don't have visitors and I get by with the help of the doctors.'

He caught me off guard. I had given prescriptions to many liars. Was it right to say no to the only sincere one? On the other hand, abetting this small offence would make me an accomplice of Shorty's and goodness knows how many others in the future. I refused his request, with a touch of remorse:

'Shorty, until now I didn't know this market even existed. From now on, I won't prescribe vitamins for anyone.'

'If that's how it's going to be, for no one, then you have my respect,' he said.

From that day on, I never again prescribed vitamins and I earned Shorty's respect. I also learned that one of the secrets of that place was not to make any exceptions: if you do for one, it's hard to say no to the others.

Another time, I treated a man of Arabic descent, who had a large nose and was dripping with chains, which were tangled up in his chest hairs: 'Doctor, I need a prescription for Biotônico Fontoura, which I've taken ever since I was little, so my family can bring it when they come to visit.'

I didn't even know the so-called revitalising tonic was still being produced and gave the prescription to the Turk, who, years later, escaped through a tunnel dug in Pavilion Seven. The tonic would be supplied by visitors, but needed a prescription to avoid being barred at the gate.

After this request came others; always the same old story about the Biotônico Fontoura that their mothers used to give them. Even after finding out about the vitamin racket, I didn't see anything wrong with prescribing the tonic, seeing as it was the families who bought it, and if the inmate later decided to sell it, it was his problem.

One afternoon, as I was crossing Divinéia, I ran into the head of the medical service, my former teacher:

'So you're treating AIDS with Biotônico Fontoura now, are you?'

'Er . . . Why the joke?'

'Hasn't anyone told you it's prohibited? They drink it mixed with *maria-louca*, the hooch they make on the sly here. A few years ago, after hearing about this *maria-louca* with Biotônico for so long, I decided to try it. A prisoner brought me a full mug of it, telling the men in the gallery that Dr Mário's strong coffee was coming.'

'What does it taste like?'

'Like sweet fire!'

The next morning in the infirmary, I complained to my helpers: 'Here I am prescribing Biotônico for inmates to put in their *maria-louca* and no one says anything!'

They laughed sheepishly, except for Pedrinho, who answered seriously: 'Doctor, you help us and we treat you nicely. You can trust us, but don't expect us to grass on our guys.'

Leptospirosis

There are so many different situations that present themselves in a prison that a lifetime isn't enough to know them all. The lesson in humility given by the more experienced prison staff helped me to relax and develop defensive techniques so as not to be duped all the time.

To assess the veracity of subjective complaints such as nausea, anorexia, weakness and diarrhoea, I started weighing the patients at each consultation. It is rare for someone claiming lack of appetite and diarrhoea five times a day to gain weight, just as it is unusual not to hear something when listening to the lungs of someone complaining of coughing and bloody phlegm, for example.

Pedrinho's admonition that I couldn't count on my helpers to expose the fakes made me pay closer attention to facial expressions. While the patients were speaking, I'd look them straight in the eye, without speaking, and would hold my gaze for a few seconds after the end of each sentence. When in doubt, I'd allow silence to fall, lower my head over their medical records as if about to write something and quickly glance at the nurses and whomever else was nearby, to catch their disbelieving expressions.

With the experience that repetition brings, I gained confidence as a doctor and spontaneity in my dealings with the inmates, who in turn stopped showing up with cock-and-bull stories like the one about the Biotônico Fontoura.

Slowly, I learned that prison infantilises men and that dealing with prisoners requires paediatric wisdom. It often isn't enough to let them complain or simply agree with the intensity of the suffering that they claim to feel. The angry manner with which many of them appeared for their consultation would disappear after I had palpated their bodies and listened to their hearts and lungs. By the end, it wasn't uncommon to find a tender look in their eyes. The patience of listening and the contact of the physical examination disarmed them.

Nevertheless, daily events made it clear that the complexity of that work required constant attention and discernment in order to work out what couldn't be said.

One rainy day, a thief from Pavilion Seven came in wrapped up in a blanket like a Bedouin in the desert, with only his eyes visible. His lips were split from fever, his conjunctivas were a reddish-yellow and he felt such intense muscular pain that he cried out when I squeezed his calf.

It was leptospirosis, a disease transmitted through rat urine which was common at that time of year, when it rained every afternoon, the Tietê River overflowed onto the Marginal Tietê motorway and traffic in the Carandiru region became infernal. With so many rats and blocked drains, a few cases here and there weren't anything out of the ordinary. That morning, however, was atypical: in two hours of consulting, he was the fourth man with the same symptoms. It was too big a coincidence.

As the inmate was speaking, I took a peek at the records of the three previous patients and saw that they were all from Seven, precisely the pavilion closest to the wall. When he finished relaying his symptoms, I jokingly asked him:

'Are you working on the tunnel too?'

What an inopportune joke! The guy grew even whiter and his yellow eyes bulged as he stared at me. As if he had become deaf, Edelso, the fake doctor, left the room. I realised that I had imprudently crossed a dangerous barrier. In prison, certain subjects burn the tongues of those who speak and the ears of those who listen.

It seems that we sat there for hours, tense, in that silent stare, until I broke the silence:

'I'm sorry, I was joking. I've never seen so much leptospirosis as I have today. You're the fourth person.'

'Now, Doctor, you've put me in an awkward position.'

Caught off-guard and uneasy, he didn't deny or confirm his work on the tunnel. I tried to reassure him:

'Look, I'm no copper. I'm here to look after the sick. You can trust me.'

'For the Love of God, Doctor, this could bring trouble for me and the other men who came here today.'

'I have no idea what you're talking about.'

Slowly, his face brightened. I suggested that he be admitted to the infirmary, but he refused; he preferred to take antibiotics in his cell. He said he could count on the help of his cellmates.

Two or three weeks later, at home, as I was having breakfast, I opened the newspaper. The headline read: 'Inmates Escape through Tunnel in Carandiru.'

The hole, hidden behind a statue of Our Lady Aparecida, was opened in a room in labour, an area where the prisoners work, on the ground floor of Seven, passed under the wall and ended in the dining room of a house on the street next to the prison. There were those who claimed to have travelled in the opposite direction: from the dining room to labour, in Seven.

Oblivious to the risk of cave-ins, the men had crawled more than one hundred metres through the flooded tunnel with drowned rats floating in it. One of the first through had knocked down a light bulb, which, in contact with the water, electrified the passage. In the darkness, squeezing their way through the tunnel's narrow walls, receiving electric shocks, sixty-three men escaped to freedom.

The only reason more hadn't escaped was because an obese inmate had got stuck in the mouth of the tunnel. Cork, as he came to be known, was quickly transferred out of the Casa de Detenção so he wouldn't be killed by the frustrated inmates who were behind him in the queue.

Angels and Demons

The cleaners were the backbone of the prison. Without understanding their organisation, it is impossible to comprehend day-to-day events, from the ordinary moments to the most exceptional ones.

It was their job to distribute three daily meals, cell by cell, and do the general cleaning. The number of cleaners varied depending on the pavilion. In those with fewer people, as was the case with Four, Six and Seven, there were approximately twenty; the more populous ones, such as Five, Eight and Nine, pavilions with over a thousand prisoners each, had a requirement of 150 to 200, split into those who served food and those who took out the rubbish, swept and washed everything.

The cleaners had a military-like hierarchy. Newer recruits took orders from older ones and on each floor there was a head cleaner who reported to the pavilion leader. Depending on the severity of a problem, there was occasional contact between the leaders, but the command was separate in each pavilion; there wasn't an overall chief cleaner for the whole prison.

It didn't fall to prison administration to choose the cleaners; rather, the corporation itself recruited its members. In order to be accepted, a candidate couldn't have informed on a fellow prisoner or have been responsible for anyone's arrest. He couldn't be in debt, have threatened to kill an enemy and not followed through with it, have been punched in the face, or taken the blame for somebody else's actions. In short, he couldn't have problems with other inmates. One of the cleaners in the infirmary once summed up the prerequisites in broader terms: 'A cleaner is a human being just like any other inmate, but he has to have a clean record with the criminals. He can't play dirty.'

The corporation was especially selective when it came to the sexual conduct of its members. Rapists were never accepted and if a cleaner was found to be one, their lives were at risk. An inmate who had been sexually abused would only be admitted if he had killed his offender. If he was homosexual: 'That's where he's even less likely to get in. It isn't right for a person who does things with his ass to be handling people's food.'

When a member was recruited, the older cleaners would explain the rules: do not get into debt, respect other people's visitors, assist those in need, help resolve disagreements and obey the group's decisions. In the event that he received an order that he considered unfair, he had first to do what had been asked of him, then respectfully discuss it with his superiors. If the order was extreme, he had to take it up with his colleagues with a knife. The cleaners were a family: if you messed with one, you had bought yourself a fight with them all.

The cleaners' togetherness ensured their unquestionable authority. To take them on, one would have had to organise another, stronger group capable of sparking an internal power struggle, which was highly unlikely, though not impossible, as we will see later.

The prison administration had a rather Darwinian view of the process, as a former director, famous for his boxing matches with the stronger prisoners, explained: 'In competition, the more able prisoners dominate the weaker ones. It's inevitable. We don't impose a leader on them – it would be great if we could. What we *do* do is take advantage of the natural selection of the leader, getting him to command the others through their organisational structure. If everyone did as they pleased, who would control all of this?'

Dialogue between administration and the cleaners was fundamental in maintaining order. One afternoon, the director of correctional services met with the pavilion leaders to put an end to the recent trend of inmates taking prison staff hostage at knifepoint as a means of forcing their transfer to another prison. The director of correctional services promised to speed up the bureaucracy of transfers and the cleaners agreed to calm desperate inmates. As if by magic, peace spread its mantle over the Casa de Detenção.

A meeting between a director and a pavilion leader was like one between a company chairman and executive manager: in low voices, each would explain what he wanted and how far he was willing to go. A commitment made was a commitment fulfilled.

The cleaners were absolutely fundamental in keeping internal violence in check. If an inmate didn't honour a debt, his creditor couldn't knife him without first consulting the pavilion leader, who would listen to both parties and set a deadline for the resolution of the situation. Before this time was up, woe was the creditor who dared attack a debtor. Without the acquiescence of the pavilion leader, nothing could be done. 'He's the one who keeps a handle on everything that happens in the pavilion. At that moment, they might be digging a tunnel, planning an escape, and a poorly timed stabbing throws a spanner in the works.'

Once, Zico, a well-known criminal from the district of Vila Guarani, recognised a newcomer to Pavilion Nine and went to see the pavilion leader, a black man by the name of Moonface with a long career as a thief.

'I'd like permission to teach that scumbag a lesson. He's a rapist. He abused my sister's friend, over in Vila Guarani!'

Moonface listened in silence and when Zico had finished he said, 'If this is for real, that he violated the girl's honour and that her mother filed a complaint at the police station, there must be a police report. It's easy. Write to your neighbour and have her bring over a copy of the report, and you'll get your permission.'

Zico followed his instructions to a T. The complaint had in fact been filed and the photocopy confirmed his story. He was authorised to kill the rapist.

When he received the authorisation, however, Zico talked it over with his friends and decided that perhaps it wasn't the best thing to do. There was no fall guy on whom to pin the crime: he would probably get many more years behind bars, precisely now when he was about to be transferred to a semi-open prison.

A few days later, Zico was summoned to Moonface's cell in the presence of witnesses.

'Zico, what's goin' on? What're you waiting for to sort things out with that scumbag?'

'I just got semi-open approval and I reckoned it was better to let it go for now and get him on the outside.'

'Now you've disappointed me, Zico! You ask for permission to kill the guy, you bring proof of the rape and then you change your mind? Pack up your things and head on over to Five, 'cause Nine just got too small for you. You're no con, you're a joke.'

At Zico's own request, the warders endorsed Moonface's decision and had him transferred to Five. A patient in the infirmary at the time said: 'The cleaners help as much as they hinder. They're angels and demons.'

Becoming a cleaner was a dangerous survival strategy: on the one hand, there was the protection of the group; on the other, a cleaner had to blindly obey orders from his superiors, no matter what was asked of him.

Those who made it to the top of the hierarchy had to be well respected and to have been behind bars for a few years in order to know the ropes. Age was irrelevant and individual physical strength didn't matter much among the inmates, contrary to what many people might think. I once met a frail 25-year-old who ran a pavilion of 1600 men. And the biggest thug in the prison was murdered in his sleep by an obstinate little man weighing only forty-four kilos.

A dull-witted or cruel person was never appointed head cleaner. All of the pavilion leaders I ever met were men of few words and extreme common sense, who became leaders thanks to their ability to resolve conflicts and form coalitions.

Abrão – the stocky former owner of a sleazy bar in the port of Santos, doing twenty-five years for killing a client who had beaten one of the prostitutes in his harem – told me the qualities that a pavilion leader had to possess:

He's got to have clout, express himself well, listen lots and say little, to keep people at arm's length. He's got to have a balanced view of things so he can say, 'That's right,' 'That's wrong,' or 'Pack up your things and head on over to Five.' In here, it's not like on the outside, where a lunatic can be a head of department, a business manager, or even make it to president like you-know-who, who they say used to snort coke and certainly looks like it. In here, the leader is a man who knows how to listen to reason, debate with his fellow cons and join forces with others to gain strength.

A pavilion leader's daily routine was arduous. From the moment the cells were unlocked until lock-up, he had to stay alert. To step away from the pavilion for even five minutes, he had to leave an assistant in his place. This precaution was justified: 'A lot of bad things can happen in a prison in five minutes.'

The leaders were always busy. In the infirmary, I treated two of them with visible symptoms of stress, as if they were high-ranking executives in a multi-national corporation or, as Moonface preferred to put it, judges. 'I wake up to a pile of problems: one guy wants to get even for something that happened on the outside, another wants to kill some low-life, dig a tunnel, collect a debt, someone else heard someone say somethin' he didn't like, and so on until lock-up. I have to put out so many fires, Doctor, it's as if I'm a father of ten. Things only calm down for me at night, after they're all in bed.' During some of the pavilion's most agitated phases, Moonface didn't even find peace in bed: 'In the silence of the night, my mind carries on working regardless 'cause the final decision is mine and a man's fate depends on it. I'm the judge of the pavilion. Except that a judge on the outside puts in his hours and his driver takes him home; I work forty-eight hours a day. He only has to decide if the accused goes to jail or give him a longer sentence at the most. I sign death sentences.'

The Warders

At first, I had the impression that the warders didn't trust me. Then I was sure of it. They were aloof, they told me later, because they thought I might be involved with human rights associations or have political interests.

During the first few years, with the exception of Waldemar Gonçalves who became a close friend and two or three others, they would change the subject whenever I arrived. If, out of curiosity, I asked a question about the most mundane occurrence, they would answer evasively.

After a talk in the cinema of Pavilion Six, I passed a young man covered in blood heading for the infirmary and asked the warder escorting him what had happened. 'A roof tile fell on his head,' was his reply.

On another occasion, I found a commotion in Divinéia. People were entering and leaving the packed body search room, all looking worked-up. Someone had no doubt been caught trying to smuggle in something prohibited. When I asked the short warder who guarded the gate to Divinéia – where he later met his death, crushed by a dump truck in a cinematographic attempted escape – what was happening, he answered in all seriousness, 'Someone took a bad turn due to the heat.'

Their mistrust wasn't personal. I hadn't said or done anything that could justify it. The truth is, warders don't like strangers in their working environment. Reality is disconcerting in a prison; what seems right is often wrong, and apparently absurd things have a logic that stems from their circumstances. Naïve visitors can jump to conclusions without knowing the facts and make indiscreet comments that eventually make it to the ears of the Inspector General, who investigates cases of abuse of authority, or to reporters.

Members of human rights associations and Catholic Prison Pastoral Care are generally ill regarded. According to the warders, they are only concerned with the rights of the criminals.

'Doctor, in the time you've been here,' one of them once said to me, 'you've lost count of the number of times a colleague of ours was taken hostage at knifepoint. There is no greater humiliation for the head of a family. Only those who have been through it can say. Have you ever seen someone from human rights or one of those Pastoral Care priests come offer a warder their support?'

It was true, I hadn't, I told him.

'A man who'd never hurt a fly, like João,' he continued, 'died under a dump truck at the gate to Divinéia in that attempted escape. Did anyone go offer his widow words of comfort? Now, go slap a bloody con and you'll see the lawsuit they'll spring on us!'

Journalists, in turn, are masters of misfortune, and can find enemies anywhere. Fearing that a former victim might recognise them and that new suits will increase their sentences, prisoners avoid camera lenses like the devil flees the cross. Point a camera at them and they will cover their faces and disappear faster than they would from a military police officer's machine gun. Warders also avoid the press, saying that it only serves to criticise and distort what is said.

Once, six inmates took a group of warders hostage in the laundry, next to Pavilion Six, to demand a transfer to another prison, which had become routine after the massacre in Nine (which I will discuss later). When I arrived at the prison, there were cameras, microphones and TV crew cars everywhere. When I went inside, I asked one of the directors who was participating in the negotiations what all the commotion was about.

'They're vultures, Doctor,' he replied. 'They land here when they sense something sordid that might help sell their newspaper.'

Time eventually broke down the warders' resistance to me. Aparecido Fidélis, an experienced warder, told me over a beer at a bar next door to the prison: 'As the years went by, we realised you'd come to help.'

From that point on, I was free to come and go as I pleased. I was even able to circulate in the high security areas, such as Yellow and the Dungeon. Walking alone amid the inmates gave me a sense of self-confidence that wasn't limited to the hours I spent inside the prison.

There were warders who acted as pleased to see me as I felt when I ran into them. We would talk about work, health problems, financial hardships (of which they had their fair share), family difficulties and misunderstandings with women. Our mutual respect reinforced the ties that held me at the Casa de Detenção.

The life they lead was tough. Their salaries weren't enough to get by on. Those who didn't succumb to corruption had to hold second jobs as security guards in banks, supermarkets, shops, nightclubs and brothels.

Much of this work was on the side, without worker's rights. They weren't even given weapons and had to use their own revolvers, generally unlicensed, since the job didn't afford them the right to bear weapons. In a robbery, if they were wounded or killed a robber, the company could shirk responsibility. They did not have formal work contracts. If they were killed, their families would have to make do with a state pension.

Their shifts were interminable. Those who did night duty headed straight to their day jobs at seven a.m. They would only sleep the following night, while on break at the prison. Those who worked during the day did the opposite. The ones who worked every day from eight to six were worse off: they would catch a few hours of sleep while on the job and that was it. The only time they would actually lie down in a bed was when they had the weekend off. Their absence from home complicated family routines, destroyed marriages and paved the way to double lives, in which they divided their time between their wives and other women. To bear the tension inherent to their work and the tiring nights, many overindulged in alcohol. Alcoholism and obesity were prevalent among the warders. They drank heavily; it wasn't easy to keep up with them.

One night, after distributing the fourth edition of *Vira Lata*, the erotic AIDS-prevention comic book, I called together the team who had participated in the project and we went to a bar across the street from the Casa, called Alcatraz.

When we arrived, at around eleven p.m., we found a group of warders from the day shift who had been drinking since they clocked off, at seven. It was a typical bar setting: the counter cluttered with beer bottles and plates of food, jukebox music, people talking and cigarette smoke. When he saw me, one of the warders shook my hand and, speaking as if with a plum in his mouth, made a small speech:

'Doctor Varella, what an honour to find you here, with this humble warder, who is, nonetheless, a human being with as much dignity in his heart as your scientific self and who, in this informal setting, insists on offering you a glass of *cachaça*, which you will be so noble as to accept.'

In spite of the persuasive vernacular, I hesitated; I had been so busy with the distribution of the comic book that I hadn't eaten since breakfast. Hard liquor on an empty stomach wasn't going to do me any good. Seeing me pause, one of the warder's more sober co-workers came to my rescue:

'Leave him. The doctor isn't the sort to drink *cachaça* at a bar.'

His remark piqued my pride. I replied that I was the one who would be honoured to drink in such distinguished company.

A glass brimming with a generous dose of firewater appeared before me. With all eyes on me, I took a man's gulp like the rest of them. The liquid blazed through my oesophagus, hit the mouth of my stomach with a jolt and instantly made my head spin. I felt a shiver run through me.

Then Waldemar suggested a serving of *frango a passarinho* – fried chunks of garlic chicken, the house speciality, accompanied by beer and the melodious voice of Alcione singing '*Nem morta*' ('Not Even Dead'). When the song was over, someone would put another coin in the jukebox and '*Nem morta*' would play again. It was as if Alcione and the full glass were on a loop.

I arrived home and got into the shower with the taste of the Alcatraz's oily chicken in my mouth and images of the prison in my mind. In the middle of my shower, I was surprised by my wife's voice.

'Is this the hour to be listening to samba at that volume?'

'The radio isn't even on!'

'Of course it isn't, I just turned it off. Didn't you even notice?'

It isn't my intention to paint a romantic portrait of these men, not least because some don't deserve it. They became involved with the criminals, took bribes in cell transfers, charged tolls at the doors of the pavilions, went along with trafficking and sold knives for self-defence. Petty corruption is universal in prisons and impossible to eradicate. They probably also took part in more serious infractions, such as facilitating escapes (one director general who took over shortly after the massacre in Nine ended up doing time in the Criminal Observation Centre for involvement in several) or allowing firearms in, a risky practice that prompted aggressive reactions from co-workers, whose lives were placed at risk as a result.

Those who did such things became indistinguishable from the criminals. As their more honourable colleagues would say: 'He who keeps company with pigs eats slops.'

Long-term contact with criminals, a chronic lack of money and the bureaucracy of the Brazilian justice system encouraged corruption.

A former director once received a tip-off that the employee responsible for ensuring that the inmates' paperwork was duly processed at the central court was charging under the counter for his services. If an inmate didn't give him money, he could rot in jail. The director gave him a dressing-down, transferred him to Pavilion Nine to guard the gate and appointed someone he trusted to the strategic function, because when transfers to semi-open prisons and releases ground to a halt, the prison atmosphere would get heavy, ready to explode.

Weeks later, amid the prisoners' mounting discontent, and unable to get any paperwork processed at the central court, the honest employee came back to the director and said, 'Sir, can I give you a word of advice? Put so-and-so back on the job. Only he knows how to get things moving down there. If you don't grease palms, things just sit there gathering dust.'

The director, a practical man who had started out in life as a policeman dealing with troublemaking drunks in the port of Santos, decided not to beat his head against a wall and summoned the conniving employee.

'Look here. You've been opening and closing the gate for cons for a month now. You've had time to learn your lesson. Now go back to the court and do whatever it takes to get the men's papers moving, before the situation here gets any worse.'

To be fair, however, there were many honest prison guards, despite the bad rap they got in the press, the ridiculous salaries, the risk of contracting tuberculosis, being taken hostage or getting killed. If it weren't for them, it would have been impossible to run the prison.

According to the tradition of the Brazilian public service, in the Casa de Detenção there were many ineffective employees and very few productive ones. Additionally, low salaries had caused many experienced men to leave the profession, forcing administration to hire younger recruits without adequate training.

Once, next to the gate between Six and Two, Chico Butt, an inmate who had been in and out of the prison several times and was an inveterate joker, called my attention to the new guard in a low voice.

'Doctor, it isn't right to put a boy like that to look after us. He's yellow with fear.'

These factors, along with absenteeism, created surreal situations. During the day, for example, a mere ten to twelve warders would watch over a pavilion like Eight, with over 1500 repeat offenders; at night, the number would drop to six or seven. Overseeing the 1600 inmates in Five, it was the same.

How such a small group of unarmed men were able to control a prison of that size was one of the mysteries of the place. Perhaps the biggest. The structure was so fragile that the only possible reason why there weren't spectacular escapes, the sort that empty out entire pavilions, was explained by Reinaldo, who worked at the front gate: 'We're lucky the cons don't see eye to eye.'

Reduced to its essence, the warders' job was to divide up the convicts in a Machiavellian manner. As Bonilha, the former director of Five, who once paid out of his own pocket for a packet of cigarettes that one inmate owed another, just to avoid another homicide in his pavilion, used to say: 'I spend the day throwing sand on them.'

Fidélis, with many years as a warder under his belt, said that the secret of the job was to take advantage of conflicts of interests among the prisoners: 'Doctor, crime is a profession. A real villain comes here to do his time in peace, get out as quickly as possible and go back to thieving, 'cause that's his life. He keeps his companions calm, doesn't get involved in escape plans, drugs or knifings, so as not to jeopardise his objective of leaving. Without realising it, the biggest villains end up being our allies.'

The ability to forge alliances with the right people, the leaders of the prison population, was essential to the smooth functioning of the prison and the physical safety of the employees.

Daily contact with the prisoners gave rise to solid friendships. For the incarcerated men, the warders represented contact with the outside world – the only contact, in the case of those who didn't have any visitors. An inmate could come to feel great regard for a warder who had done him a small favour, given him support at a difficult time or had the patience to listen while he let off steam. Mutual respect was a part of the balance of forces that was established in the prison and was decisive in preserving lives in moments of irrational violence.

In the tumultuous days following the 1992 massacre, convicts who were well respected by the other prisoners went as far as to escort warders to the exit, to avoid possible reprisals from the prison population.

As well as having the right friends, a good team of informers was fundamental to internal peace. Grasses are as old as prisons themselves. They informed for personal gain: a transfer, the payment of a debt, revenge, envy, a dispute over a woman or to take out a competing dealer, according to Florisval, who started out as a warder and made it to director: 'When a grass appears, I try to see if the information he brings is worth what he wants in exchange.'

Luisão, a legendary former director of the Casa, swore he was able to identify those in whom grassing was an innate quality. 'There are born grasses, Doctor,' he once told me.

Grassing was a high-risk activity, punishable by summary execution. Nevertheless, to the despair of the prisoners, as Not-a-Hope ruefully admitted, 'There's always a grass hanging around, Doctor.'

In the prison, because each narrator gave his version of events, no one ever knew where the truth resided. If you listened to ten people, you would hear ten different stories, and separating truth from fiction was a puzzle that required intellectual training. Experienced warders would notice everything that went on in the prison environment, even insignificant details. When a problem arose, they would listen to the well-informed, talk to the head cleaners, debate it with their colleagues and summon their informers. Until they made their final decision, they were walking on thin ice: 'The smallest slip-up can lead to a death.'

When he wanted to discover who was guilty of something, Jesus, the director of security, said he avoided making brusque movements. 'I would poke around a little, then wait to see what came out in the wash.'

They were shrewd, artfully confusing the inmates, who were not a united front.

Pavilion Eight once spent the whole day locked up because of a rumour that a tunnel was being built. On such occasions, no food was served and bad moods grew as the day went on. Late that afternoon, when 120-kilo Jesus crossed the pavilion courtyard, he heard someone shout from a window:

'You're going to die, Jesus!'

'And you're not, scumbag?' he shot back.

Alongside those who believed in more civilised techniques, however, there were more radical warders: 'Clubs and transfers are what keep a jail in order, Doctor, the rest is crap. Find your man and transfer him to the penitentiary in Presidente Wenceslau, almost on the border of Mato Grosso. Then see if he doesn't come back with his tail between his legs.'

In the Casa de Detenção, aggression towards prisoners, a strong tradition in the Brazilian prison system, never disappeared, but it did become less common over the years, as Luisão explained: 'When I started, the thing was to knock them about; then it was to lay off them. Warders adapt to the times. If you take your wife to a dance, Doctor, and they play a waltz, are you going to try to dance samba?'

Curiously, the older prisoners considered Colonel Guedes, a director in the 1970s, during the time of the military dictatorship, to be the best director of all. They spoke of him with great admiration:

His motto was clubs and cells, but there was respect, on our part and the part of the warders. He'd walk alone through the whole prison and everyone would put their hands behind their backs when he went past. The man was a fascist, he didn't go easy on us or the justice system. With him, both sides had to obey the law. He'd call up the authorities and tell them that so-and-so had finished his sentence: they could either send over the release permit quick-smart, or he'd put the guy on the street anyway. The judges were all afraid of the colonel.

Given the prison's conditions, it was impossible to put an end to the aggression, as their constant dealing with criminals had made some employees so callous that they didn't see any other way to impose order. How could anyone keep tabs on them in the middle of the night, in a hidden corner of a dark prison?

Once, in a conversation with Lourival, an experienced warder, about a scandal in which two prisoners had complained to a priest that they had been beaten with an iron pipe and the complaint was relayed to the Inspector General's office, he said: 'I doubt anyone sits the public exam to become a prison warder just so they can beat up inmates. It's the environment here that makes men like that.'

The cycles of prison violence invaded the warders' lives. When the inmates were settling matters among themselves and a group decided to finish someone off, the warders had orders not to interfere. Those who had to die would die. They couldn't intervene, as they worked unarmed. 'At times like that, Doctor, there's nothing to be done. It's like trying to break up a dogfight.'

A 30-something-year-old warder who had a second job as a security guard at a brothel, which he swore was a respectful place and insisted that I visit, told me that the image of the first prisoner he saw die, five years earlier, would come back to him when he least expected it. 'Eight men arrived in the cell of a certain Alagoas carrying knives and clubs. He saw me and started yelling, "Help me, Paulo, for the love of God!" The only thing I could do was ask them not to kill the boy. It made no difference. He took over twenty blows. It's ugly, Doctor, a human being screeching like a pig being slaughtered and you can't do a thing.' Over the years, Paulo witnessed other, similar deaths, but the first one made a lasting impression on him. 'To this day the expression of terror on that boy's face comes back to me, at a family birthday party, in bed with my wife or watching TV with my children.'

On my part, I can confirm that the influence of the environment was no trivial thing. Regardless of the fact that I am a doctor, I often felt like hitting someone in the prison, not because they had treated me with disrespect, which never happened, but out of indignation at the perversity with which one prisoner was treating another.

The Flock

Catholic priests, evangelical pastors, mediums, Candomblé and Umbanda high priests and priestesses and even Satan worshippers frequented the prison to lead the stray sheep to the Lord. Belief in divine help was, for many inmates, their last hope for spiritual comfort, the only way to help them establish some kind of order in their chaotic personal lives.

The Protestant preachers, who offered a path to heaven through knowledge of the Bible and a clear division between Good and Evil, were more successful than the Catholic priests.

Of the born-again Christians in the Casa de Detenção, the most cohesive group was that of the Assembly of God, which had close to a thousand men in its ranks – over 10 per cent of the prison population. In Pavilion Nine alone there were 200; on the fifth floor of Five, next to Yellow, 180. They wore long-sleeved shirts buttoned up to the neck and carried the holy book with them at all times. They called one another 'brothers', claimed to be God-fearing and repeated biblical jargon in a monotone.

In practice, with the born-again Christians, I always had a hard time distinguishing between those who had converted to the way of the Lord and those who had donned the stereotype to avoid reprisals from the prison population. Rapists, contract killers, drug users with unpaid debts, informers and thieves who had cheated their partners when dividing up the loot from robberies sometimes pretended to have converted in order to obtain the protection of the religious group. Because they wore the same clothes, carried the Bible and dropped the Lord's name into every sentence, it was impossible to tell them apart from the real ones.

The other inmates complained of the same difficulty. They respected the born-again Christians but demanded consistency. Once, in the infirmary, I treated a member of the Universal Church who had been beaten up by his fellow inmates in Pavilion Nine when they caught him sneaking a cigarette. The guy had welts on his back, a bruise over his right eye and a knife cut on his arm. My nurses justified the aggression: 'If he wants to be a born-again, we respect his choice, but he can't mess around with us. It's his job to spend the day prayin' for God to protect us criminals.'

To bring in new recruits, the brothers would even go as far as to pay off recent converts' debts. It was often an inglorious task, explained one of the pastors from Five – a barrel-shaped man doing time for selling lots in the middle of Billings Dam and other scams aimed at the poor: 'Because the Bible itself says to pacify, Ecclesiastes 10 and 4, we pay his debt. But some aren't sincere and, after we've paid, they go crazy again and insist they're wicked and goodness knows what else. While they're among the wolves, they're sheep; then they come here and want to play the wolf in God's fold.'

In Pavilion Five, the head pastor ran the wing, aided by three others. The pastors had to be married, have a good testimony and a spotless reputation with the prison directors. They were chosen over time, after moving through the ranks of co-operator, deacon and presbyter and were kept under observation for three to four years before they were nominated, according to one deacon with a pious gaze doing time for robbery, selling crack and participating in a mass murder in the *favela* of Heliópolis: 'They keep an eye on 'em to see if they're spiritually elevated, if they know the Lord's word and if they lead a life of prayer, because this one might not be totally sure of his faith, that one might have a bit of a temper on him, and another one masturbates; in other words, not cut out to be a man of God.'

The path of recent converts was arduous, as all eyes were on them. There was no escaping the group's constant supervision and the omnipresent gaze of the Lord. Valente, a guy condemned to 130 years for the deaths of seven people, justified the need for this rigour:

'The problem is that we can get some pretty good actors here. Really big-time fakes! So a team of deacons watches 'em forty-eight hours a day. It's not like we're the police and investigate them; it's the Holy Ghost who warns us that that person did this or that and doesn't want to stay in the flock.'

The behavioural code was severe and born-again Christians had to stand out from the crowd for their exemplary behaviour. They had to give up slang, women and their swaggering ways, dress formally, with polished shoes, bathe regularly and comb their hair. People in common-law marriages weren't allowed to live in the Assembly of God gallery, only single men and those who were legally married. Gay men were accepted, but with one proviso: 'They have to give up their lives of sin and go back to being normal citizens.'

The born-again Christians believed that rapists – universally hated in the prison – deserved the Lord's pardon, because they had problems. 'Mental and diabolical problems,' according to Valente.

Those who joined the ranks of the faithful hoping for an easy life were mistaken. The paths to God were thorny, the deacon with the pious gaze told me: 'The Church routine in here leaves no time for slacking off.'

At eight o'clock in the morning, as soon as the doors were unlocked, they would all leave for the first prayer, which lasted sixty minutes. At nine, the prayer meetings would begin: eight to ten men would gather in their cells to pray for another hour. Half of the meetings were dedicated to prayer, fifteen minutes to praise and fifteen to 'The Word', when everyone spoke at once and their voices rose up to God. Anyone passing through the gallery at that hour felt as if they were in the tower of Babel, with them all talking simultaneously. The brethren could work up quite a sweat and lose their voices from so much elevating themselves to the Creator.

After this prayer meeting, another one began at ten, in which an older brother would lead everyone in prayer until eleven-thirty. Then it was time to shower, eat lunch and quickly head downstairs, because from one to three p.m. they prayed outside, to attract new members. When it was over, they would race back up to their cells because 5 o'clock was lock-up time and they didn't like to make work for the warders, as a matter of principle.

After lock-up, there was more prayer, praise and 'The Word' until six-thirty. Then they would shower and eat dinner. Afterwards, they would pray, study the Bible or give testimony until bedtime, which was early, because television was prohibited and they were not allowed to listen to any kind of music on the radio, only evangelical stations.

The church functioned as a rehabilitation centre, perhaps the only one available in the prison. With the exception of the fakes, who – it was said – 'threw sand' in the eyes of their brethren, the others were happy, in the pastor's opinion. 'We feel God working in their existence,' he told me. 'Here there are bars and walls, there's no escaping, but you look at the sky and see God. His presence brings peace and, with your heart flooded with faith, you pray with devotion to leave this malignant place.'

Yellow

Next door to the faithful, on the top floor of Pavilion Five, was Yellow, one of the gloomiest parts of the prison. Over five hundred men, most of them sworn to death, inhabited cubicles thick with cigarette smoke, in which five or six inmates, often more, lived in cramped conditions. A strong smell of prison filled the atmosphere. The cells were in a very poor state of repair. Sometimes there wasn't any water, and there were often clogged drains, leaks and floods. The inhabitants of a cell could spend the entire night standing in water.

The inhabitants of Yellow were almost permanently locked up, and releasing them was an operation that meant keeping the rest of the pavilion in their cells. Nevertheless, as a precautionary measure, the warders limited the unlocking to Saturdays, which was visiting day in Pavilion Six, next to Five. One hour was all they got and then back they went. It was wise, since the presence of families in the building next door ensured peace in the courtyard of Five. Even so, there were some who felt it was more prudent to pass on the sunshine and stay behind bars: 'Better safe than sorry, Doctor.'

Yellow was never painted yellow: the name came from the skin colour of its sun-deprived inhabitants.

The biodiversity of the sector was rich: insolvent crack-heads, informers, contract killers, rapists, the losers of disagreements, men who had run into enemies from the outside in the prison and many others, including those who were unable to buy a decent cell or who had sold the one they had.

I once treated a thief from Yellow, dressed in old trousers and a tattered T-shirt, whose body was covered in tiny contagious sores. He requested a medical certificate for his wife, a lawyer, to send to the central court. I asked if his wife couldn't help him get out of Yellow and he answered:

'Doctor, more help than she already gives me? She's already brought me the money for a cell five times. And I smoked it every time.'

Smoking crack and being almost constantly locked up were enough to drive the occupants of Yellow crazy, according to Dionísio, a thief with incurable tuberculosis, whose wife had left him because she was tired of his promises to get straight: 'You're under lock and key day and night, surrounded by men who are out of it and neurotic. You go to sleep next to a stranger and five minutes later he's at your throat. There's no rest. It's psychological torture, Doctor.'

Days in Yellow were spent in absolute idleness, with the prisoners lolling about on mattresses, when there were enough to go round. No one read or watched television. For the final of the 1998 World Cup, Waldemar Gonçalves had a plan to put a TV set in the gallery and allow them to watch the game. It didn't work out; the directors warned him off it for security reasons.

To broaden their visual horizons, the inmates would climb up to their cell windows, sit with their legs hanging out and hold onto the bars. They would stay like that for hours at a time, giving the facade of Pavilion Five a unique decoration, with a row of legs hanging from the top floor. For this reason, they were disparagingly known as 'the shins'.

From the windows on the outside wall of the pavilion, the shins were able to watch football matches in Eight or talk to passers-by on the path between pavilions by shouting. Those who occupied the cells facing the inner courtyard were less fortunate; there was only a view of the clothes drying in the windows of the cells on the opposite side.

The inhabitants of the inside cells established a curious symbiosis with the members of the Assembly of God, who attended the open-air prayer session in the courtyard. While the brethren were praying to convert infidels to the way of the Lord, the inmates from Yellow would fasten a plastic bag to an old trainer to weight it down, tie it to a piece of string and throw it down towards the faithful. They did this with great skill; the string was exactly long enough for the bag to hover a metre above the ground. As patient as fishermen, they would hold the string until the faithful publicly demonstrated, with bananas, bread rolls, sweets or clothes, the love that they professed to feel for their neighbours.

Sweet Talk, a dealer from Eight deserving of his nickname – who used to smuggle cocaine from Bolivia and threatened to kill distributors who mixed it with other products because he had a name to protect – once explained the origins of the high-security wing: 'Yellow exists 'cause we got no invoicin' department, which leads to misunderstandings. Doctor, if I sell a rock of crack and the guy doesn't cough up, I got no judge to complain to or promissory note to claim. If I let it go I become a doormat, see, nobody pays me anymore and my supplier doesn't give a rat's ass. It's a chain reaction; one man's debt brings consequences for the next man.'

Security in Yellow was relative, however. Florisval, the director of correctional services, unanimously considered by his colleagues to be one of the people who best understood the Casa, was realistic: 'We do what we can, but unfortunately nowhere here is safe. When they decide to kill someone, it's very hard to stop them. In a jail, death doesn't respect geography.'

Mário the Dog – a thief who used to break house windows with a car jack, found twelve kilos of gold bars one time and was later arrested with a blonde in the Northeast of Brazil – showed up at the Incarceration office in Nine one afternoon, claiming he had received death threats from enemies in the pavilion and asking to be transferred to the secure wing. In Yellow, his behaviour was exemplary, he earned the warders' trust and was integrated into the team of inmates who served meals to their partners in misfortune.

A few days later, a certain Ronaldinho, bald like the football star, sentenced to prison for having raped a mother and her daughter among other serious crimes, arrived at the Casa. With this past, he insisted that there was no possibility of his living with the masses and he was sent straight to Yellow. As it happened, Mário the Dog was the son and brother of the violated women and had requested a transfer to Yellow in advance because he had heard that the rapist was being held at a police station and was to be transferred to the Casa de Detenção.

At breakfast, Mário the Dog opened his enemy's cell. The first stab punctured the right eye of the rapist, who tried to find the exit in vain. When I saw his body, I was struck by the number of stab wounds and, in particular, the punctured eyes and two deep, symmetrical puncture wounds in the soles of his feet. An inmate standing nearby said: 'Mário the Dog worked with the stealth of a cat.'

Jeremias, nostalgic for the good old days, said that if he were ever invited by the governor to take over as director general of the Casa de Detenção, he would do away with Yellow as his first initiative: 'That'd fix the problem, seein' as a guy can get into debt and then ask to go to Yellow. That's not how a real man does business. If he knew there was nowhere to hide, he'd take responsibility for his actions. Without Yellow, a few would die here and there, but it'd be good 'cause there'd be more respect like there used to be.'

The first time I treated the inhabitants of Yellow was on a winter night. I took Julinho, a helper from the infirmary who was later transferred to Pavilion Nine when it was discovered that he was diverting inmates' medications from their intended destination, most likely in cahoots with one or two prison employees.

We went up to the fifth floor and improvised a consultation room in a cell in the born-again Christians' wing. One by one, the patients were brought to us. There was widespread tuberculosis: the men were underweight and complained of fever, night sweats and coughing, scattering droplets of secretions throughout their crowded cells. In that poorly ventilated environment, the only thing that couldn't complain about its living conditions was Koch's bacillus.

Most of the sick scratched so much that it was hard to watch them. They had little blisters on their legs, forearms and lower torsos, and the weary look of sleepless nights. The scratching broke open the blisters, allowing their crystalline contents to ooze out. This made the itch better, but the blisters would start to sting. In the place where the blister had been, a thick crust would form and when it fell off it would leave a dark, permanent scar. Their contaminated fingernails would sow new blisters and the infectious process would go on for months.

It was almost ten o'clock at night when we finished. At the end, the head pastor came up to us ceremoniously:

'Doctor, I know you must be very tired and need to rest in the Lord's peace, but there's a transvestite with some inflamed silicone in her rear end. She's in pain and insisted I ask you to see her.'

'No! That's enough. My work here is never-ending. Besides, I know nothing about silicone.'

'Of course, Doctor. I'll tell her to be patient and to pray with faith for Jesus to intervene in her life.'

I gave in to the blackmail in the Lord's name and told him to send her in. Today I thank the pastor for having introduced me to Veronique, a character we will meet in another story.

After this time, I returned to Yellow regularly, which earned me prestige among the prison staff because many of them, out of fear, refused to work in that sector. I treated the sick in a little room with a window that faced the entry cage. There was no privacy; to examine anyone without their clothes on, I had to ask them to go into the little adjoining bathroom. This staff bathroom had a toilet and a sink and its floor and walls were wet from the constant leaks. In order to wash your hands, you had to turn the shutoff valve and quickly jump back to avoid the water that squirted out of a pipe in the wall. Merely opening this valve would cause the water to gush in the sink and the toilet to flush on its own.

Later, in Yellow, I gained the assistance of Paulo Xavier, 'Black Paulo', a nurse from the Sírio-Libanês Hospital who had volunteered his time to help me with the sick inmates. Paulo organised my consultations with the help of a prisoner by the name of Lúcio, a strong young man with different-coloured eyes.

Lúcio cared for the sick with dedication and was gracious with me. One day he told me that he had been arrested after a street fight. He was walking along unarmed, when an arch enemy with many killings under his belt appeared holding a sharp knife. His enemy stabbed him three times, but Lúcio managed to grab a piece of wood and smash it over his head. Then, taking advantage of the knife and the fact that his assailant was unconscious, he cut off both his arms so he would never stab anyone again.

One Saturday, Black Paulo, Lúcio, Manoel – a thick-bearded employee of the pavilion – and I, decided to attack the scabies epidemic that was making the inmates' lives hell. The operation started at seven. The entire pavilion started the day locked up so the men from Yellow could leave their wing. In the cells of the sector, the inmates piled up their belongings on the ground so they could be sprayed with insecticide. Downstairs in the courtyard, next to the side wall of the prison, a pipe of cold water was waiting for them.

The prisoners lined up in front of the pipe, while an inmate sprayed their cells. It was cold. Manoel, with his twenty years of experience, warned me:

'Prepare yourself, Doctor. Convicts are like cats: they're water-shy.'

He was right, there was no shortage of complaints. They claimed to have a cough, tuberculosis, pneumonia; some had bronchitis and others simply refused to take a cold shower. I explained to the queuing men that those who didn't wash and apply the medicine they were given would spread scabies to the others, which would affect them all. It was a convincing argument: the inmates would never risk being accused of harming their fellow prisoners in any way.

As they were bathing, I noticed that they all stood under the pipe with their backs almost touching the wall. I mentioned this to Manoel, who explained:

'Criminals never turn their asses towards one another, Doctor.'

After showering, purple with cold, the men went and stood in front of a fellow inmate charged with spraying them with scabies medicine from head to toe. When they were dry, those with dermatological infections were separated by Lúcio and Black Paulo and brought to me.

The job, involving over five hundred men, was finished by midday, the time to lock Yellow and release the rest of the pavilion. Anticipating a few asthma attacks triggered by the insecticide, I left ten ampoules of cortisone for Lúcio to medicate them with and left with Black Paulo. We were pleased with the success of the operation and chuckled about how the inmates had taken their cold showers with their asses against the wall.

All On The Spoon

Crack invaded the prison in the middle of 1992. One afternoon, on the football pitch of Eight, I saw a guy who was completely out of it. He was talking in an intimidating tone of voice and gesticulating at an imaginary figure in the window of a second-floor cell. At the door to the pavilion, a corpulent guard who suffered from hypertension gave the diagnosis and a bitter prediction:

'Look, Doctor, it's crack arriving at the Casa. That's all we need.'

I was surprised. In my naïvety, crack was something in American films, a problem in the Bronx, never in Carandiru.

In the prison, crack was prepared by hand. They would mix cocaine with sodium or ammonium bicarbonate on a spoon, under which they would hold a lighter to heat up the mixture and melt it. When it turned to liquid, an oily base would rise to the surface, which they would push to the edges of the spoon with a matchstick to cool and solidify. The resulting rock was smoked in improvised pipes.

Sad, a dealer on the inside who spent his nights preparing it and who was once caught with 300 grams of rocks ready for consumption, complained that the process was hard work: 'People say I'm makin' easy money, but no one sees how hard I work. On the outside it's easy, the crack comes ready-made from the lab; in here, it's all on the spoon.'

Crack swept injectable cocaine off the map. It is a compulsive drug; there is nothing left for the next day. When experiencing withdrawal symptoms, if an addict sees pure cocaine, a crack rock or someone under the effect of it, they will feel awful: they experience heavy sweating, a racing heart, abdominal pain, diarrhoea and vomiting.

Ronaldo – a thief with AIDS who escaped from a penitentiary hospital and was smoking crack in the street forty hours later – told me that while holding up a draper's in downtown São Paulo, he had suddenly felt ill when the manager opened the till: 'When I looked at the money, I got this image of myself buyin' coke at the den. My stomach started churnin' right then and there and I left the hold-up halfway through it, vomiting.'

Cocaine can be snorted, injected or smoked. When snorted, the powder sticks to the mucous membrane of the nose and is gradually absorbed; the effect increases, reaches a peak and then decreases. When injected intravenously, it passes straight into the circulatory system, through the lungs and to the brain; the euphoria comes and goes quickly; users feel a buzzing in the head and a rush to the brain. With crack, the effect is even more instantaneous, because the cocaine goes straight into the lungs and doesn't lose time in the circulatory system.

Ronaldo, who had learned to smoke crack with his wife, the mother of his four children, told me that the quality of the cocaine in the prison had fallen: 'It used to give you a long twing in your ear. Now it's a quick twong and it's over.'

Injectable cocaine users, or 'slammers', aren't interested in the slow effect of snorting, which they consider 'square'. Crack, however, gives users a similar feeling to that of slamming, with certain advantages: it is cheaper, doesn't leave scars on their arms and, above all, it doesn't transmit AIDS.

Within a matter of months, cocaine injecting in the Casa was limited to a few die-hard slammers, who later died of AIDS in the infirmary in Four. Slamming had gone out of fashion in Carandiru as silently as it had entered.

In January of 1994, we repeated the prevalence study we had conducted four years earlier. We found that 13.7 per cent of the inmates were infected with HIV (compared to 17.3 per cent in the 1990 study). The only explanation we found for the decrease in the number of inmates infected in the four years between the two studies was the reduction in the number of intravenous cocaine users. In 1998, of 250 volunteers tested, 18 were HIV-positive (7.2 per cent).

As the years passed, many former users of injectable cocaine told me they had switched to crack because of the talks in the cinema. If it is true, I am happy. Maybe even crack has a good side.

To Bring Down the Cons

Everyone recognised that crack had shaken up the prison. It is a treacherous drug. The first few times the effect takes a while to wear off; however, with daily repetition, it ends in seconds. It is rapidly addictive; in the infirmary I met people who, after their first contact with the drug, were never able to stop, not even locked up in the cells of Yellow, indebted, with their lives at risk.

With time, cocaine users develop symptoms of persecutory delusion every time they use the drug. In the prison, those who suffered from this syndrome, commonly referred to as paranoia (or 'noia', in prison parlance), moved through the galleries terrified, locked their cells from the inside, curled up like children under their beds, screamed and ran away from imaginary enemies.

Ronaldo, the father of four who had vomited during the hold-up and who died of tuberculosis in the infirmary six months after being recaptured, used to describe the paranoia that tortured him like this:

Crack is so devastatin' to the mind that I smoke locked in my cell and convince myself that someone's under the bed with a knife waitin' to kill me. I get terrified. I want to look but I'm afraid if I look he'll stab me in the eyes. It takes me ages to work up the courage to sneak a quick look. Of course there's no one there. I'm alone in the locked cell, but even so I'm still not sure: there is someone there, I just didn't see 'im properly. I look again, even though I'm afraid he'll stab me in the eye, and I don't see anythin'. But it doesn't make any difference, I'm not convinced, and I look again. And so on, ten, fifteen times. When the effect starts wearin' off, I realise it was all just noia: how can there be someone there if the cell's miniscule and the door's locked? Before I have another smoke, I look under the bed and check to make sure the door's properly closed; sometimes I even take a peek in the crapper. Fine, I'm gonna have another smoke and this time the noia isn't going to attack me. The minute I take another puff, Doctor, it happens all over again: there's someone under the bed, he's gonna kill me, if I look he's gonna stab me in the eye . . .

Finally, Ronaldo summarised the existence of crack users: 'We have a miserable fate. If there's hell on earth, it's the life of a crack-head.'

It was impossible to know how many smoked crack

in the prison. The inmates estimated at least 60 per cent. I once asked Lúcio, the nurse from Yellow who had cut off his enemy's arms so he would stop stabbing people, how many of the inhabitants of Yellow were crack users. He answered: 'All of them, Doctor. When one shows up who isn't, I take him out of here and ask the pastor to accept him in the born-again gallery.'

The old-time warders used to say nostalgically: 'I miss the good old days of joints, Doctor! There was more respect among the inmates. They'd have a puff and sit quietly in a corner thinking, then they'd eat and go to bed. No one lost their family home because of marijuana. We were happy and didn't know it.'

Crack shook the internal power structure, the inmates' morale and generated more violence. Addicts compulsively spent what they didn't have; then they would blackmail family members claiming to have received death threats. When their family was depleted, they would sell their personal belongings and, when they had nothing left of any value, they would steal, get beaten up, stabbed, take the responsibility for crimes committed by others and even work as hit men in exchange for a rock to smoke.

Addiction liked financial ruin. One of the techniques I used to identify those who didn't smoke crack was to look at their feet: if they were wearing new trainers, they weren't a crack-head.

Carlão, who smoked crack non-stop for a year on the outside and two inside before giving it up, reached an extreme: 'Crack came to bring down the cons. Because of it I even sold my revolver – my work tool. I was caught muggin' someone with my aunt's kitchen knife.'

Debts in the Casa were not forgiven: if an inmate didn't pay up, he could run, get beaten up or die. The only way out was to ask the warders for protection. If they were convinced of the seriousness of the case, they would transfer him to Yellow. There, in the high-security wing, the crack-head would run up new debts, ask for another transfer and end up in the Dungeon in Pavilion Four, his last chance at survival.

Asking the warders for help was demoralising for the inmates. I once found the infirmary in a flap because Júlio – a big-time criminal doing twenty years for killing three rivals who had ambushed him in the alley of a *favela* – had sought refuge in Yellow because he owed thirty-eight *reais* to a drug dealer half his size. In the end, an inmate admitted to the infirmary with chronic boils in both armpits, which forced him to hold his arms out like wings as he walked, summed it up: 'Crack does away with a man's sense of shame.'

On another occasion, Xanto – who had shot his drunk uncle in the chest because he didn't know how to shoot anyone in the leg – was upset with a fellow prisoner who, during a visit, had offered his own wife to the dealer to pay a debt. The fact that the girl worked as a prostitute in a bar didn't attenuate matters. 'It doesn't matter how she makes her livin' out there. In here, among us, she's a fellow con's wife and deserves respect. Offerin' her like that takes a lot of piss.'

Xanto wasn't the only one who felt that way. The day after the visit, the indebted crack-head was forced to pack up and move to Pavilion Five: 'He didn't deserve our respect.'

Goal Net, a skinny dealer from Eight, attacking forward on the pavilion's football squad, house burglar and father of two little girls whom he maintained in a private school, would give crack-heads two weeks to cough up and not a day longer. In five years of prison and dealing, he had sent many a man to Yellow, although he recognised how useless it was: 'What good is it to have the fools locked up there, hanging their shins out the window, and me here without my money?'

One day, the wheel of fortune span and Goal Net was transferred to a penitentiary in the interior of the state. There he found three former prisoners from the Casa whom he had sent to Yellow. He died the night he arrived, his throat cut.

The prison became a very different place to the one I had found when I first arrived, in 1989. Crack subverted the internal order. Like people, prisons also change with time.

The Inside Deal

Drugs go looking for addicts, the inmates used to say.

Two trips abroad convinced me of it. The first was during a visit to Rikers Island, New York's biggest prison, when I passed the door of a communal bathroom situated in the wing that is shown to visitors and caught a strong whiff of marijuana. The second was in the icy outskirts of Stockholm, in a model prison which exclusively housed fifty young ex-drug users, guarded by 350 trained warders (seven per prisoner). Each morning, when their private cells were opened, the inmates had to go down to the infirmary and, in the presence of a doctor, urinate in a glass for a toxicological exam. The laboratory would often detect heroin, cocaine, alcohol, marijuana and even everyday shoemaker's glue in their urine, mysteriously smuggled into the model institution.

Shorty, the lisper who had killed four police officers, didn't believe that drugs could enter the Casa without the collusion of prison employees or the guards on the wall: 'Can an inmate go out to get cocaine, Doctor?'

It would be unfair to generalise, however. Most of the warders were never involved in trafficking, in spite of their low wages and professional disenchantment. Additionally, the prison administration was always rigging traps to catch those who had 'crossed over', and when they were caught the punishment was harsh: five or six years in prison.

Smoky, a well-liked teller of tall tales in which he was invariably the protagonist, knew first-hand that drugs weren't a problem exclusive to Carandiru: 'I've been in the system for eighteen years, in several different prisons, and in all of them I was able to smoke a joint or crack – which I've been off for two years now, 'cause there's no future in it – and, back when slammin' was the thing, the only reason I didn't do it was 'cause I don't care to jab myself over and over. It's funny, Doctor. I don't mind other people's blood, but I start to black out when I see my own.'

Shorty said: 'If coke corrupts free society, why would it be any different here inside, where there are lots of thieves, dealers and users? Here of all places, where it costs double what it does outside!'

In the consulting room, when inmates came to see me with tuberculosis, I would forbid them to fill their lungs with smoke, be it from marijuana, normal cigarettes or crack. It wasn't hard to get them to see that the smoke was harmful to their inflamed lungs. In the following weeks, when I asked if they had stopped, most had given up marijuana and even crack, but few were able to quit cigarettes. I saw so many similar cases that I became convinced that nicotine is the most addictive substance of all.

Inmates who could get drugs into the prison could sell them. It wasn't like on the outside, where dealers owned a specific spot which they guarded with bullets. According to Horácio – whose wife had left him after he had lost the movement in his legs when he crashed a stolen motorbike into the back of a truck, with a blonde sitting behind him: 'The dealer distributes to the guys who work for him. If he pays four thou a kilo, he's gonna sell it to us middle-men for seven or eight thou, to double his capital. And I'm gonna want ten a gram, 'cause of the risk. If you get caught it's a serious crime, which is terrifyin' for a man who's already tallied up a lot of years.'

According to Lenildo, a thief who never dealt on the outside but started in jail in order to support his two wives, three children and rheumatic mother, it wasn't easy to deal in crack and come out alive: 'You have to be tough, be careful what you say and weigh up the consequences of what can happen. One wrong move and I could end up on the tip of a knife, like that guy you examined last week. I counted more than thirty stab wounds. For Christ's sake, Doctor, I felt like givin' up crime!'

I had indeed seen the body. He was a strong young

man with a tattoo on his chest: Saint George on a horse rearing up in front of a fire-breathing dragon. The saint was thrusting his lance down the dragon's throat with great flourish. There was a stab wound in the warrior's waist, another in the dragon's arrow-shaped tail, and another through the plume in the saint's helmet, in addition to many others. There may well have been more than thirty.

It had all been the consequence of a routine transaction. A regular user had gone to buy five *reais*-worth of crack on credit, saying he'd pay that Sunday. Suspicious that the user was insolvent, the guy with the tattoo had told him he didn't have any goods. The peeved buyer mentioned it to his friends and they sent someone else to make the same kind of purchase. The guy with the tattoo didn't suspect anything and sold on credit. He never should have given someone else the credit he had denied his old customer. It was a fatal mistake.

I had seen so many similar cases that I couldn't understand why they didn't just do away with all credit. I once tried to call together some leaders among the prisoners to propose this measure. My hopes were dashed by a black man with dyed blond hair who had done time in the Casa on a number of occasions: 'There's no way it'll work, Doctor. An addict who owes twenty *reais* will hand over his TV for that price. It's very lucrative. It's just like with the banks outside. You owe 'em 20,000 and they take your house that's worth 100. No one throws away that kind of business.'

Lenildo, who prided himself on supporting his two wives and mother without them wanting for anything, explained that dealing in crack obliged dealers to take extreme measures, even though they might not want to: 'I get sixty grams from my dealer and owe him four hundred. I package it up, sell it here and there, and some pay me and others ask me to wait 'til the weekend. Come Monday, my supplier wants his money. If I don't pay, my goose is cooked.'

Within this scenario, self-preservation spoke louder: 'As a result, so I don't get a knife in my ribs, 'cause I've got a family to support, I have to stick it to the guy who owes me, with a knife, a club or boiling water, so he sees that I don't let things slide. And that's how it goes, each man lookin' out for his own hide.'

There were situations, however, in which it was more advantageous to cut one's losses: 'The buyer didn't pay up? Let it go. Except that then, if somethin' goes wrong and I find myself in a bit of a spot, he's the one who's gonna knife me, to clear his debt. Otherwise it'll come back to bite him in the ass, unfortunately.'

In spite of attempts to repress it, trafficking was firmly rooted in the prison. Each big dealer headed up a group of associates, who sold to the addicts desperate for drugs. It was an invisible, secret network: 'like the mafia', someone once told me.

Idleness

The inmates themselves used to say that an idle mind was the devil's playground. Contrary to what one might imagine, most preferred to do their time working. They said time went faster that way, and at night: 'When your body's tired, you're less likely to sit around reminiscing.'

It also allowed them to learn a trade and gave them some kind of perspective in life when they finally went home. Releasing them poorer and more ignorant than they were when they came in wasn't going to rehabilitate them.

Sérvulo – a thief who ran the medical room in Eight and used to pack the waiting room with patients, and who I later discovered was charging two packets of cigarettes to get them a consultation – saw another advantage to working: 'Prison would be less dangerous with those malignant minds occupied.'

As an incentive, the law established that a person's sentence could be reduced by one day for every three worked, though the mathematics weren't always respected for those without a lawyer. Even so, many vied for the few jobs available. Others, however, were more orthodox: 'Work? Not even on the outside, with my dad on my case. In here, never. It's a matter of principle.'

One Venezuelan naturalised as a Brazilian – who used to go into the Amazon jungle to receive drugs and then kill the delivery man because it was cheaper than paying him – was adamant: 'The only way I'll work for society is after I'm dead, if they cremate me and put my ashes in an hourglass.'

To be fair, however, with the exception of security-related activities, the prison's other tasks were all done by the prisoners – they cooked, distributed meals, cleaned everything, collected tons of rubbish, fixed things, made deliveries here and there, and organised football tournaments and the Winter Clothes Campaign.

The inmates kept the Big House running and without them it would have been chaos.

Some companies employed inmates to sew leather balls, flip-flops, insert spirals in notebooks, spokes in umbrellas, screws in hinges and similar jobs. Theoretically, the prisoners should have been paid for their services, which could have helped support families left without breadwinners or gone into savings for when they were released. In practice, however, there was so much bureaucracy involved in receiving the money that many of them accepted payment in packets of cigarettes, the prison's traditional currency.

Because there was only enough work for a privileged few, most spent their days lazing about, spinning yarns to their mates in the courtyard, lifting weights at the gym, practising *capoeira* in the old cinema, walking up and down the stairs, inventing anything at all to entertain themselves and, above all, getting into trouble.

The Venezuelan concerned with the fate of his ashes warned me as I walked unawares among the groups of men that formed in the football pitch of Eight: 'You hear so many stories of muggings, revolvers and gunfights, Doctor, you should walk through 'em with your head down 'cause of the stray bullets.'

Running parallel to the organised work, which reduced sentences, was an informal economy of unregistered work. Some inmates offered clothes washing services, others sewed, cut hair, built sailboats decorated with football team emblems, cooked (there was a pastry shop in a cell on the third floor of Pavilion Eight and an ice cream parlour in Pavilion Two), distilled *maria-louca* and set up stalls in the gallery, where they sold general supplies, used trainers, clothes, battery-operated radios, TVs and photos of naked women.

Goods were purchased by bartering or paid for with packets of cigarettes or, discreetly, with actual money. Internal trade was fundamental to the vitality of the economy; it was how goods were redistributed, merchandise circulated and debts were paid. In a place in which the men were only given food and beige trousers, all the rest was up to them: 'There's a cost of living inside.'

Coming from the lowest echelons of Brazilian society, not all of them had outside help. On the contrary, most had wives, children and elderly parents to support, which is why men who never would have got involved with drugs when they were free became dealers in prison in order to continue supporting their families.

In the cells of Yellow and Solitary Confinement, full of cigarette smoke, locked the entire time, the men would spend the day chatting and when they ran out of things to say, they would stare at the walls. In old Jeremias's experience, idleness could drive a man crazy: 'In the past, when I was in Solitary, I saw lots of men go in OK and leave there straight for the insane asylum.'

He spent three months alone in one such cell, in total darkness. To occupy himself, he would throw a marble at the wall and feel about on the ground until he found it. He once repeated the operation 177 times on the same day: 'But, thank God, I came out of there with my wits about me.'

Capital Punishment

Rapists were hated by all, as I've said. The inmates accepted everything: physical violence, swindling, theft, white slavery and heinous murders – except rape. Their loathing for this crime was shared by the warders themselves and society in general. In a poor district of São Paulo, a man sexually abused a boy and killed him. The newspapers published photographs of the murderer and the child. One Friday afternoon, as the result of an apparent bureaucratic slip-up, a group of prisoners was transferred to the Casa without administration realising that the murderer was in their midst. From the moment he got out of the police van in Divinéia to his death in Pavilion Five, exactly fifty minutes passed. He was stabbed so many times that his right arm was almost disarticulated.

Marcolino, an illegal lottery operator and counterfeit money vendor, who was about to be released, told me that the rapist's arrival in the pavilion was no surprise: 'We were more than prepared. There were newspaper clippings with a photo of him on every floor. The men'd stab him then pass the knife onto the person behind them in the queue. He was stabbed more than sixty times and, believe it or not, he died without a sound. It was weird!'

On another occasion, Gilson, a 30-year-old sales representative, gave a 15-year-old schoolgirl a lift in his vee-dub and did everything he could to convince her to go to a motel with him. When he realised she wasn't going to go with him, he pulled out a revolver and crying or saying she was a virgin didn't help her. With the girl at gunpoint, he drove to a deserted place and raped her. That night, as he was watching the nightly news with his little boy asleep on his lap, while his wife and mother-in-law washed up after dinner, the doorbell rang. It was the police.

'Was the vee-dub parked outside stolen today?'

He answered no. Then they asked if he had lent it to a friend. Gilson again said no and was handcuffed.

Down at the police station, he told his cellmates that he had held up a market stall. The next day, an illiterate crack-head asked Gilson to write a letter of apology for him to his mother, who had promised to abandon him once and for all if he was arrested again. The sales rep, with great style, began the missive: 'Beloved Mother, I am down on my knees, with a bleeding heart, to beg your forgiveness. I have erred, I cannot deny it, but I regret it with every part of my being . . .'

When he finished, he read it out to the crack-head,

who, moved by the beauty of the words, was unable to stop himself crying.

As he was reading, the police officer on duty arrived holding a half-empty bottle of whisky:

'Which one of you is Gilson? What's your article? What are you in for?'

'Article 157. Holding up a market stall.'

'Market stall, my ass! You raped a 15-year-old girl while holding a gun to the poor thing's head. If there was any half-decent con in this cell, he'd give you a good workin' over and get half a bottle of Drurys for his trouble.'

It was irrefutable. He had the police report with him.

The crack-head went first. With tears still in his eyes, he stood up and kicked him in the face. Then came the other occupants of the cell – there were eighteen of them. He was beaten until he lost his senses.

He woke up with a bucket of dirty water in his face. He was tied to the bars of the cell: 'They made me hold a light bulb in my hand and touched the bars with a bare electrical wire. They had doused me with water to conduct the current better. Two hundred and twenty volts. They only turned it off when the light bulb came on in my hand. There was a horrible jolt in my body and my tongue rolled up, then the flash of the light bulb. I thought I was going to die. I just prayed to God that it would be fast.'

When they tired of the game, Gilson fell to the ground half-conscious, covered in blood and with a deformed face. That was when they urinated on him.

Then Belly – a thief who had been caught stuck in the skylight of a house in which he had hoped to find a fortune in smuggled jewels – pulled down Gilson's trousers: 'Now you're gonna feel like the girl you raped!'

Gilson claimed that Belly wasn't able to penetrate him. Cilinho – a thief from Five who had killed his unfaithful mistress and back-stabbing partner who was planning to run away with her and the money from a robbery – had witnessed the scene at the police station and discreetly gave his version of events: 'Yes he was. Even in the state he was in. Doctor, Belly is more of a man than you and I both!'

The prison administration tried to protect rapists by keeping them in Pavilion Five, Yellow or even the Dungeon. Security was relative, however, as Not-a-Hope once told me: 'One day we find out. It might be a Nosy Parker who takes a peek at his file, someone who knows his dirty secrets or a screw who doesn't like 'im. All sorts of ways. He hasn't got a hope.'

Often, rapists were given the opportunity to live peacefully among the other prisoners for long periods. But one day, in the anonymity of a rebellion, the angry mob would take out its pent-up hatred on them. On these occasions, they were thrown off the roof, stabbed to death or tortured with sophisticated cruelty, like a man I once treated in the infirmary, whose tongue had been burned with a scalding-hot knife and was infected with the microbes present in the excrement he had been forced to eat every thirty minutes.

The unpredictability of this settling of scores meant that rapists had to be constantly on guard. Anything that wasn't routine could be the harbinger of capital punishment.

In a place where the murderer of a defenceless father deserved respect, this aversion to rapists may seem disproportional. Lupércio, who prided himself on never having stolen anything, although he had spent most of his life behind bars because of marijuana, and who, years earlier, in Eight, had seen a rapist impaled on a broomstick that was driven in with a sledgehammer, explained the philosophy: 'You can't have men like that around the place 'cause our wives, mothers and sisters visit us here. A man who's done somethin' that vile might have a relapse and be disrespectful. I'm against the death penalty in this country, but I'm in favour of it in the case of rapists.'

Fall Guys

'Fall guys are the pathetic individuals who
take the rap for other people's cock-ups.'

A fall guy was the one who would come forward to
take the blame when a warder found a hidden
knife, a coil used to distil *cachaça* or a lifeless body. Many
were recruited when they arrived in the distribution
cells. For someone whose family brought supplies, there
was no shortage of friends and a corner he could call his
own; others were lucky enough to find friends from the
outside in the pavilion. As for the recent arrivals who
were poor and unknown: 'For every ten cells they ask to
live in, they get eleven no's. There's only one way out of
distribution for a guy who's in a bad way financially: to
become a fall guy, 'cause the men have him take the
blame for everything that happens in the cell.'

The majority of fall guys, however, were recruited
from the ranks of the crack users. Many addicts
would take the blame for crimes committed by others

in exchange for drugs. Dealers didn't need to do the dirty work.

When someone lost his life on Rua Dez, the warders would lock all of the cells until the guilty man stepped forward. The technique was infallible; no prisoner dared allow an entire pavilion to be caged up because of him. In the end, the one who claimed responsibility was almost always a fall guy.

Although the warders knew he wasn't really the one who had committed the crime or offence, there was little they could do about the code of silence that governed life among the criminals.

I once treated a man called Needle, thin as a rake, who used to work the traffic lights on Avenida Paulista. Every wallet, watch and chain he stole, he smoked in his crack pipe, until his arrest. A compulsive user, he smoked sixty *reais* more than he could afford in the pavilion. One day, his dealer called him to his cell:

'Needle, you've been owin' me for a few days now. When are you gonna pay up?'

'At this exact moment, I haven't actually got the cash, 'cause my mother didn't come to visit me, 'cause she's in hospital with my sister, who got shot in the chest along with my brother-in-law, who was murdered . . .'

The dealer interrupted him:

'Needle, here's the thing: later this afternoon, a stiff's gonna show up on Rua Dez on the fourth floor. You head down to Incarceration and take the rap. Say he

offended your mother who's in the hospital lookin'
after her widowed daughter.'

Needle took the blame for the crime, which had
actually been committed by six inmates, and was sent
straight to Solitary Confinement, on the ground floor
of Five. Later, he described the thirty days he spent
there, sharing the space with five others: 'I wanted for
nothin', 'cause my cellmates took me food, joints to
smoke and even *cachaça* to work up the courage to face
the food.'

Because Solitary Confinement was on the ground
floor and the window was covered with a perforated
metal plate, his companions in the courtyard outside
would pass a long straw through a hole in the plate and
into the cell, where Needle would suck *maria-louca*, the
locally produced firewater, straight from the straw, the
far end of which was dipped in an innocent-looking
coffee pot held by one of the true murderers as he
absent-mindedly leaned against the wall.

Needle signed the confession when he had served
two years and three months of a forty-year sentence.
He paid his debt to the dealer, but it cost him twelve
years more of prison.

Another time, I arrived in the consulting room and
noticed a strange atmosphere. The nurses were pulling
out the patients' records in silence and exchanging
enigmatic glances. I asked them what was going on and
they said it was nothing. I waited five minutes and
repeated the question. Their answer was identical to

before. I started seeing the patients, and they remained as quiet as tombs. I decided to be more incisive:

'Are you going to tell me what's going on or am I going to have to find out for myself?'

Their leader, a skinny thief who was merciless with his enemies and whose greatest disappointment was the fact that his younger brother had joined the police force, smiled wanly:

'A knife we had stashed in the steriliser fell out. A small one, just for self-defence.'

They had removed the back plate of the steriliser, hidden the knife and screwed the plate back on. It was unlikely that the warders would have discovered the hiding place without the help of an informer. When I asked them who had taken responsibility for the offence, they replied that it had been Fethry, a guy in the final stages of AIDS, committed to the infirmary, who could barely stand.

'Judges don't want to know about fall guys. They give 'em heavy-handed sentences with no privileges,' 82-year-old Lupércio told me. Once a fall guy went down to Incarceration and took the blame for a death, there was no turning back. If he denied in court what he had previously confessed, his life would be at risk when he returned to the prison. Even if he was transferred to another prison, it was dangerous. 'He'll die there too, 'cause we all talk to each other. Every day people come and go from here, bringin' news. It's the Iron Mouth radio.'

The Iron Mouth radio was so powerful that even after his release, a fall guy who had gone back on his word wouldn't have any peace on the outside: 'That's where he's gonna die even more!'

Although the number of fall guys in the prison increased significantly in the crack era, it was not an exclusively modern phenomenon, according to Philosopher, a career con artist whose glasses were patched with plasters: 'There's always been the sort who'll take the responsibility for a death, and then, in the twists and turns of fate, he ends up getting killed himself, while another fall guy takes the blame for his death. Lots of mothers lose their beloved sons that way, leavin' only tears rollin' down the face of human sufferin'.'

Good Guys

'Everyone out of the cell with his hands on the gallery wall.'

Bebeto was already fast asleep when three warders gave the order. He was worried; he had only been in the prison for three days and barely knew his cellmates. All seven of them came out in silence and the warders searched everything. They were about to give up, when one of them pulled up the bottom of a cupboard next to the wall and found two knives. Bebeto was surprised: 'I had no idea two blades like that could even fit in that space.' The warders wanted to know who they belonged to. 'There they were, all pretendin' it had nothin' to do with them. Am I gonna say it's not mine? First of all, the screws won't buy it, and second, I'll get a reputation as a grass, 'cause if it ain't mine, it's theirs.'

Solidarity cost him thirty days in Solitary. All things considered, he felt it had been worth it: 'I came out with a reputation as a good guy. Life inside got easier for me.'

It was better to pay for someone else's crime than

turn in a fellow con. The accused was allowed to claim innocence; but name the person responsible, never. In the event that someone else was unfairly punished, the real guilty man would pay a debt of gratitude, at the very least.

Gypsy, a tattooed thief who worked in the infirmary for a while, received a letter from his wife. Troubled by possessive feelings, he went looking for some *maria-louca* in Pavilion Eight. Cidinho, his supplier, was sorry he couldn't help him, but he was out of stock after a riot squad raid. Feeling sorry for his friend, however, Cidinho got him a bottle of Dreher for fifty *reais*. Gypsy paid twenty, assumed a debt of thirty and took the bottle: 'To make up the difference, I sold a few shots, which is where I got unlucky. A guy got drunk and was disrespectful to a screw. They found out where the cognac had come from and said that if I gave them the supplier, they'd let me off.'

Gypsy told them that the bottle had mysteriously appeared that morning at the door to his cell. He got thirty days in Solitary, but spared Cidinho – who had once thrust a dagger so hard into the hand of a business owner who had refused to open his safe that the blade went through his bones and buried itself in a table. The police had shown up immediately afterwards and when they saw the man with his hand stuck to the table, beat Cidinho and his two partners so badly that he lost the hearing in his left ear and all of his front teeth.

Gypsy's gesture did not go unnoticed by Cidinho: 'He's a good guy. If he'd turned me in, it would've complicated my legal situation, 'cause I've already asked for a transfer to open and I can't put a foot out of line, otherwise I'll lose the benefit. But I didn't let it go unthanked. I used my understandin' with a screw to get a tin of *goiabada*[1] to him in Solitary, 'cause in there it's a month eatin' the food straight from the source, without doctorin' it up.'

This kind of respectful recognition didn't apply to fall guys, who were looked down upon for taking the blame for someone else's deeds – for what were considered the wrong reasons: cowardice, to settle a debt or some other form of immediate reward. The difference between a good guy and a fall guy was often very subtle, as it involved the reason behind the act, explained Chico – a former sailor who had killed his brother-in-law, been arrested and had never seen his children again, because, in retaliation, his wife had told them he had died in the penitentiary: 'Fall guys take the blame in exchange for some kind of immediate benefit. A good guy helps his mate without knowing if he'll ever be rewarded for it; he deserves our respect because he's an altruist.'

---

[1] Guava jelly.

Transvestites

In the beginning, with the transvestites, I had a problem with their identity. A man with breasts and delicate gestures whose medical record had him as Raimundo da Silva, but whom everyone called Loreta, would sit before my desk. As a doctor, how was I to address this person? Raimundo, take this medicine, or should it have been Loreta, dear?

I quickly realised that Loreta was the right choice. Treating them as women didn't offend them; much to the contrary.

Transvestites live their lives on the margins of Brazilian society. They all come from the poorer classes, and when they go out at night, with their large breasts and tight skirts, they are automatically considered dangerous, regardless of what they have done. When they are arrested, they are taken to police stations, where the district chiefs try to place them in special cells, but when there isn't room, what can they do? Squashed among men, in a situation in which many a brave man is at risk, curiously, transvestites find strength in their female fragility and command respect.

In the Casa de Detenção, most lived on the fourth floor of Pavilion Five, but there were others scattered throughout the prison. Things were not all rosy among them; they would fight and bitch about one other, but their survival instinct brought them together in the face of danger.

Old Jeremias said that the prison used to be different: 'There were less trannies and more fags.' He remembered a long-haired transvestite known as Índia who used to do the nails of the director general – the feared, iron-fisted colonel. 'She was beautiful. When her sister came to visit, you couldn't tell 'em apart.' When younger inmates asked, and only then, Jeremias, a survivor of many conflicts, would give them the following advice: 'If you're walkin' along in the gallery and you see a faggot comin', you'd best keep your head down. I've seen many a man die 'cause someone said he was eyein' up someone else's faggot.'

He was right, the husbands were jealous. Prison wives never circulated through the galleries and only went down to the courtyard accompanied. In order to marry, the husband had to be in a good financial position, because it was up to him to support the household, while she had to be submissive to the provider. Some disapproved of it in a veiled manner, but this kind of relationship was socially respected.

The passive partner wasn't considered a male. In the

surveys we conducted, it wasn't enough for us to ask if they had homosexual relations. We had to add: what about with a prison wife?

Before intimate visits were instituted, homosexuality was prolific. I once told a toothless thief that he had tested positive for AIDS and asked him if he had ever shot up drugs in the past. 'Never,' he answered. 'I got this thing shagging prison ass. Lots of ass, Doctor!'

Single transvestites could move about among the inmates without danger, as long as they knew their place. In the event of one of them disagreeing with another inmate they were allowed to defend themselves verbally, like women, but they could never get physically aggressive like the other men.

Once, two dealers from Eight went to Five to collect a debt and had a misunderstanding with the debtors and their friends. They were stabbed. Among the attackers was a transvestite. The men in Eight didn't let it go and wanted to invade Five. It was a conflict of serious proportions (both pavilions were crowded and the conflict could easily have escalated), which was only overcome thanks to the shrewdness and persistence of the pavilion director.

The outrage in Eight wasn't because of the physical aggression, which was commonplace in debt collection, but because a transvestite had participated. Zacarias, a chronic asthmatic and cleaner in Eight, complained to Valdir, a warder in Five: 'Look what this prison has come to. Nowadays even fairies stick their knives in cons!'

When they arrived in the Casa, the transvestites had already been estranged from their families for quite some time. Without any help in the prison, they either had to marry or continue working as prostitutes, as they had done on the outside. In the latter case it was for a pittance, in exchange for a tin of cooking oil, a good piece of chicken or a rock of crack.

Patrícia Evelin, with her false eyelashes, had wound up behind bars because she had killed a client who didn't want to pay her. What had upset her most was that he'd been rude and had kicked her out of his car like a dog. Once, Patrícia had asked the cleaner distributing lunch for an extra banana and received an indecent proposal: 'Only if you give the bad guy here a bit of somethin'.' She later laughed about it and said it was the least she'd ever charged. 'What was I to do? I was dyin' for a banana.'

AIDS was devastating among the transvestites in the Casa. They would show up in the infirmary with advanced tuberculosis, perineum sores, shrunken breasts because they had stopped taking hormones and their wasting muscles infiltrated with industrial silicone. Enough suffering for any woman. In the end, bedridden, they would still smile with feminine sweetness. I lost count of how many died there.

Innocence

The prison was overflowing with innocence. An observer would be convinced by an initial conversation that no one was guilty. They were all victims of police set-ups, informers, sleazy lawyers, judges, ungrateful wives or bad luck.

Paulão was a plump 40-year-old mulatto with a friendly smile and thick beard who was always moving back and forth through the infirmary. For months, our contact was limited to the coffee that he would bring me in the middle of the afternoon, in a glass with gold stripes and an Indian girl in a leopard skin on the side. The first time, I raised the coffee to my lips with ceremonious concern, which, to my surprise, was unnecessary: the coffee was strong and bitter, a pick-me-up in the interminable afternoon of consulting. One day, he brought the glass with the Indian girl on its side in an interval between patients.

'Paulão, I want to thank you for your kindness. Freshly brewed coffee every time. I'm going to bring you a packet. It's not fair that you're using yours.'

'Don't, Doctor, it'll make me feel sad. It's my pleasure.'

'How long are you in for, Paulão?'

'I still haven't been judged.'

'Robbery?'

'No way, Doctor! I'm awaiting judgment for a guy who died on my street.'

'Was it you who killed him?'

'My brother was murdered. A few days later, the murderer himself had an encounter with death. I became a suspect. Some say I did it, but they didn't see nothing, and others say they saw it and it wasn't me. And with all this business of some thinking it was me without seeing nothing and others seein' that it wasn't, here I am waitin' to see what the judge decides.'

A few months later, at his trial, the judge sentenced him to thirteen years and four months.

Lover Boy

It was a moonless night. A police van pulled up in Divinéia and eighteen handcuffed prisoners got out. The night guard grumbled: 'And they say they're going to deactivate the Casa.' In protest against overcrowding, the newcomers had destroyed the cells at the local police lock-up where they were being held: 'It's always the same old story: they solve all the problems with the System by dumping more on us.'

In the darkness of Divinéia, with one warder in front and two behind them, the procession turned left into Pavilion Two, in silence, stopped by Incarceration for the usual bureaucratic processing and was sent to distribution, on the ground floor. A warder stopped at the door and waited until they were all together. He opened it. The light was on.

One of the prisoners, Zildenor, who, ironically, had been arrested in a toy shop while buying a train set for his children with the money from a robbery, couldn't believe that the warders were going to lock them in

185

there. 'It was hot as hell,' he said. 'More than thirty cons lyin' on the floor.'

Some were sleeping on foam mattresses, others on tattered blankets. Strings stretched from one wall to another served as clothes lines for wet washing. There were plastic bags holding personal belongings hanging from nails on the wall. A privileged few, known as 'bats', had strung up hammocks and were hovering above the others.

The occupants of the cell were outraged by the arrival of the newcomers. 'When they saw there was eighteen of us, the ruckus started. There was lots of complainin', people sayin' it wasn't right, there wasn't room for anyone else, they'd have to kill one of us to prove their point. But the screws stuffed us in there 'cause they don't give a rat's ass about cons sufferin',' said Zildenor.

One warder justified it, saying, 'It's so no one can complain that there's no human warmth here.'

Inside the cell, the newcomers explained to their irate cellmates that they didn't want to be there; they had destroyed the holding cells at the police station. 'We were all victims of the same thing: overcrowdin' in the country's prison system,' stressed Zildenor.

It wasn't easy to calm tempers, as the heat was relentless and the men were kept locked up all day long, being bitten by the body lice hiding in the folds of their clothes. Eventually things quietened down and the eighteen newcomers settled in around the toilet, according to the law of priority. It was actually a relief for them: 'We were in all sorts of bother at the station. You had to take turns to sleep: some of us would lie down while the rest would stand there, trying not to touch the next guy, 'cause it was wall-to-wall men.'

The next night, a short, fair man with blue eyes arrived in distribution with his belongings wrapped up in a sheet of newspaper. He entered quietly and took up position next to the toilet.

A short time later, a man lying near the window identified him as his wife's lover.

It was a serious matter: men who went out with inmates' wives were the object of everyone's hatred in the prison. I saw countless murders result from these love triangles: the husband would go to jail and the wife would take a lover, who later ended up in the same prison as his disconsolate rival. The former warder Aparecido Fidélis told me that wives were more likely than mistresses to abandon their men in jail.

From his spot by the window, the spurned husband shouted: 'That's it! I know who you are: you're the one who was fucking my girl. Now you're gonna die!'

He started over towards his usurper, but some peacemakers intervened:

'Drop it, man, or you'll get a bunch of years inside. Your sentence is too short. Get the bastard on the outside.'

Their common sense appealed to the betrayed husband, who decided to get revenge in a less radical manner: 'OK, I won't kill the fucker, but lover boy here's gonna have to pay tit for tat for what he did to my wife. I'm going to ride him from behind!'

The lover humbly tried to dissuade him: 'Not a good idea, man. I'm HIV-positive. I'm gonna die anyway, but do you want to get AIDS too?'

At this point, a fat, toothless inmate, who had been in and out of the Casa several times, stood up and said: 'Leave blondie-boy to me. It's no problem, 'cause I'm HIV-positive too!'

According to Zildenor: 'Blondie-boy was forced to go along with the fat guy in the corner.'

The next day, realising that Zildenor was also new to the cell, the lover let off steam to him: 'Jesus, man, that business about being HIV-positive wasn't true. I just made it up.'

Zildenor comforted him: 'Don't worry, Mr Big in the corner isn't either.'

This hatred of the figure of the lover was mercilessly incited by a military police officer who used to guard the wall behind Pavilion Eight. Whenever he was on duty, at ten o'clock at night on the dot, he would come out of the sentry box, find a dark point along the wall, near the windows of the pavilion, and rap on the wall three times with his helmet: clang . . . clang . . . clang . . .

'Hey con, here you are, all locked up, while the wife's off having a fuck.'

There would be a long silence, invariably broken by the same tenor: 'Fuckin' pig!'

It was the cue for a fiery crescendo of swearing:

'Fuckin' cunt of a pig!' 'I'm gonna tell your sister when she visits on Sunday!' 'Hey motherfucker, I had your lady on all fours!'

The shouting would reach an unintelligible peak and slowly subside until the last voices had silenced. Unperturbed, in the penumbra, the police officer would wait until silence had returned. Then he would beat the wall again with his helmet: clang . . . clang . . . clang . . .

'Hey con, here you are, all locked up, while the wife's off having a fuck.'

The Power Puzzle

One winter, many years ago, things got tense in Pavilion Five. The director of correctional services received complaints that the cleaners were charging protection money for rapists and drug debts directly from visitors. 'Here's the thing, ma'am: if you don't bring the money next weekend, your son's gonna die!'

In the face of this inadmissible breach of the inmates' internal code, according to which a prisoner, no matter how close he was to a fellow con, could only approach his family members if he was invited to do so, Luís, the director of correctional services, called Jocimar, the head cleaner in that pavilion:

'I've been getting complaints that the cleaners are extorting money from prisoners' families, and I won't allow it. To avoid unpleasant consequences for your personnel, you'd better get order in the pavilion.'

Luís wasn't at all pleased with Jocimar's reply:

'I think your story's wrong. Besides which, I can't control everything that goes on here.'

The following Monday night, the silence was interrupted by shouting in the cell of an asthmatic on the second floor. The warder doing the rounds looked through the window in the cell door, saw that the man was blue in the face and having difficulty breathing and opened the cell. The six occupants came out holding knives, took the warder hostage, then went down to Incarceration and overpowered the five warders on the night shift. They said they had received death threats from their enemies and wanted to be transferred to another prison.

In these situations, despite the tension, a gentleman's agreement would be established: the warders wouldn't react and the inmates wouldn't be overly violent, to avoid future consequences. On that occasion, however, everything was different; the mutineers were rough with one of the hostages and stole money from the others. There were two cleaners among them.

The negotiations stretched into the small hours. When the day staff arrived, things got worse. Indignant at the humiliation to which their colleagues were being subjected, the warders pressed administration to let them resolve the situation with force. It wasn't easy to contain them.

Finally the negotiators reached an agreement with the rebels. At the prison gate, the warders flanked the police van that was to take them to another prison, as they had demanded.

At this moment, with the acumen that the passing

years bring certain people, Luís, a large, bespectacled man, planted himself in front of the door to the police car and told his colleagues, who were blind with rage:

'Look, boys: what they did is unacceptable. We're going to give 'em a workin' over, but I'm takin' the first swing. I'm the director of correctional services and no one touches 'em before me.'

As well as having the undeniable moral authority of one who had started out as a warder when he was barely a boy and made it to director, Luís was holding a convincing length of metal pipe.

In the courtyard, the prisoners came out using their hostages as shields. The agitated warders formed a circle around them, while military police officers guarded the prison entrance with machine guns. When the prisoners arrived at the door of the police van, Luís, still holding his length of pipe, quickly shoved them inside with a brusque movement and locked the door, without giving the indignant warders time to react. At that same instant, he turned to face them:

'We're professionals. It's over, folks. Everyone inside. It's over. We're professionals.'

Rumour has it, though no one knows for sure, that during their transfer to a prison in the interior of the state the prisoners got the beating that the frustrated professionals had wanted to give them, from the heavy hands of the military police who were transporting them.

When this episode was over, the director of correctional services found himself facing the following dilemma: to speak with the pavilion leader again would be interpreted as a display of weakness on the part of administration; on the other hand, deposing him and putting someone else in his place wasn't within his power. It was the inmates who chose the leader of the cleaners, not him.

Luís, grandfather of two and son of a woman with a head of white hair who had spent her life worrying about his safety, realised that it was imperative he did something. His humiliated subordinates wanted revenge; the inmates were silently waiting to see what the next move would be.

To buy time, which wasn't a bad thing in a situation like that, Luís made a bold play: he transferred the pavilion leader to the State Penitentiary and declared his post open. With this measure he showed firmness in his command, appeased the warders and gave the cons a scare.

Two or three days went past without a leader and the inevitable impasse arose: who was the substitute going to be? In Luís's opinion, the cleaners would probably choose someone who would uphold the status quo of extortion, coercing visitors and disrespecting warders. In the following nights of lost sleep, looking after his wife who had just had an operation, Luís considered a radical measure: transferring the entire group of cleaners, scattering them throughout the system.

He shelved the idea because a dangerous vacuum of power would appear; in the dispute to occupy it, many could lose their lives. Additionally, it couldn't be forgotten that the cleaners carried out important duties in the prison routine. The very next day, who would distribute breakfast and lunch? And what if, out of fear, solidarity or some other reason, no one agreed to take on the tasks of those who had been transferred?

According to old Lupércio, a pothead from the days in which one could calmly smoke a joint in downtown São Paulo because passers-by thought it was a rollie: 'A jail without food is dynamite with a lit fuse, Doctor.'

Luís's many years as director of correctional services had given him time to organise an intricate network of informers which extended throughout the entire prison (if he hadn't had the competence to put it together, he wouldn't have held onto his position).

Through the grasses, he was able to better assess the atmosphere in the pavilion. There were prisoners who were angry at the cleaners' conduct, people who had had money extorted, who had been humiliated or who simply disapproved of what they did for moral reasons. He discovered that within the cleaners themselves there was even a group who didn't agree with the methods used by their colleagues.

Machiavellically, Luís remembered String Bean, a grass who had made a career of informing at a downtown police station, providing information in exchange for part of the goods seized from the thieves he turned in. His dirty past had led him to seek protection from the director as soon as he got to the prison. Luís had been willing to talk to him, promised discretion and gave him his word that the other inmates wouldn't get access to his criminal record. At that moment, he didn't ask him for anything in exchange, but one day, who knew? The future belongs to God, was Luís' philosophy in running the prison.

String Bean, tall, thin and with a wandering eye, ran the warders' kitchen in the pavilion with a group of other inmates. Weeks earlier one of them, in prison for rape, had been stabbed to death by six cleaners as he was leaving the kitchen.

Luís invited him into his office and offered him a coffee.

'String Bean,' he said, 'ever since you set foot in here I've protected you. I've been good to you, I saved your life. If anyone heard from my lips about your past as a police informer, God help you; you'd be a dead man. Well, the hour has come for you to show your gratitude: I want you to head up the group that is going to take over the cleaners.'

String Bean was intelligent. Luís didn't need to explain everything. He merely helped him regiment those who were discontented and those over whom the directors had power. Proceeding with caution, in a matter of days he had managed to unite 300 dissidents around the new leader, and did his sums: 'There are approximately two hundred cleaners. The numbers are in my favour.'

In spite of his numerical advantage, the director

knew that the overthrow would be traumatic. By this time, he could have transferred the entire group of cleaners and put String Bean and his followers in charge, but it would have been evident to the inmates that administration was behind things, and the group put together with such great shrewdness would be considered by all to be a bunch of traitors. Many would pay with their lives for such a miscalculation.

The old director concluded, then, that the only solution was for the new group to take over the cleaners' cells, expel the losers and make the pavilion respect them, the best way they knew how: 'Against force there is no resistance.'

Luís was walking on eggshells. You can't be careful enough, he thought: 'Violence is a difficult remedy to measure.'

The day of the final battle went like every other. At five everyone went upstairs. On the floors, as happened from time to time, the rumour on everybody's lips, no one knew where from, was that there was going to be a general search for knives, alcohol and drugs. Those who had any ran to hide them.

At the usual hour, the warder rapped on the bars with the padlock. Men hurried back to their cells, and there were sounds of metal, TV and a singer playing a ukulele. All entirely routine, except for one detail: the head count, sacred in the prison, wasn't conducted.

Baianinho – a thief with over one hundred robberies and two deaths on his record, who lived for free in one of the six cells with a TV owned by Jocimar, the leader who had recently been transferred to the State Penitentiary, with the condition that he hide eight knives in the cell and take responsibility for them if they were found – thought it was very odd that there hadn't been a head count: 'But because they were sayin' there was gonna be a bust, I thought that was why. It was OK. The screws weren't gonna find anything in our cell; we'd hidden all the knives in the shower.'

The slightest disruption in the routine of a prison makes the men apprehensive. That night, the rumour about the bust and the fact that there had been no head count created an atmosphere of expectation in the cells. A deep silence fell. Bad sign.

At eight-fifteen, movement was heard in the poorly lit gallery. Roberto Carlos – a thin thief with Our Lady Aparecida tattooed on his chest and a blind right eye, who had been discharged from the infirmary two weeks earlier – looked nervously through the window in his cell door: 'I didn't like what I saw: cons wandering the gallery at that hour, ten or twelve of 'em. If there was gonna be a search, why was it that they were out there and there were no warders around?'

Behind the ten or twelve came another two hundred. Their faces covered with ninja-style hoods, they formed a double corridor along the entire gallery where the cleaners' cells were, on the second floor. They came holding knives, pieces of wood and metal piping, and the keys. They opened the first cell; precisely the one

Roberto Carlos was in: 'They told us to come out in just our underwear, 'cause we all thought we were big shit, we took money from visitors and we were gonna die. Of the eight of us, no one wanted to be the first one out. We were sure our days had ended. We tried to sit tight, but we didn't have any means with our knives all stashed in the shower.'

If they had known that the plan was to overthrow the cleaners, they wouldn't have hidden the knives and, above all, they would have disobeyed the order to return to their cells at lock-up.

More experienced than his cellmates, Roberto Carlos took the lead: 'Seeing as we were gonna meet our death, let it be free, runnin' through the gallery and not like a chicken cowerin' in its coop. I stripped down to my underpants and came out, 'cause when the ship's goin' down, the man without initiative drowns first.'

In his thirteen years in the system, Roberto Carlos had never seen as many knives as he did when he left that cell. He confessed that he was scared: 'Those rows of men must have been hit men, rapists, all worthless shits, and the odd thief who had somethin' against us. There was no way to even try to fight back, or explain that we didn't know what was goin' on. I took three steps and got a thump in the head that filled my eyes with stars. Even so, I tried to get out of there with my friends behind me.'

By the time he got to the stairs, Roberto Carlos had been hit seven or eight times with pieces of wood and pipe. When he got there, a new surprise was waiting for him: 'Every two steps down there was an enemy waitin', lookin' like a ninja. One of them, ironically, was holding one of the knives that Roberto Carlos had personally hidden in the shower and thrust it at his chest: 'How's that for bad luck? I hide the knife, some-one finds it and sticks it to me of all people, aimin' for my heart, except it got my shoulder. I don't know if he missed 'cause he was all worked up or if it was the work of the saint tattooed on my chest.'

He was kicked and beaten as he ran down the stairs until he reached the pavilion door, where he took a relieved breath because he was still alive. But because an imate's happiness never lasts, on the pathway between pavilions Five and Six there was another row of beige trousers and ninja hoods. Some say that among them were warders holding lengths of pipe, because it was the shift of the same team that had been taken hostage and abused fifteen days earlier. The fifty metres of pathway separating the two pavilions seemed inter-minable to Roberto Carlos: 'It felt further away than Rio de Janeiro.'

One by one, the cleaners' cells were opened and their occupants kicked out at stick-, pipe- and knife-point. The intention was to evict and frighten the cleaners, with no fatal accidents. Black and blue, but alive, the cleaners and company were taken into the entry cage of the neighbouring Pavilion Six. From there, they were transferred to the safety of the Dungeon, in Four.

The events of that night were avidly watched from the windows of Pavilion Eight, with a partial view of the expropriated cleaners' floor.

The next morning, String Bean, as leader of the victorious group, and two direct subordinates crossed over to Eight on a diplomatic mission: to debate the conditions for recognition of the new order with that pavilion's cleaners. With the support of the men in Eight, they thought, the pavilion of the older inmates, most of whom were repeat offenders, they would win the respect of the entire prison.

They met in a cell on Rua Dez, out of sight of the warders. The dialogue was somewhat tense:

'Now the three of you are going to die. First you, String Bean, for startin' this circus. We don't like you, 'cause you defend rapists, like that friend of yours that they had the good sense to kill. Besides, if you wanted to take over the cleaners, fine, it's your right, but it should've been by the light of day. By night, with the men locked up, that's just gutless.'

They grabbed the men, brought a rubbish bin and put String Bean in it with his hands tied behind his back:

'You're gonna burn to death and then we're going to quarter you as they did with Tiradentes[1].'

Under such extreme circumstances, String Bean

---

[1] The martyr José Joaquim da Silva Xavier, who was hanged and quartered in 1792 for his role in the conspiracy known as the *Inconfidência Mineira*, which favoured Brazil's independence from Portugal.

demonstrated his ability as a negotiator, without which he would never have made it to where he was:

'Do you know why you're not gonna do that? 'Cause if the three of us don't make it back to Five safe and sound in fifteen minutes, your seven mates over in Solitary are going to die the worst of deaths.'

After moments of indecision, String Bean and the other two were released with the threat that they would meet their death in any prison within the system to which they were transferred.

Santão

During the time when I was giving talks in the cinema, I met a thief and receiver of stolen goods by the name of Santão, who had had a falling-out with a childhood friend and killed him because he had called him Dumbo. Santão, who had been born missing the outer part of one ear, had been angry about it: 'Dumbo has two ears, but they stick out. My case is different.'

Santão was the eighth child of a grocery carrier at the Central Market and a laundry woman. By the time he was seven, he was already making his own way in the world: he worked in downtown São Paulo shining shoes, cleaning car windscreens and selling roses, to help out at home. He looked older than his age and decided to change paths at the age of thirteen: 'Curiosity got the better of me: I started stealin' wallets and pickin' pockets.'

Whenever he was arrested, the police never believed that a muscular mulatto like himself, unmanageable and missing one ear, was a minor and they would send

Communal cell in Pavilion Eight.

Corridor in the general infirmary.

The skull with dagger through it is associated with cop-killers.

Pavilion Four.

Inner courtyard of Eight.

The surgical centre of the infirmary in Four.

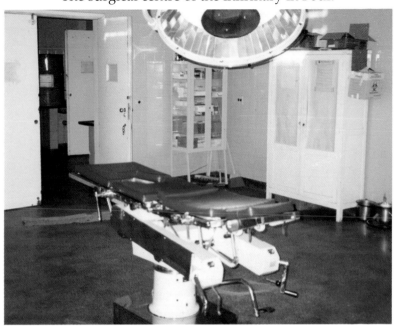

An offering in the Umbanda centre in Pavilion Nine.

The last page of the comic book *O Vira Lata* ['The Stray'].

AIDS : ASSIM PEGA

AIDS PASSA DO HOMEM PRA MULHER.
AIDS PASSA DA MULHER PRO HOMEM.

AIDS PASSA PRA LÁ E PASSA PRA CÁ.
VÍRUS NÃO RECONHECE MACHEZA

QUEM TOMA BAQUE NA VEIA VAI PEGAR O VÍRUS.
SE NÃO É HOJE VAI SER AMANHÃ OU DAQUI A SEIS MESES.

ASSIM NÃO PEGA

Prisoners arriving in Pavilion Seven.

A lawyer talks to an inmate.

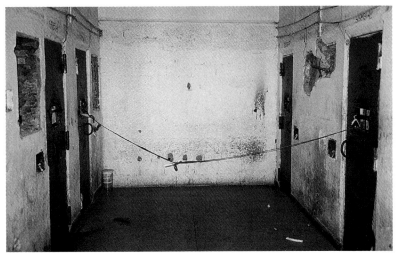

Communication between cells in Yellow.

Communal cell in Two.

Mounted Military Police officers guard the entrance to the
Casa in a moment of tension.

Riot squad conducting a search.

Burial after the 1992 massacre, at the Vila Formosa Cemetery.

him to the DEIC[1], like an adult: 'I'd be held with the hardcore villains, gettin' worked over by the cops, who wanted to know what my crimes were, but all I'd done was pick pockets, pinch things from shops and snatch wallets as people were payin' for things.'

His strong body was a disadvantage. The police saw him as a dangerous criminal; his older companions as a small-time thief in a big body. At the age of sixteen, hanging head-down in five sessions of *pau-de-arara*,[2] he decided to change his life. 'That's when I said: I need to do somethin' more serious so I've got somethin' to give 'em the next time they string me up.'

He left the downtown area and started robbing houses and holding up supermarkets and delivery trucks. He ended up in Pavilion Nine of the Casa, sentenced to eighteen years. In jail, he eventually came to accept his lot: 'If I'd kept goin' the way I was, I'd be dead or paralysed by now. When you're in crime, you're high on success.'

That was his background. When the story I am about to tell took place, we had just finished the study showing that 78 per cent of the transvestites in the Casa were HIV-positive. Staggered by the number, I arranged with Waldemar Gonçalves to have a talk with the

---

[1] State Department of Criminal Investigation.

[2] A torture method in which the prisoner is hung by his knees from a metal bar with his hands secured around his lower legs with a rope and then tortured with electric shocks, beatings and cigarette burns.

transvestites. It was scheduled for a Friday at eight a.m., in the cinema.

On the day in question, I arrived in the cinema half an hour early. I was lucky I got there when I did, because the sky grew dark and a loud thunderstorm caused a power outage in the prison. No one was there yet. I entered alone, in the half-light, and went to the window opposite the door to watch the rain. My gaze became lost in the water falling on the wall and the front of Pavilion Five.

At a particular moment, I noticed a tall mulatto in a white T-shirt at the door of the cinema, some twenty metres from me. He stood there a while in silence, staring at me. Then he turned and left. Still standing by the window, I pretended not to have noticed him.

A short time later, two others arrived and leaned against either side of the door frame. Then the first one came back and stood between them, his weight on one leg, the other casually cast out to the side. The three of them didn't say a word. I was afraid, alone in the dark with the deafening storm outside.

I lost track of time. The inmate in the white T-shirt started walking slowly towards me with a criminal's swagger. The other two remained in the doorway. When he was half way across the cinema, I gave up trying to pretend nothing was out of the ordinary and turned to face him.

He lifted his chin at me. I did the same with a racing heart and waited for him to reach me. When he was closer, I shifted my weight and put my hands on my hips, facing him, chin up, matching the expression on his face, which I was now able to see.

When he was two steps away from me he smiled and held out his hand.

'How's it goin', Doctor?'

'What's up?'

'It's like this, Doctor. I'd like to help you out here in the cinema. I admire what you're doin'!'

'Do you know how to work sound equipment?'

'I can get by, Doctor. On the outside, I used to deal in electronics.'

We arranged that he would start the following week. He shook my hand vigorously and smiled again. I asked how I could find him.

'Just ask for Santão, everyone knows me.'

Women, Motels and Partying

Santão started helping set up the sound equipment. One day, after a talk, he came over to me and said:

'Doctor, I don't want to take advantage of the prestige your friendship brings me, but do you think it'd be possible to take a look at Ezequiel, a mate of mine who's got a problem with his lungs, over in Eight?'

Ezequiel's cell was lined with colourful women. There were so many that they merged into one, forming a mosaic that covered the wall and door. He was lying in the lowest bed on a bunk, his front teeth missing, dehydrated, with a high fever, pain in his chest and sweat running down his face.

Ezequiel told me he had done time in a penitentiary in the interior of the state for trafficking and receiving stolen goods. One night, in the penitentiary, he saw two warders remove an inmate from his cell. The next day, the guy was found dead. They claimed he had tried to escape. Ezequiel couldn't accept it and reported the warders to the prison director. Years later, when he had been transferred to a semi-open prison, Ezequiel came face to face with the same warders, who had been relocated there as a result of the case he had reported. 'Open isn't a bed of roses like they say,' he said regretfully.

Anticipating the worst, seven days later, Ezequiel left for work and didn't return to the prison afterwards, as he was supposed to. 'I thought one thing, but fate had somethin' else in mind for me.'

He found his family struggling to get by, living in a house vulnerable to flooding, on the banks of a creek in a poor district of São Paulo. His parents were aging and his older sister had moved in together with her four children after being abandoned by her husband. He took charge of the family. Because he was on the run he kept no fixed address, but would show up at his parent's house for lunch or dinner. He would have barely finished eating when he'd be back on the streets again: 'There's one thing I know how to do well: I've been in crime for a long time and the cops have never busted my home. I don't give 'em the chance.'

To help him start over again, a friend lent him 200 grams of cocaine. He quickly found his feet as a dealer and only had to sleep in downtown hotels with low-class prostitutes on a few occasions; most of the time he spent his nights in the homes of female cocaine users in the cities of São Paulo, Santos and São Vicente. 'Life on the run is busy: women, motels and partyin'. In the middle of the night, you're in a club having a drink and you hear a siren in the distance and think it's the cops. Or you're in the city centre and a police car goes past and you get a shiver down your spine. Some men'll run and get caught for something silly, when they weren't even after them. You're always on edge.'

He made good money. He'd buy a gram for 250 and resell it for 600 or 700. He delivered it by motorbike, personally. His customers would invite him in and offer him expensive imported drinks. They trusted him so much that they even paid him with cheques. Ezequiel deposited them in a bank account belonging to his sister, who had looked out for him ever since he was a child. He slowly raised his family's standard of living, with a little house on higher ground, a stocked pantry and good clothes for his sister's children. To spare them any worry, he told them he was in the business of buying and selling automobiles.

'Meanwhile, I got myself a girlfriend who worked for a phone company and knew society people, lawyers, doctors, a stock market manager and a guy who did adverts on TV, first-world people who liked me 'cause I only sold the purest, uncut merchandise. One client of mine, the biggest lottery man in the south of the city, whose name I can't name, used to say that I was a very honest guy.'

One day, one of his customers was arrested and things got complicated: 'They must have given him such a workin' over that he gave them my name as his dealer. He even gave them the licence plate of my motorbike, which was in my dad's name. They investigated who his children were and my name came up, with a debt to the justice system and all.'

A few days later, he was sitting on his motorbike eating an ice cream, when two revolvers appeared behind him: 'Hey, Ezequiel dos Santos, how's our fugitive doing?'

One of the police officers, wearing a pair of dark sunglasses, searched him, while his bearded partner kept a distance. Ezequiel was unarmed.

Once he'd got over the initial shock, he asked if there was any way they could come to an understanding: 'They wanted 800 or I'd be back inside. I told them I'd already done ten years, I'd seen hard times, the oldies depended on me and so on, plus my sister and her children. I said they weren't gonna gain nothing by arresting me and that I wasn't doin' society no harm, since I only sold to people who wanted to buy. So, we cut a deal where they took the motorbike, which was worth 400, in exchange for my freedom.'

Without his motorbike, it was harder for him to service his clientele and sales fell. He went into debt with his supplier who brought him cocaine from Bolivia.

The solution to his crisis came through the stock market manager, in a São Paulo nightclub. The man snorted a fresh line, stretched, placed his arm round Ezequiel's shoulders and whispered: 'You're a good guy, you only bring me the purest snow. Know what? I'm going to give you an opportunity worth half a million dollars. You deserve it!'

He told Ezequiel that his girlfriend was secretary to a money changer in the district of Jardins who kept $500,000 in a safe in his home. The broker gave him the money changer's address, told him he had three children and that his wife was bound to a wheelchair because of an accident. 'I decided to do a really good job plannin' the heist. I spent ten days followin' the guy.'

He discovered that the money changer left his office at six p.m. every day and went straight home. At first, he thought he'd grab him as he was leaving, take him home and force him to open the safe. He abandoned the idea, however, as he thought it would be complicated to kidnap someone on the busy Avenida Faria Lima at rush hour. He decided it would be more prudent to enter his future victim's residence late in the afternoon, take his wife, children and two maids hostage and wait for the money changer, who would have no alternative but to open the safe for him.

To carry out the robbery, he needed a partner and a fast car. He remembered Alcindo, from the city of Santo André, who had done time with him in a prison in the city of Presidente Wenceslau. 'Alcindo was known as the best driver around. He was even nicknamed Ayrton Senna.'

They arranged everything for a Thursday. The day before they would steal the getaway car, which they'd keep hidden at Alcindo's house. They would paint 'Rosa Gardênia Florist' in white letters on the door of the vehicle, and, at the scheduled hour, would go to the money changer's house to deliver flowers. They rehearsed everything several times. It was all perfect. They were already planning what they were going to do with the money. As at the open prison, however, fate had something else in store for him.

On the Tuesday, they went car-hunting. It wasn't easy. Alcindo was demanding about the quality of the vehicle. After a lot of walking, they found a couple arguing in a car that Alcindo considered adequate for the job. They each appeared with a revolver at the front windows. The man didn't react in any way; he only asked that they leave his fiancée alone. They explained that they were only interested in the car and drove away.

They turned three or four corners and, as they were about to give a sigh of relief, a police car appeared from nowhere with a wailing siren and squealing tires. The chase began: 'The cops were hangin' out of the windows with their guns pointed. The only reason they didn't fire was because there were lots of cars around them. Then I found out that Alcindo didn't have a drop of Ayrton Senna in him. He was all over the place like a headless chicken. The other cars were makin' way because of the siren and he kept bumpin' into them. He was a bundle of nerves and whiter than an ambulance.'

When they got on a viaduct, they collided head-on with another car, in which a man was taking his pregnant wife to the doctor. The impact knocked Ezequiel unconscious. 'I woke up at the door of the hospital, but they clouted me across the chin with a nine-millimetre Luger and I blacked out again.'

He was released that same night. When he got to the police station, he was told that the owner of the stolen car worked for ROTA, a military police tactical force, and had called in the theft himself, initiating the chase. To make matters worse, the man whose car they had crashed into, with his pregnant wife in it, was an investigator with the State Department of Criminal Investigation. The double coincidence made his punishment even worse: 'I lost seven teeth and then had to pull out the only one I had left in the front. They strung me up on the *pau-de-arara* and kicked me so many times in the back with their boots that I still have problems in the cold weather.'

The police kicked him and one said: 'If that man's child dies, we're gonna finish you off good, you useless piece of shit!' He swore that he loved children, that he was crazy about his nieces and nephews, especially the youngest, his godson, and that he'd never intended to kill an innocent in its mother's belly. It was no use. He was kicked in the mouth, in the ribs, and they used a stun gun to give his wet body electric shocks.

'It was an unlucky day, Doctor. Stealing the wheels for the getaway from a ROTA officer; crashing into the investigator's car, with his pregnant wife in it to boot; and the only thing Alcindo had in common with Ayrton was his nickname. My fault for believing it. How can a guy raised in a *favela* be a good driver at the age of twenty-two? He's never even had a car!'

His past successes were no consolation: 'It's hard, Doctor. I get out of breath climbin' the pavilion stairs, doubled over like an old man, and I feel horrible knowin' my family's suffering without me, experiencin' hardship.'

Maria-Louca

Ezequiel recovered from his tuberculosis and we became friends. He was the most highly respected *maria-louca* distiller in Pavilion Eight, and his famous product attracted customers from the entire prison.

Maria-louca was the prison's traditional bootleg *cachaça*. According to the older prisoners, it was as old as the Brazilian penal system itself. Despite the punishment in Solitary if one was caught, large-scale production persisted. The high alcohol content made the men violent. They would fight, knife one another and disrespect the warders who tried to keep them in line.

Ezequiel wasn't exactly modest about his art: 'I only sell the very best. If you put my *cachaça* on a spoon and light a match in the dark, it'll give off the purest blue flame. Lots of blokes make it, but it doesn't even catch fire; it's a kind of vinegar. I make whisky.'

The popping corn that his mother would bring him, unaware of its intended use, was Ezequiel's raw material: he would pour five kilos of corn, with sugar and the peels of fruits such as honeydew melons, papayas, oranges and apples into a large drum he had bought in the general kitchen. He would then cover the top of the drum with a clean cloth and put the lid on tight: 'That's the secret! If it leaks, the smell creeps out into the gallery and the screws come after it, 'cause they have it in for *cachaça*. They say the men are rude to them when they drink. The way I close it, Doctor, a squadron can march down the corridor with their noses in the air and they won't know what goes on in this cell from the smell.'

The mixture would ferment for seven days. 'On the seventh, it's so fermented that the drum'll sometimes move on its own. It looks like it's alive.'

Due to the internal pressure, one could not be careful enough when opening it. Once open, its contents were strained through a cloth and the solids thrown away. At this point, the solution tasted like beer or a dry wine. One sip of it would numb your oesophagus and send a shiver through you. Every five litres would become one litre of *cachaça*, after the mixture had been distilled.

During the distilling process, the liquid was transferred to a large tin with a hole in the top, through which ran a little hose connected to a copper coil. The tin was placed on the cooker and its contents brought to a boil. The steam would rise through the hose and pass through the coil, which Ezequiel cooled constantly with a mug of cold water. When the steam came into contact with the cooled coil it would condense, a phenomenon of physics that impressed him: 'The force of the thermal shock! The steam turns to liquid!' After passing through the coil, the *maria-louca* would drip into a bottle. Five kilos of uncooked corn or rice and ten of sugar yielded nine litres of the drink. 'It comes out clean and it's absolutely divine. The best there is. My *cachaça* doesn't make you thirsty in the middle of the night, or need to go to the toilet, and it doesn't make your feet swell up.'

When he started, Ezequiel was one of the few distillers in Eight. He worked hard, from eight o'clock at night until three-thirty in the morning, because it wasn't the kind of work one did by the light of day. It earned him a reputation: 'I used to sell it for ten a litre. Nowadays any old lazy arse can make it. They produce this bitter vinegar and it costs an arm and a leg: thirty, forty a litre. It's abusive.'

Ezequiel was very careful when practising his trade and was never caught due to negligence: 'The three times I was found out, it was because someone had grassed.' The first time, he spent ninety days in a cubicle with eight other inmates, in the heat of summer. The other two times, he only got thirty days.

Proud of his work, Ezequiel only stopped producing *maria-louca* when he fell seriously ill. He was shrewd and never took an interest in the easy profits of cocaine: 'Doctor, I've been convicted four times for 157: robbery. I've never been caught with drugs. If I got convicted of selling crack in here, I'd wind up in 12: traffickin'. It's a completely different article, and even worse if you're caught doin' it on the inside. The judge could call it a continuous crime, he could say I glorified crime. He'd say I can't be rehabilitated and deny me all benefits.'

Eight, the repeat offenders' pavilion, was traditionally the prison's biggest *maria-louca* producer, followed by Five. In May of 1998, 1000 litres of it were found there in a single raid. I was surprised when I heard how much had been seized, but a warder reminded me: 'It might seem like a lot, Doctor, but don't forget there are 7000 inmates.'

Indeed, those 1000 litres didn't break the record of a previous raid: 1200 litres, distilled and ready for sale.

Miguel

Miguel used to carry out armed robberies with his partner, Antônio Carlos. They trusted each other so much that they agreed to look after each other's families should one of them be arrested. They did well out of a supermarket job and invested the money in cocaine, which proved to be prosperous for them. They decided to stay in that line of business, as small retailers in the municipality of Taboão da Serra, part of Greater São Paulo.

One day, as they were travelling with two companions in the back of a truck loaded with furniture, with two kilos of cocaine hidden in a cupboard, they ran into a police barricade. In the ensuing shoot-out, one of the companions in the back of the truck was killed. Miguel went to break the news to his widow in person.

Marli paled as she listened in silence, then burst into tears. Miguel said he was sad too. He gave her her husband's cut from the job and told her to contact Antônio Carlos or himself if she needed anything.

He left, enchanted by her beauty. He had never seen such beautiful legs, not even on TV, and dreamed of them at night. Miguel left his family for Marli and fell headlong in love for the first time in his life at the age of thirty-eight; she was twenty-two.

One afternoon, when they had been together for almost two years, Antônio Carlos, who lived a block away, showed up at Miguel's house. Marli had gone to visit her mother. The conversation was truncated and weird, until Miguel interrupted him:

'What's up, Antônio Carlos? Talk to me, what brought you here?'

'Your wife's fucking a cop.'

'Who told you that?'

Antônio Carlos gave him the name of the motel where Marli and her lover met and said he'd seen them himself, fooling around in a police car in the centre of Taboão da Serra.

Miguel felt as if he'd been stabbed in the heart. It occurred to him to kill the officer, but he discarded that idea; he'd have to skip town. Kill Marli? How? It isn't easy to kill your beloved, he realised.

He packed her clothes into a suitcase, put it on their doorstep and locked the door. When Marli got back, she knocked loudly:

'What's this, Miguel, have you gone crazy?'

At first, he didn't even answer, but she insisted, saying she had the right to know what it was all about. If he was in love with someone else, she would leave, because she wasn't the kind of woman to share her man with some slut. Then she complained that the neighbours could hear everything and he opened the door.

In the living room, she saw her husband was shaking and was surprised. She took the glass of alcohol that was in front of him and tipped it down the sink. In a low voice, she tried to calm him down until he was able to speak:

'You're a whore, a slut. I gave up my wife and kids for you, I've given you a comfortable life, affection and friendship and you repay me by cheatin' on me. I know about the cop you've been meetin' at the motel behind the petrol station on Raposo Tavares for over a year, while the idiot here was out riskin' his hide to fill up your wardrobe.'

Marli listened impassively, then asked: 'Who told you?'

'None of your business.'

'Course it is. Someone tells you a story that wrecks our home and I don't have the right to know who it is?'

He refused, saying that she was a worthless slut and that she was lucky he was a good man, otherwise he might have done something crazy. She ignored the verbal assault.

'Who told you?' she insisted, and kept on asking until Miguel confessed:

'It was Antônio Carlos. Why?'

'Well, you're gonna make him repeat it in front of me. Then I'll get my bag and go to my mother's.'

Antônio Carlos repeated the whole story in front of Marli and Miguel, and even mentioned details that he had spared his friend: 'I saw you nibblin' his earlobe in the police car!'

She listened quietly, sitting on the couch, until he had finished. There was another silence, which she broke:

'You forgot the best part.'

'What do you mean?'

Marli, who had been staring at the trinkets in the crystal cabinet as she listened to the story, got up from the couch, stood in front of Antônio Carlos and, looking him straight in the eye, said:

'You didn't tell him that you asked me to leave Miguel and run away with you. And that I refused because I love my husband and I'm friends with your wife.'

Antônio Carlos called her a liar and said that if it weren't for his respect for his friend, he'd smash her face in. He said she had a diabolical mind. She didn't answer and just stood there like a statue, then got her bag and left.

Antônio Carlos turned to his friend:

'Miguel, you didn't believe that lyin' bitch, did you? We've been friends for four years and I've never done nothing behind your back.'

'Forget it, Antônio Carlos.'

Antônio Carlos noticed a certain hesitation in his voice.

While this conversation was going on, Marli went

and rang Antônio Carlos's doorbell. A platinum blonde appeared in the window. It was Dina, his wife.

They talked in the living room, standing up.

'Dina, is Antônio Carlos a faggot?'

'What a question, Marli!'

'Sorry, but he went to Miguel with some story about me seein' a cop, which is a complete lie. He's tryin' to destroy my marriage. So it got me wondering: either he wants me to leave so he can have Miguel to himself or he wants Miguel to leave so he can have me to himself.'

'What you talkin' about? Antônio Carlos can't stand faggots.'

'Well then, darlin', it's me he's got the hots for.'

She took the bus to her mother's house.

Antônio Carlos was something of a ladies' man and Dina was the jealous sort. She had once come to blows with a prostitute that he knew, and it had taken two men and a woman to separate them. When Antônio Carlos got home, Dina sunk her fingernails into his face:

'You bastard, I always said you had a thing for her. And you always said I was crazy. Can't you even stay away from your friend's wife, asshole?'

The next morning, Antônio Carlos knocked on Miguel's door.

'Did you sleep with a cat?' asked Miguel, when he saw the scratches on his face.

'You won't believe this. When your wife left here,

she went to my place and put it into Dina's head that I've got the hots for her. When I got home, Dina flew at me.'

Miguel inspected his friend's injuries and said, ceremoniously: 'Antônio Carlos, the hand of suspicion's come to rest on our friendship. It's time each of us went his own way.'

His friend tried arguing, saying that their partnership was advantageous for both of them, but it was no good. The next day, Miguel went to get Marli at her mother's house. She agreed to come back on the condition that they forget the entire episode and go back to the harmony they had enjoyed before. He promised and kept his word, in part. He began to follow her; he would tell her he had to leave town, then return home in the middle of the night; and eventually he hired someone to trail her: nothing. Her behaviour was exemplary.

A year later, with business going well, they moved into a bigger house, which they put in Marli's name because Miguel couldn't have anything in his name. He was no longer suspicious of her. As for his partner, they didn't see each other anymore. Antônio Carlos had been arrested and was doing time in the Casa de Detenção.

Around this time, Miguel raised $40,000 in a kidnapping and decided to triple his money. He told his wife that they'd buy a house in the countryside afterwards.

He took a coach to Santa Cruz de la Sierra, in Bolivia.

From there, he took a smaller bus – the sort which people get on carrying crates of chickens – and alighted in the main square of the town, in front of the hotel that belonged to his cocaine supplier's mother.

Miguel made a 50 per cent down payment and the Bolivian sent his cocaine off for refining. It took two days, but he didn't mind. He took the opportunity to go fishing with the producer's brother, who was fond of telling funny tales. Once in possession of his order, Miguel headed back, avoiding the most heavily policed route. Instead, he took a bus to Brasilia, then to Belo Horizonte, São Paulo and Santos, where he sold the cocaine. He wore a navy-blue suit and shirt buttoned up to the top and carried a Bible, which he read the whole way back: 'As a disguise.'

He arrived home with almost $100,000. He opened the door and walked down the dark corridor. The dog barked and wagged its tail. He drank some water from the filter and headed for the bedroom. Marli was asleep in her underwear and a skimpy top. He lay down beside her warm body and nibbled delicately on her neck. Miguel was happy again.

The next morning, she woke up early and went to the bakery to buy some bread. She made a call from the public phone at the bakery: 'The bird's come back to the cage. He's brought a bag of birdseed.'

The police surprised Miguel on the toilet. Marli's lover headed up the operation. Then he took her on a holiday to the Northeast of Brazil.

Miguel

Miguel arrived in the Casa de Detenção and wallowed in crack. He caught tuberculosis, didn't treat it properly and died in the infirmary. From sadness, said Antônio Carlos, who looked after his friend until the end.

Disappearing Act

Claudiomiro said the only reason he was caught was because he had a wife and child. The chief of police had investigated the city's health clinics and found his son's vaccination records, with his mother's address on them. He had her followed. One night, she took a bus to the town of Leme, in the interior, with the boy and went to stay at her aunt's place. The police set up an observation post in the district. Three days later Claudiomiro showed up, having been missing his family.

I met him due to a procedural requirement of the Casa: every prisoner summoned to testify at a police station had to have been examined by a doctor before he left. I asked him to remove his clothes. He had a strong body, with three old scars and no signs of recent violence. I asked if he had been beaten up.

'Not here. Let's see what happens now down at DEPATRI.'[1]

---

[1] Department for the Repression of Crime Against Property.

'What are you facing down there?'

'They want to pin sixteen bank and eight armoured car robberies on me.'

'How many are you going to plead guilty to?'

'None, Doctor. I can't. I've already got more than fifteen years to serve.'

Two days later on the news, I saw that a group had attempted to escape from DEPATRI. Claudiomiro was one of the leaders and was sent back to the Casa the same night. I ran into him on the path between pavilions.

'So how many did you plead guilty to down at DEPATRI?'

'They didn't get around to interrogating me.'

'Can you make good money doing banks and armoured cars?'

'You can, but it's only worth half, sometimes less.'

This enigmatic reply was followed by a conversation about his profession.

'It takes a lot of discipline, Doctor. At eight p.m., I turn in. I don't hang out at bars or nightclubs, because the police might pick me up in a routine bust. I go to bed early and, at my place, I'm the one who wakes up the rooster.'

Claudiomiro helped his wife with the household chores and shopping, changed nappies and told his son bedtime stories. Whenever he was in hiding, not even his wife knew where he was. But he never fooled around behind her back during his absences: 'There's no shortage of women for bank robbers. Except that lots of them wind up inside or in a trap set by another con, 'cause a woman whose pride has been hurt is capable of evil things.'

According to Claudiomiro, precise information was fundamental: what time the armoured car passed, how many thousand were in the bank safe, the number of guards, every last detail. He obtained this information cautiously from the guards themselves, who worked for security companies. 'You can't just walk up and say, "Hey, man, give us the rundown." You've gotta approach them through a friend, a family member, in a bar, over a beer.'

On one occasion he spent six months tracking down the information he wanted. 'I became friends with the guy, lent him money; I even went to his son's christening. You have to win their trust first, and raise their awareness later. You explain that he's risking his life to protect other people's money and makin' peanuts, that these security companies exploit their employees, that if he dies on the job, his wife and children are gonna be hard up.'

It was a slow indoctrination. 'Until he spills the beans.'

Weeks or months were then spent planning the heist. If it was a bank, a sketch would have to be made, showing the locations of the cashiers, the safe, the internal closed-circuit cameras and the guards. When it was an armoured car, they had to time its trajectory over a number of consecutive days, prepare a map of the nearby streets and determine the exact time they were going to make their move. It was slow, solitary work. 'Just me and God. I wear a suit and tie, carry a leather briefcase, and in some cases I open an account at the branch with false ID, to justify my goin' there every day.'

With the plan in place, Claudiomiro would start looking for men to hire. This was the worst part, according to him. 'You need to know how to deal with thieves.' A robbery of that scale could require up to a dozen men and Claudiomiro didn't work with a set gang, for security reasons. He felt it was more prudent to outsource certain tasks, with the exception of those carried out by two partners who had been with him for many years. 'Even so, they don't know where I live, or who I live with. When I have a job, I go find them. We meet early and I tell them the plan two days before the heist, but I don't say where it is and they don't ask. It is only on the day, half an hour before we set out, that everyone finds out.'

The three of them would analyse the sketch and calculate how many men should be hired and for how much. Some were paid a set fee, others a percentage. The calculations had to be done well. 'Otherwise it becomes a free-for-all; no one sets his eyes on the loot.'

After the meeting, Claudiomiro would return home and the other two would put together the team and steal the getaway vehicles, which were later abandoned not far from the site of the robbery, because the occupants would change cars, sometimes even with normal people in them, as a disguise. 'Some people will even put a fat old lady in the driver's seat and a child in the back. I don't put innocent people in danger, 'cause when the police come after you, they don't want to chat.'

On the scheduled day, Claudiomiro would head out at four-thirty in the morning to pick up the weapons: repeating rifles, machine guns and imported revolvers. Only he knew where they were hidden. In the world of crime, weapons were power. 'I generally leave 'em with people who are above suspicion: a man of faith or a churchgoing widow.'

The person would provide the service in exchange for rent money, groceries or help in a time of need. This complicity bred emotional ties: 'At five o'clock in the morning, when I show up to get the tools, there's an old lady who serves me coffee with boiled manioc and corn cake. The funny thing is that I show up without any warnin', and the table's set, with a clean tablecloth, cake and milk on the stove. As I'm leavin' she says, "God protect you, my boy!" At that moment, it's comfortin' to hear those words from an old lady.'

The most dangerous period was from five a.m. to ten a.m., with the weapons in the car. The police were familiar with the makes of cars that thieves preferred and knew when to move in. 'After the job, in possession of the money, you're a goner if they catch you.'

The work required a cool head. The tension didn't let up even when everything went according to plan. The robbery would put the police on the streets and stir up other criminals. 'When I get a decent sum, I evaporate. I move house, change cars, and I don't have visitors over to show off my TV, my new fridge, the comfort my family enjoys. It's better than hirin' guards, as a lot of people do, and losin' my family's privacy.'

The news could even travel as far as the prison: 'So-and-so's got a new car. He's loaded now. Thinks he's a big shot. He got lucky but he's a fool. He won't get far. What, a small-time thief like him with that kind of money? I can have a chat with my cop friend and get him arrested and he'll be done for.'

Claudiomiro was once approached by two armed men who searched him and demanded $30,000, for their boss, who would leave him in peace if he paid. Claudiomiro told them the money was in the safe at the bank and took them there. One of the blackmailers stayed outside with the revolvers and the other one waited in the bank foyer. Claudiomiro went to the safe and came back holding a package. He pumped three bullets into one of them and two into the other, without opening the package. The dead men never could have imagined that there was a revolver in the safe.

Claudiomiro didn't brag about his cunning; he hadn't actually wanted to do it. 'It would've been better to pay the thirty thou, since I'd made seventy-four in the heist, than to kill the two of them in the middle of that crowd, runnin' the risk of being shot by a security guard or the police, who were all over the place in no time. Except that I don't want to get known as easy pickings because then everyone'll come knockin', and I've got a wife and son to support.'

Claudiomiro always kept $50,000 handy in case he was caught. If the police approached him, his first question was if there was any chance they could come to an agreement. 'If I see that he hesitates, I point it out: look, you make 700 . . . 800 *reais* a month, you pay rent, and you can't afford a toy for your son or support your mother or mother-in-law. What are you gonna get if you arrest me? For me, it's cheaper to settle with you than pay a lawyer, who'll get me off further down the track.'

That was why he said his money was worth half.

On another occasion he obtained a healthy figure robbing a branch of Bradesco. He rented a three-bedroom apartment in the São Paulo district of Bixiga, and furnished it according to his wife's taste, with all the electrical appliances she wanted.

'I didn't even enjoy twenty days of comfort.' One afternoon, as he was leaving the supermarket after shopping for groceries, he noticed a man in a baseball cap at the news stand next door. Instead of crossing the street, Claudiomiro turned right. At the next set of traffic lights, before crossing the street, he glanced around: the man in the cap was coming in the same direction. Claudiomiro was certain:

'Cops. I can smell 'em from a distance.'

He went home as if nothing had happened, changed into a pair of Bermuda shorts and flip-flops, got his wife, baby, pram, the bag with the baby's bottles on top of the money, and they left. The man in the base-ball cap was at the service station across the street. He must have thought they were taking the baby for a walk and waited for them to return, in vain. 'As soon as we were around the corner, I hailed a taxi and we were out of there.'

They left everything behind. 'TV, video camera, double bed and all the rest. Even my new Ford Verona in the garage, properly registered and everything. My wife didn't say a word. It wasn't the first time we'd left everythin' behind, nor would it be the last, but that day it broke my heart to see the tears on her face.'

Months after I heard this story, Claudiomiro was transferred and escaped from prison. He continued his life of crime until he was brought down by bullets from a police car that happened to be passing in front of the bank he was robbing. He was thirty-five years old. He was survived by his pregnant wife and young son.

Deusdete and Mané

When I arrived in Pavilion Four one time, the sun was shining brightly on the ground-floor cage. Shorty was chatting with a warder by the stairs. I asked if the lift was working. He replied with his characteristic lisp:

'As usual, no, Doctor. Have you seen the bodies?'

In a bathtub-come-morgue, on the ground floor, lay the bodies of two young men. One of them, wearing Bermuda shorts, was horribly burned. His body was covered in blisters, especially his face and chest; some had burst, exposing deeper layers of dark, moist skin. The other was riddled with stab wounds.

The bodies belonged to Deusdete and Mané, who had grown up in the same neighbourhood and had been inseparable friends until they were fourteen, when Mané got a job at a junkyard and left school. At around the same time, Deusdete's father was killed when he fell off the back of a train on which he had hitched a ride. Deusdete started working during the day and studying by night. But Mané became involved in crime and lost interest in his hard-working friend's life.

One night, Deusdete's middle sister Francineide was hounded by two criminals on her way home from the bakery. One invited her to sit on his face. 'Ask your mother to sit on your face, you sleaze,' she replied, insulted. They beat her and she arrived home with a torn dress and swollen mouth. When he saw his sister in that state, Deusdete hurried down to the local police station. He waited over two hours, only to hear the clerk say that he'd go crazy if he had to file a complaint for every case of aggression in the district.

A week after the incident, on the bus, a neighbour warned him that his sister's attackers knew he had gone to the police and were after him. Deusdete asked for an advance on his pay and went out to buy a revolver. It didn't take him long to find one.

Although he was now armed, he changed his route to school anyway. It made no difference; they found him on his way back, alone, on a dark street.

'Where does the grassing pupil think he's goin'?'

'I don't want to fight. Let me go home.'

'You're going running to mother, you faggot, but first we're gonna give you a bit of lovin', like we did with your little sister.'

The first to approach him was holding an iron bar. He was so sure of himself that he didn't notice that Deusdete had pulled out the revolver. He took two bullets and fell down dead. His companion, who was holding a knife, took off running. Deusdete fired, missed and gave chase. Three or four corners later, the fugitive ran into a street bar. Deusdete waited crouching behind the fence of a house, until his enemy came out, looked around suspiciously and crossed the street, coming right towards him. The man took the last three bullets in the barrel, to the surprise of two fellows who were playing snooker in front of the bar and who later testified against Deusdete in court.

When Deusdete arrived in the Casa de Detenção, he was taken in by Mané, who was doing eight years and six months for cargo theft and conspiracy and who owned a cell in Pavilion Five. With the help of his friend, Deusdete, sentenced to nine years for double homicide, found his feet among the inmates. He taught at the pavilion's school, wrote letters for the illiterate and typed up appeals for fellow prisoners.

This harmonious existence, however, was shaken when Mané discovered crack. His friend's advice was useless; Mané smoked away everything he had.

On the night of the tragedy, Weasel appeared at the window in the cell door.

'Mané, I've got some rocks for us to smoke.'

Deusdete lost his patience.

'Enough! You're not smoking with me in here. If you want to kill yourselves, be my guest, but do it tomorrow, after I'm gone!'

Weasel didn't stay.

'Forget it, Mané. Talk to you tomorrow.'

Mané felt diminished in front of Weasel, but didn't say a word. That night, while his childhood friend was asleep, he filled a large pot with five litres of water, a tin of oil and a kilo of salt and lit the cooker. When the mixture was boiling, he poured it over his cellmate.

Deusdete died in the infirmary of Pavilion Four early the next morning. At midday, his angry friends met with the cleaners from Five, for a 'debate', as they say, which involved more than forty people. They decided that a group would wait near the pavilion entrance and another would block the stairs on the first floor. When Mané entered, the group near the entrance came up behind him.

His body was taken to Four on a food trolley. There, one inmate took him by the arms, and another by the legs and they laid him on his side in the corridor between Deusdete and the wall. Mané's inert arm fell on his friend's waist.

Mother Dear

'Jail is a place where a son suffers and his
mother doesn't see it.'

Night had fallen. I was in the consulting room,
anxious to leave, when a tall, strong man slowly
entered, walking with his legs apart and holding his
testicles with his hands. He needed two nurses to help
him onto the table.

The guy had a reputation as a fearless robber, with
illegal lottery connections and a scar on his right
eyebrow, and he was the second-in-command of the
cleaners in Eight, the repeat offenders' pavilion. He had
an abscess in his scrotum the size of a large peach. Red
as fire, its contents were liquid, and the skin was so taut
in the middle that it actually shone.

'Look,' I said, 'this needs to be lanced to drain the
pus. I'm going to refer you to Mandaqui Hospital.'

'Doctor, I've been sufferin' for eight days now,' he
replied. 'I've already been referred to Mandaqui three

times, but they haven't had a van free to take me. They ended up takin' me yesterday after I begged 'em, 'cause I was desperate, but I didn't even get out of the van 'cause the cops said it was gonna take too long and they weren't nursemaids for scum like me. Isn't there any way you could do it here?'

'We've only got the most basic material here. Besides, you've got no idea how much it hurts. It's hard to take without an anaesthetic.'

He tried to smile.

'C'mon, Doctor. You're talkin' to a man with four bullets in his body. I've been strung up more than twenty times. I got beaten with a metal pipe for two hours and didn't give the cops what they wanted. If it's just the pain you're worried about, forget that: I'm your man!'

In terms of suffering, I thought, perhaps he was right. Referrals to outside hospitals were complicated, as the regulations required inmates to be transported in vans that weren't always available, with a military police escort to deter attempted escapes or attacks by gangs to rescue the prisoner. The long wait when they got to the public hospitals only made relations with their police escorts even tenser. And I had seen many a death in the infirmary while the patients were waiting to be transferred.

On the other hand, doctors could find themselves facing legal problems when somebody pretending to need outside treatment, referred by them, escaped. It had happened to me twice. The first time, a former mechanic with AIDS-related cachexia had managed to get his shrivelled hand out of the handcuff attached to the bed and disappeared. The other time, Romário, a crack user with advanced tuberculosis, had jumped the fence of the Central Hospital, situated behind the Casa de Detenção, while the guards were watching Brazil play Germany on TV, spent fifteen days on the streets smoking crack and was brought in again; he died two months later in the infirmary.

If the patient was willing to undergo the procedure in the prison without a general anaesthetic, why not? Because there was no surgeon present I called for Lula, a bank robber who often performed small operations in the infirmary.

When Lula arrived with the material, I positioned four inmate-nurses around the table, to hold the cleaner's arms and legs. I carefully lifted the swollen testicle and placed a wad of cotton underneath it. The slightest movement of the inflamed region was intensely painful. Sweat was beginning to run down the man's forehead. When everything was ready, I showed Lula where to make the incision.

Wearing gloves and holding a surgical knife between the forefinger and middle finger of his left hand, Lula made a deep cut in the inflamed skin and in the same movement tossed the knife onto the tray and squeezed hard, from the outside of the abscess towards the centre. He kept a firm grip, without letting up. The pus squirted out yellow and thick.

The incision itself appeared to be painless, but the compression elicited a deep howl from the cleaner. His body stiffened like an arch supported by his head and heels. If it weren't for the determination of the four nurses, the table would have overturned. Lula continued squeezing impassively.

The cleaner's guttural spasm only ended when he had exhausted the air in his lungs.

'Aahh, for the love of God, get off . . . Aahh, mother . . . Watch over me, mother dear.'

Lula continued squeezing pitilessly until the yellow secretion stopped flowing and blood stained the cotton. He let up the pressure, and then gave it another three hard squeezes to be sure of a job well done. When he finally let go, the convict's chin was trembling like a leaf. Pale and dripping with sweat, he was still obsessively repeating: 'Aahh, mother dear . . . Aahh, help me Blessed Virgin . . . Watch over your son, mother.'

A few minutes later, relieved, the cleaner humbly thanked everyone.

'Thank God, it's better. God bless you all. God bless you, Doctor. God Watch over you, Lula.'

Professionally gathering up the instruments with a scowl on his face, Lula interrupted him.

'OK, enough! Leave Him in peace now. Too much God in a con's mouth ain't right!'

In slow motion, the cleaner climbed down from the table and hobbled back into the gallery with his legs apart. When the door closed, Pedrinho, who was washing the table with a soapy cloth, muttered quietly, 'Christ, a big-time bank-robber like that, who's held up armoured cars, second-in-charge of the cleaners, begging for his mother like that!'

Edelso

Of all the inmates who worked in the infirmary, Edelso was the one who had the most talent for medicine. He was the inmates' favourite when it came to giving injections, bandaging up wounds and, when they were suffering in the middle of the night, for prescribing the best treatment for their symptoms. With his experience, he learned to diagnose tuberculosis better than many doctors. He would bring the patients in with treatment already under way:

'Doctor, this guy here has a fever, pain in his chest and night sweats. He was prescribed a drip with vitamins and ampicillin, but I've already started him on the triple therapy.'

Pleasant-mannered, with well-cared-for teeth and clothes, he stood out in that environment of poor men and bodies marked by violence.

Edelso had been in and out of jail for vehicle theft. He came to the Casa sentenced to eight years and seven months, having been found guilty of a number of crimes: receiving stolen goods, conspiracy and misrepresentation. He was arrested because he had assumed the identity of a recently deceased doctor in the city of Mogi das Cruzes. With fake documents, he rented a two-storey house in a neighbouring town and set up a medical practice, with a sign on the door, a prescription pad and a medical licence number.

'I used to buy stolen cars at a chop shop in São Paulo and would re-sell them on the Paraguayan border.' As a disguise, the role of doctor fit like a glove for Edelso, who had studied to be a nursing assistant. 'It's normal for doctors to always have new cars.'

He moved into the residence-come-medical practice by night. His neighbour even helped him carry in the furniture. The next morning, he awoke to the doorbell ringing. He looked out of the bathroom window and saw the police officers, a tall one with a greying moustache and another mopping the sweat off his forehead with a handkerchief. 'I'd barely moved in and things went south!' said Edelso.

He thought about escaping on foot through the back. It wouldn't be the first time he'd left his belongings behind. He hesitated, while the doorbell kept ringing. In the end, he decided to pretend he didn't know what it was about and calmly went downstairs, with his revolver stuffed into the waist of his trousers. Through the little window in the door, he asked what the police officers wanted.

'Doctor, there's a child in a bad way down at the

public health clinic and the doctor hasn't arrived. Can you help us out?'

When Edelso arrived at the clinic, there were several people standing around a seven-year-old girl who had a roaring fever and sore throat, lying on a stretcher. They looked poor. A woman in black who appeared to be the girl's grandmother explained that she had been complaining of an intense headache. Edelso thought it was odd.

'A small child with a headache?'

He placed his hand behind the girl's neck and tried to bend her neck to make her chin touch her chest. She cried out with pain.

'A stiff neck!'

The neurological symptom was enough for the fake doctor to make a diagnosis.

'Meningitis! You need to get her to Emílio Ribas Hospital. This place isn't equipped to deal with it.'

At that moment, as Edelso was telling her family what to do, the real doctor arrived, described by the charlatan as: 'A weird sort, chewing gum and dressed in white, with a hairy chest. He walked in, didn't speak to anyone, only looked at the little girl's throat, prescribed Keflex every six hours and turned his back.'

Edelso kept quiet, looking for an excuse to leave. His business was something else and he didn't want to take any chances. As he was leaving, the girl's father came after him.

'Doctor, you think it's meningitis and the other doctor

said it's just tonsillitis, but he didn't even examine her. What should I do?'

'If it were my daughter, I'd take her to Emílio Ribas.'

The father's common sense prevailed. The diagnosis of bacterial meningitis was confirmed at the hospital, where the girl was admitted and cured.

Edelso's reputation grew and the clinic prospered. He charged only small fees or nothing at all, according to what his patients could afford. He didn't depend on medicine to survive, as he made $2–3000 for each car he took to Paraguay.

'Those trips are hard, Doctor. You have to do all your driving by night to avoid being picked up, and you're alone, because you can't involve friends or an innocent woman in a scheme like that. What if the cops pull you over? Do you drive through their barricade, stop and get arrested, or hand everything over to them?'

One day things really did go south. A general practitioner in Mogi das Cruzes treated a patient with a prescription given by Edelso in the name of the deceased physician and reported him to the police.

Edelso's career in the infirmary ended one weekend. The director of Pavilion Two had him transferred to Seven, because when a drug dealer's cell was raided his name was found on a list of debtors, with ten *reais* against his name.

Months later, I ran into him on the path between pavilions. He looked well, having had a rest from his work with the patients. He was making plans for when he was released. 'I'm getting out of this business of cars, chop shops, and Paraguay, because there's no future in it. With the medicine I learned from you, I can't wait to set up my own practice in a simple place and live a peaceful life looking after my patients.'

Lula

Iwas introduced to Lula in the consulting room because of a freckled inmate with a knife wound in his buttock. The guy, who had a tattoo of an eagle with its wings spread on his back, was brought in lying face-down on a stretcher, with his trousers down and underwear torn from the stabbing. The knife had reached his deep muscles but had spared the most important nerves and blood vessels; it just had to be washed and sutured.

With a queue of patients to see, I thought I should send him to an emergency room, which Edelso imme-diately warned me off.

'At this hour, forget it, Doctor. He'll have to wait 'til tomorrow. Why don't you authorise Lula to stitch him up?'

Lula was a thief with a long history. He had arrived in the prison after his photograph was shown on the popular TV variety show *Fantástico*, having been shot down in the foyer of a branch of the Banco Itaú, in a robbery in which two of the other thieves were killed. He and the gang leader, a short fellow by the name of Ferrinho, arrived in Carandiru amid great admiration.

Bandeco, a popular character in Five, who spoke like a machine gun, said that nothing was as satisfying as that. 'Arrivin' in jail and your mates treatin' you with all the respect in the world is the most beautiful thing in a criminal's [robber's?] life.'

Less than a month later, Ferrinho, tortured by depression, hung himself with a sheet from his cell window. In his trouser pocket was a photograph of a small boy and a blonde woman wearing bright lipstick.

Edelso had just left when Lula walked in, wearing white shoes and a shirt unbuttoned at the top showing a silver chain with a crucifix against his chest. He was in a hurry. Without paying me much attention, he examined the wound and pushed the edges of the cut together several times.

'It can be done, Doctor. It hasn't damaged any nerves. Stabbings in the rump are just to rough the victim up a bit.'

That was our first contact. I impressed upon him that the secret was to anesthetise the wound and wash it well with soap and water. When he was done, he called me over to discharge the patient. The suture was excellent, the distance between the stitches perfect, and the blood had been carefully removed.

I don't know who had trained him, but he was truly talented. With the most basic of instruments and thick cotton thread, he made delicate sutures which left imperceptible scars, drained abscesses, extracted projectiles from bodies and, with great skill, removed flecks of dirt from eyes with the tip of a hypodermic needle.

Lula once brought me a patient with an enormous lipoma on his back. It was a soft, fatty tumour, fifteen centimetres in diameter. He wanted me to authorise its excision. I thought an operation like that would be difficult without a general anaesthetic. I told him both he and the patient were crazy. He replied that he had already done bigger operations, in less accessible places.

Months later, I ran into the patient in the courtyard of Seven and, smiling, he lifted up his shirt to show me the scar. It was perfect, in the shape of a Z to relieve tension in the skin that was pulled over the cut. I asked him who had operated on him.

'It was Lula. It's good, isn't it?'

'How, if I didn't authorise it?'

'He asked another doctor.'

Lula and I worked together for many months. I taught him the principles of asepsis, notions about the lines of force in the skin to guide him when making incisions and I lent him an anatomical atlas, which he leafed through with eyes shining with curiosity and never returned. I came to admire his surgical ability and the delight he took in learning. With time, we became friends.

At the end of one year, I noticed that his behaviour

had changed. His spontaneous laugh had disappeared; he was agitated and tense. He glanced around suspiciously in the galleries. He would sometimes disappear when he was supposed to be working. He grew thin and his face marked.

One morning, I saw him in the corridor.

'Lula, I'd like to talk to you in private,' I said.

We entered a room in the surgical centre. He locked the door and put the key in his pocket.

'You're smoking crack.'

'What, Doctor? I can't afford to, especially doin' all these operations.'

'Lula, that wasn't a question: you're smoking crack, every day, and lots of it.'

He denied it again, but I insisted that it wasn't good for adults like ourselves, family men, to muck around making fools of one another.

'Yeah, Doctor, I started about six months ago. At first it was every now and then. I'd go for a whole week without smokin'. But for a while now it's been every day.'

'All day long.'

'Truth be told, it is all day long. I wake up just itchin' to go down to Eight to get some rock. Sometimes I say, this ain't doing me no good, I'm gonna give it a rest. But it don't last. After one or two days, I'm off to Eight all neurotic. I spend about twenty or thirty a day on the bloody stuff.'

'How do you pay for it?'

'It comes from my surgeries. Nothing's free in here, Doctor.'

'But you operate on people and then smoke that poison: you'll lose your dexterity.'

'I'm sorry, but that's where you're wrong. I don't smoke crack after I operate. I smoke it before.'

'You're crazy, irresponsible. Crack takes away your control over your movements.'

'Wrong again, Doctor. Sometimes I have to do a big, difficult suture. I go to my pad for a smoke. Then I come up, inject the anaesthetic and wash the wound with soap and water, just like you taught me. I wash it slowly. Sometimes I spend up to fifteen minutes under the tap scrubbin', lots of suds, and I don't worry about the blood. I dry it well, and when I operate, it's amazing: I can see the blood vessels glowin', fluorescent. I tie them off one by one, my hand steady on the forceps, and I don't let nothing escape. And when the wound's dry, without a drop of blood comin' out of it, them subcutaneous stitches holdin' the edges close together, I suture the skin. I'm so precise that if you measured the distance between the needle hole and the edge of the cut, it wouldn't even be one millimetre, on both sides.'

Crack was Lula's undoing. A few days later the pavilion director fired him from the infirmary and had him transferred to Eight. He didn't stay there long; deprived of his private clinic, he had no way of supporting his habit, got into debt and lost the respect of his companions.

One day, he was found dead in his cell. Next to his body was a bloody syringe. The rumour that spread through the prison was that it had been an overdose. I thought it was very strange; the guys in the infirmary, who had worked with him for years, didn't know that Lula shot up.

Margô Suely

Margô spent three months in a police lock-up, in a cell with thirty-two men, and no one abused her. Despite her tight skirt, bustier and silicone implants in her thighs, everyone treated her with great respect. When she was transferred to Carandiru, she met a gangster and fell in love. He was frank with her. 'If you want to be mine, fine, but you're mine only, got it? I'll put you in a pad and I'll make sure you're comfortable, but you don't double-cross me. Keepin' a wife in here costs a fortune. Cheat on me and you're fucked.'

Margô's cell had a bunk-bed, a beige curtain and a rug with two swans and a little house embroidered on it, so she wouldn't have to put her feet on the cold floor. A blue sheet hung directly behind the door to ensure privacy, and a chequered curtain covered the window. There were clippings of famous artists all over the walls. Under the window, a crude little cupboard served as a table for the cooker, on top of which sat a coffee pot with a crocheted cover in the shape of a chicken. Next to it was a television set with steel wool on the antenna.

Cigarettes, tasty treats, afternoon joints, pills for her breasts and the other cons' respect, all provided by the gangster. On her part, just total fidelity. She never went out into the corridor. Her place was in the cell, with the door closed and the blue sheet and chequered curtain pulled to in order to avoid flirting and the spilling of blood. She was allowed out to get some sun occasionally, though never alone; three of the gangster's bodyguards would escort her down to the courtyard.

The top bunk belonged to Zizi, an older transvestite, whose face was asymmetrical because the silicone she had had injected in her cheekbones had slid out of place. She was the maid; she took care of the cooking, cleaning, washing and ironing. When the gangster visited, she would discreetly make herself scarce.

Margô fell in love because in the beginning he was good to her, protective, demanding, and made sure she had everything she needed. As for her, she spent her days watching TV, reading women's magazines and painting her nails. The other transvestites envied her.

One Sunday, when the inmates were busy with their visitors (except the transvestites, who had been estranged from their families for a long time), the gangster burst into her cell with furious eyes.

'You're gonna have to learn to shut your fucking mouth!'

And before Margô could work out what was going

on, he punched her in the chin so hard that she lost her balance, hit her head against the cupboard and with her elbow knocked over the pot of fennel tea which Zizi drank to calm her nerves. The gangster's wife, mother of his three children, had told him at her visit that she knew everything and would only come back when he dumped that degenerate.

The incident shook Margô's relationship with the gangster. Things were never the same again. The crisis came to a head when she developed a painful, moist sore in her private parts. The gangster refused to accept it.

'No sex, no luxury!'

He cut the lipstick, pills, joints, stocked pantry and, worst of all for her and Zizi, cigarettes.

When the infection got really bad, Margô Suely came to the infirmary. She spent some time there with us. The first day, the gangster came to visit and was understanding; then, never again, in spite of all the messages she sent.

Late one winter afternoon, having recovered, Margô was discharged and returned to Pavilion Five. She arrived in time for the head count. She was still a little weak and climbed the stairs with difficulty. In the fourth floor gallery, only two light bulbs in a row of eight were holding out. Poorly dressed for the cold, Margô headed down the corridor, turned right and ran straight into a warder.

'Where do you think you're going?' he said.

'I've just been discharged from the infirmary. I spoke to Valdir downstairs and he said I could come up.'

'What's your cell number?'

'417-E.'

'Off you go then, I still haven't locked it.'

The door was pulled to, though not locked, and light, sounds from the TV and the smell of fried garlic were emanating from inside the cell. Inside, she could feel the heat from the cooker, on which Zizi was busy frying something.

'Zizi, look, I'm back!'

Zizi swung around with a start, her eyes bulging as well as lopsided, and the spoon splattered hot oil on the wall.

That was when Margô realised that there was someone else there. Lying on the bed, wearing Margô's wool socks, was Lady Di, a fair-skinned whore five years younger than her, whom the cons all secretly admired.

'Take my socks off and get out of my bed, slut!' said Margô, shocked at the intruder's cheek.

'What're you talking about? I married your ex. I'm where I belong, you old bag.'

Humiliated, Margô turned to Zizi, who was still holding the spoon, petrified.

'Zizi, you back-stabbin' bitch! I'm gonna kill you both!'

She grabbed Lady Di's hair and slammed her head into the wall several times.

The shouting was infernal. Snoopers stuck their

heads out of their cell windows. Zizi took advantage of the ruckus and ran to the gangster's cell, all worked up.

'I had to leave. Margô Suely's smashin' Lady Di's head into the wall as hard as she can. Good God, you should see the blood! You have to do somethin'!'

'Me? Do somethin'?' said the gangster. 'Like what? Get involved in a catfight?'

Chico

Chico had killed his brother-in-law, a shifty sort. He had also killed a guy who had worked his way into the gang's good books with the ultimate objective of turning them all in to the police. And he had killed a third one whom he refused to talk about. 'He didn't deserve to live, Doctor.' The deaths brought him no remorse. 'If they were worth remorse, they wouldn't have died.'

Chico was the father of two girls and a boy whom he hadn't seen in many years. He had been abandoned by his ungrateful wife, the daughter of a family of low-lifes, who was responsible for his going into crime, according to him. He was serving a 44-year sentence. He missed his children terribly but accepted it, thinking it was probably a good thing that they didn't see the inside of a jail.

He didn't look his fifty years. 'An incarcerated man needs to exercise so he doesn't lose his dignity,' he once told me.

Ever since he had been arrested, his wife had inter-
cepted his correspondence with the children, as revenge
for the death of her brother. She told them their father
had died in the penitentiary.

Standing there with his arms folded, head shaved, a
tattoo of a skull with two daggers underneath it on his
right forearm, the weight of his body evenly balanced
on parallel feet, his posture betrayed his past in the
merchant navy. It had been a time of hard work in the
engine room, distant ports, knife fights and unforgettable women.

In the galleries, from the most hardened lag to the
lowest thief, his name was pronounced with respect.
'Chico said so . . . If Chico finds out, there's gonna be
trouble.'

When an inmate wanted to consult Chico, he would
stand nearby and wait for an invitation to approach as
he finished whatever he was doing. When the moment
came, he would glance at the inmate: that was his cue.

It would always be the inmate who spoke and gesticu-
lated; Chico remained quiet, staring off into the distance
or occupied with some small task. He would then turn to
the inmate, utter a few words in the low volume of serious conversations among prisoners and stare off into the
distance again. The conversation was over.

The General Kitchen

Zelão, Flavinho and Anorak ran the general kitchen with an iron fist. They were a scary trio, not so much for their long c.v.'s, but for the ferocious expressions on their faces. They had all been incarcerated for at least ten years and had each been sentenced to more than thirty.

They only spoke to one another when it was absolutely essential. Words were useless compared to the agility of the looks they exchanged when decisions had to be made. They shared the same cell and claimed to be willing to put their lives on the line to defend the other two, should circumstances require it. No one dared challenge them as leaders of the seventy-something cooks.

They were responsible for all of the material in the kitchen. One day, before lunch, a meat cleaver disappeared. They searched everywhere, but couldn't find it. At two o'clock in the afternoon, Anorak gave an ultimatum: 'From five o'clock on, one cook a day is going to die until the cleaver shows up!' Fifteen minutes later, the cleaver mysteriously fell from a window in Pavilion Nine and was returned to its rightful place.

The kitchen was, perhaps, one of the most vivid examples of the old prison's deterioration. It was large and leaky, on the ground floor of Pavilion Six, and water formed puddles in the floor where the blue tiles had come loose, making it impossible to keep it dry. There were eight pressure cookers, each with a 200-litre capacity. The exhaust fans above them had stopped working years earlier, so when they were all in use the kitchen had steam from eight industrial-size cookers spewed into it.

In the hours preceding meals, there was so much steam that the kitchen looked like Dante's *Inferno*. One could barely make out the men moving about the kitchen in rubber boots. They would wear a cloth over their hair that fell over their shoulders, making them look like the Foreign Legion soldiers in films. The steam was so intense that, for safety reasons, it was imperative that anyone walking anywhere with a knife in his hand held it with the cutting edge turned inward and the tip pointing down.

The cookers sat on a cement slab designed to keep them above ground level. This wide L-shaped platform was covered with the same grimy blue tiles. Between it and the rest of the floor was an open channel, where run-off water gushed towards the drain next to the entrance.

In the corners of the kitchen were the wooden trolleys with metal frames and the large pots used to transport the food to be served in the cells. Rice and beans were tipped straight from plastic bags into the pressure cookers and served as the basis for a mixture of chunks of meat with potatoes and carrots. Flour was also added to give the dish a better consistency.

Kitchens are a delicate issue in any prison. The director of correctional services told me that in a place as overpopulated as the Casa de Detenção it was even worse. 'If there's a food shortage, the prison will explode in less than twenty-four hours.'

To avoid tragedies, the prison administration let the inmates themselves run the kitchen, one of many examples of the self-management that made up for the chronic shortage of employees.

The successive administrations were never naïve enough to imagine that the system would stop supplies from being pilfered from the pantry and sold into the black market, with the inestimable collaboration of certain warders, since it happens in every prison in the world. What they intended when they handed the running of the kitchen over to the inmates themselves was to create a mechanism for controlling the amount stolen, so as not to jeopardise supply.

That was why those charged with imposing order in the environment and guarding the chopping knives couldn't be just any prisoner; they had to be men who were feared and respected by the prison population, like Zelão, Flavinho and Anorak, otherwise the pantry would have been pillaged by the more audacious inmates.

Zelão had committed over two hundred robberies and killed two members of his gang; he was thin, short-haired, cordial in manner and had a reputation for violent reactions. Flavinho had arrived in the prison at the age of eighteen with three deaths and a number of escapes from juvenile detention on his c.v.; short and thin, his physical stature didn't inspire respect, unless he was crossed and his black eyes would stare into those of the person who had offended him. The third, Anorak, who had earned his fame and lost his front teeth for resisting successive police interrogations without informing on his companions, swore he had matured in jail and regretted having stolen from the poor. He intended to turn over a new leaf when he got out, and promised he'd only hold his revolver to the heads of corrupt politicians. His greatest desire was to hold up two former state governors of São Paulo.

Because the carpentry workshop in Pavilion Six was on the same floor as the old cinema where we held the talks on AIDS, from a distance I often observed Zelão, Flavinho or Anorak chatting with the head carpenter, Chico – the old sailor who had killed his brother-in-law and two others who hadn't deserved to live. The dynamic of these secret conversations respected the ritual described earlier, when the inmates would go to Chico for advice: the heads of the kitchen would wait for Chico to give them permission to approach, then they would speak quietly, listen to his advice and leave. It was clear that it was Chico who ran the kitchen from the carpentry workshop.

In 1995, the prison administration deactivated the kitchen and hired an outside company to supply meals. The era of takeaway containers had begun. 'It's hard to stomach, Doctor,' the inmates told me.

Reunion

One rainy afternoon, the telephone in the Incarceration office of Pavilion Eight rang. An employee answered and took the message in a low voice to Pires, the pavilion director:

'There's a phone call for Chico. It's a woman.'

Because outside calls to inmates were against regulations, the director went to see who it was.

'Who wants to talk to Chico? We don't take outside calls in here!'

On the other end, he heard a timid voice:

'I'm sorry, sir. I'm twenty years old and I have a sister who's eighteen and a brother who's seventeen. We're Chico's children. The last time I saw my father I was five years old, and my brother was so small he doesn't even remember his face. We thought he was dead. When I found out he wasn't, I got together with my brother, sister and the pastor of our church without our mother knowing, and we decided to look for our father. It was really hard to speak to anyone here, but today I

266

managed to explain it to the telephonist, who felt sorry for us and put the call through.'

Her voice was filled with fear. The director sent for Chico, who entered Incarceration warily. He glanced around; everything seemed to be running according to routine, with employees and a few prisoners busy with bureaucratic work. Pires, with grey hair and a pencil behind his ear, was sitting at his desk reading a report.

Facing the window, with his back to everyone, Chico took the phone, said hello and then fell silent for a long time. From where he was sitting, Pires noticed the tears in his eyes.

For several days the pavilion director observed Chico's solitary behaviour. Unaware of the reason, the inmates kept a respectful distance from their saddened leader. A few days later, Chico went to find him.

'Pires, I'd like to ask you a favour that I'll make a point of never forgetting,' he said in a serious tone of voice.

He told him what had been going on all those years: his wife's revenge for the death of her brother, the returned letters, being dead to his kids, and the conversation he had had with his eldest.

'I'd like you to authorise me to meet them outside, at the bandstand in Divinéia. I don't want my children in a prison.'

'You've put me in a spot now. Imagine if the other 7000 ask me the same thing. Still, seeing as it's a special situation, after so many years, I'll make an exception, but you can't stay more than twenty minutes.'

On the scheduled afternoon, Chico headed for the bandstand with two inmates carrying a red rug, a vase of flowers, two litres of soft drink, biscuits, pastries and a small table with a chequered tablecloth.

When it had all been arranged, the former sailor, wearing a long-sleeved shirt to hide his tattoo, crossed his arms over his strong chest and waited.

Two hours went past and his children didn't arrive. When Pires finally decided to bring him in, he found him sitting with his elbows on his thighs and his head in his hands. The two of them returned to the pavilion without exchanging a single word.

The following week, at the same time, there was a call from the telephonist: Chico's children were waiting at the entrance. All of his years working in the prison didn't stop Pires from getting choked up. He went to the carpentry workshop to give Chico the news himself. He found him sawing a bench with a chainsaw and unplugged it.

'Chico, go get ready to see your children.'

When Chico's incredulous eyes met his, they discovered a tenderness he hadn't seen in Pires before. The director, in turn, saw in the former sailor's angular face the expression of a child who has caught a balloon that has fallen from the sky.

Chico met his children at the bandstand, which had been quickly decorated with the red rug, table, snacks and a vase of flowers taken from the Our Lady Aparecida altar in the pavilion's chapel. The two girls were wearing long dresses and had their hair in braids; the boy was dressed in a blue suit and tie and was holding a Bible. The four of them embraced for a long time and cried.

Thirty minutes later, the head of Divinéia approached the group to take Chico back to the pavilion, but he didn't have the heart to interrupt the family reunion and retreated to the bandstand stairs. Pires did the same, two hours later.

A few months after the reunion, in a surprise search, the warders found an arsenal of knives in Chico's cell, including an enormous improvised scythe. The younger inmates never understood why he didn't hide them somewhere else. 'The old boy was set in his ways. He didn't adopt the modern methods. It had to be the way he was used to.'

As punishment, Chico was transferred to a prison in the interior of the state. At the same time, Zelão and Flavinho were sent to the State Penitentiary. I never saw them again, but I still got news about Chico from Anorak, who stayed on in the Casa waiting to be released so he could turn over a new leaf and finally be able to hold up the former governors.

Zé from Casa Verde

His name was Kenedi Baptista dos Santos, but everyone knew him as Zé from Casa Verde. The slang, his way of speaking, the way he'd stand with his torso leaning back, his ever-readiness to rib his mates: everything about him smacked of the world of crime.

He had been a thief since his adolescence. On his way home from dances, when the bakery opened at dawn and the staff started filling the shelves with bread, he would pinch a sweet roll and take it to his father, who was unaware of the illegal origin of the gift. He did it to get revenge on his father, an honest man who used to fight with him to get some common sense out of him.

Zé and I were once chatting in the courtyard of Pavilion Four, when an inmate with a bureaucratic role brought a piece of paper for me to sign. Zé fell silent and grew serious until the man had left.

'What's wrong, Zé?'

'I've never liked dealers. They're a devious lot. They

get involved with the cops and people who rub shoulders with the pigs tend to grass.'

His logic was Euclidean: as a thief, he would go into a bank, take everyone by surprise and make off with the money. It was the police's problem if they wanted to come after him. If they did, he'd open fire, because he'd come to take the money and had two families waiting for him. But drug dealers didn't operate like that.

'You have to have access to addicts, own a den. And a den's open forty-eight hours a day. It's a fixed place, with people comin' and goin', like a supermarket. The cops soon find out. You have to pay for their protection so you can operate. It's a big circus.'

That's why Zé from Casa Verde was categorical: 'A thief's place is with other thieves. Let the dealers try and see eye to eye with the pigs!'

Zé was married to two women, Valda and Maria Luísa. 'Valda's skin is as white as snow. She comes from a good family, who never accepted our relationship 'cause of my colour.'

They had met at a dance when she was still a virgin, dancing with a guy whom Zé thought rather dodgy. The next Sunday, as his rival was playing a game of football, Zé approached her at the edge of the field.

'Get up and come with me, 'cause I'm gonna ask your parents for your hand in marriage.'

'You don't even know me!'

He talked about how he'd seen her at the dance, her white skin that contrasted with his black skin and their mixed-race children that would all be beautiful, each one a different colour. When he had finished he went to wait for her in his vee-dub, which he had just had decked out using stolen money.

He didn't have to wait for long. She appeared at his car window.

'Are you serious?' she said.

'I've never been more serious about anythin' in my life.'

They parked the vee-dub outside the door to her parents' two-storey home. She was hesitant to invite him in and he tried to convince her of the honesty of his intentions. They were in the middle of this conversation when the boyfriend appeared on the corner, still in his football uniform, ready to fight. Zé didn't think twice; he got out of the car and fired three shots at the guy, who took off running and even lost one of his football boots in his haste. Then he turned to his beloved and said persuasively:

'Tomorrow, at eight, call your parents and sisters together 'cause I'm gonna ask for your hand in marriage. Forget that guy: if he loved you, he'd face the danger.'

The next day, at eight, her family had the worst possible reaction. Despite the souped-up vee-dub and the way he presented himself as a working man, from an exemplary family, the owner of a property officially registered at the notary's office in Casa Verde, the girl's father said he'd rather see his daughter dead than married to a black hooligan like him.

Zé's persistence caused tempers to become raised, with her father referring to his colour with increasing disrespect. When he was called an insolent nigger, Zé lost his patience. He climbed onto the table, pulled out his revolver and shouted that he'd kill the first one to react.

'I locked everyone in the bathroom and took my love with me, my black hand in her snow-white hand.'

He had four children with Valda and said they were the way he wanted them to be: 'Each one with a different skin tone, Doctor.'

They were extremely happy until he met Maria Luísa, a dancer with the Império da Casa Verde samba school. 'The percussion session was really goin' for it and there she was dancin' up front, in a short little dress with a smile that lit up the whole rehearsal area. She looked like an ebony goddess.'

At Carnival itself, minutes before the school was to parade down the avenue, with Zé dressed as Xangô, the warrior, and Maria Luísa in a sequined bikini, Valda together with Zé's youngest sister, supporting her sister-in-law, appeared out of goodness knows where and began to grapple with Maria Luísa. Once again, Zé lost his patience and pulled out his revolver. 'I clouted each one over the head with the butt of my revolver, sent all three home and sambaed down the avenue alone.'

In his double life, he had three children with Maria Luísa. He was later caught holding up a shoemaker's, not far from the Casa de Detenção itself.

On his first Sunday in prison, he received a visit from Valda. They sat holding hands on a bench covered with a blanket, by the wall. After a time, Zé heard over the loudspeaker:

'Kenedi Baptista dos Santos, please come to the entrance of the pavilion.'

He felt a shiver in his stomach. It could only be Maria Luísa! He excused himself from Valda, ran to the boiler room next door and dirtied himself with grease. He found his mulatta at the door, smiling and glad to see him. He kissed her ceremoniously so as not to touch her with his dirty hands and explained:

'My love, it was so good of you to come but, unfortunately, I can't invite you in 'cause I'm fixing a boiler that burst and the man wants everything ready by the time visitin' hours are over.'

'Zé, you're with that slut. You never worked when you were on the outside; do you mean to tell me that in prison, on a Sunday, you've decided to turn over a new leaf?'

There was no arguing with the facts, he thought, and gave in to her female logic.

'All right, it's true, but you're here and now there's no turnin' back. Today the three of us are gonna come to an understandin'.'

It was hard to convince her to meet her rival. Sitting on the bench, Valda couldn't find the words to express what she felt when she saw him arrive with Maria Luísa, offer her a place on the bench and sit between the two of them. There was a long silence.

Finally, in a low voice to avoid a scandal, Valda turned to him and said:

'How can you bring this whore here?'

'Darling, Maria Luísa isn't a whore. She works in a textile factory and is a loving mother to our three children.'

He then turned to Maria Luísa.

'And you said outside that Valda was a slut. That's not true either. She's hard-workin', with an office job down at the City Hall, and looks after the four children that we brought into this world.'

'You'd better decide now which one of us you want to be with,' said Maria Luísa, with which Valda immediately agreed. Zé was disconsolate.

'You're going to break my heart in half like that.'

According to Zé, the two of them eventually learned to live in such great concord that they would even take their seven children for Sunday walks together in the park. When he got out, he told me, he was going to realise his old dream of bringing his two families together under one roof, all living in peace.

Blackie

Blackie had a tough start in life: 'My mother killed . . .
I think it was her lover who showed up drunk and
wanted to smack us around again. My dad couldn't
know about it 'cause he was locked up in the State
Penitentiary. That was when we all rebelled and each
one went his own way.'

There were six children: Blackie, four sisters and a
younger brother. With the mother in prison, the children were placed in state care, with the girls in one
institution and the boys in another. In contrast to his
brother, who was more obedient, Blackie didn't stay
long at Asdrúbal Nascimento, an old building in downtown São Paulo where homeless children and youth
offenders were kept. He escaped with some older children and disappeared into the streets.

With all of the wisdom of his six years, Blackie lived
by his wits in the city. He slept under the awnings of
buildings rolled up in a blanket, with newspaper
stuffed inside his clothes, stole wallets, sold bags of

sweets and chewing gum and took part in *arrastões*[1] with his older companions. 'Every now and then, I'd be picked up again and taken back to Asdrúbal Nascimento. I didn't even get upset. I was learnin' on the blackboard of life.'

One day they would get distracted and he would run away again. 'So I made my way as a thief. A kid would go past, all cute and smiley, dressed up for a special occasion, others with their toys, and I had nothin'. I got kinda selfish, 'cause I wanted things but couldn't have 'em or didn't have any way to get 'em, 'cause I didn't have a mother or father to take care of everyday stuff.'

From the ages of six to eighteen, he spent almost eleven years locked up and one and a half on the streets. He was even sent to a jail in the city of Mogi with a category C classification, for more dangerous youths. He escaped from there too. When he turned fifteen, his father was released from the penitentiary, determined to reunite his family. He gathered up a daughter here; another there; the youngest son, who was well behaved; and then went after Blackie, who was making a living from crime. He found him at a snooker table in downtown São Paulo.

'Enough of this life, son. Your dad's back.'

They went to live in a modest little house and all had

---

[1] Literally meaning 'dragnet', an *arrastão* (plural: *arrastões*) is when a group of thieves, often children, moves through an area mugging everyone in sight, usually in crowded places such as the beach or busy downtown streets.

jobs except Blackie, who would bring home a steady supply of stolen groceries, sweets and soft drinks. One day, Juciléia, his oldest sister, fell in love with a worthless sort. The father, who had suffered in jail and didn't want criminals in the family, forbade her to see him. One night, when he got home from work, he found the daughter's boyfriend sprawled across the sofa holding half a bottle of beer. He saw red. 'He said he didn't want criminals in our house and the next time he'd put him back in the street with a beatin'.'

The boyfriend took it badly. 'It pissed him off and he shot me dad twice in the stomach.'

As fate would have it, Blackie arrived home at that exact moment, accompanied by his .22, which went everywhere with him. He saw his father lying on the floor and the boyfriend still holding the gun, with his back to the door. 'I just said, "What's this?" and as he turned around I shot him in the head several times.' So as not to leave the body in front of his family, in the living room, Blackie dragged it into the middle of the street and told his sisters to call the police, who arrived quickly, and an ambulance, which took hours. He was sent back to the juvenile detention centre.

His father had two operations and escaped with his life, his sister forgot the boyfriend, married and started a family, like the other three, and his brother got a job with a good company. Blackie, however, continued living out his destiny.

He arrived at the Casa de Detenção for the first time

when he was eighteen. One night, he and four friends had been taking a taxi home from their samba school rehearsal, when a police car flashed its light for them to pull over. Against his passengers' orders, the driver, who was totally innocent, pulled the car over and threw himself onto the asphalt with his hands on his head. Blackie and his friends dashed out firing their guns. 'I was shot six times. I got two in my back, one in the belly, three in the chest and one grazed my ear, which I don't even count. But I wasn't left handicapped or nothing.'

He served nine months and was released again, because the judge determined that he had acted in self-defence. After all, the police had also fired and weren't wounded.

On the outside, his happiness was short-lived, as always. The police surrounded the *favela* where he lived as they searched for him. 'I got caught, 'cause they took me by surprise. They handcuffed me, put me in the van and took me to a deserted forest. There, they made me get out with my hands behind my back, in handcuffs, and told me that I'd killed a cousin of theirs, who was also a cop, but nothin' was proved in court 'cause the witness didn't recognise me, and besides, I'd only just been released from jail two weeks before.'

This time his punishment left a mark. He was shot eighteen times: in the back, legs and arms. One bullet entered through his upper jaw, passed behind his eyeball and stopped in his brain, near another that had entered through his skull: 'The two of them are in my head to this day, but they don't affect me. Thank God, I can talk normally and think the right ideas. The only one that affected me was one they gave me in the spine, where they put the gun, fired and said, "Get up, scumbag!"' Blackie tried, but his legs didn't obey him. If he didn't die, he'd be crippled, they said. 'Then they put the .22 in my hand, and fired three times, as if I'd had a shoot-out with them. They grabbed me, swung my body back and forth and threw me back in the van and drove off slowly. I was bleeding out, my legs dead, and they were as calm as cucumbers. They only turned on the siren when we got near the Clínicas Hospital. These days I think what they did was pretty cowardly.'

He spent several days in intensive care, full of drips and surgical drains. The hospital didn't even wait for him to recover fully before discharging him; they were afraid his cohorts would show up to rescue him. He ended up in post-op care at the State Penitentiary hospital.

He spent approximately ten years in that prison, in a wheelchair, until he was transferred to a semi-open prison, where he served three months and was released.

He only spent ten days on the outside because, according to him, he was set up by the police, who claimed to have caught him with one and a half kilos of crack, ten machine guns and a thirteen-round Taurus PT: 'It went to court and I proved that there was no way – as a paraplegic, handicapped – I could have made contact with any criminal, 'cause I lived in a *favela* and didn't have a vehicle to get around in. Dunno why, but the judge didn't listen to me and sent me to a police lock-up. I got shunted from one lock-up to the next, with sores on my ass, without any way of lookin' after them and pus oozin' out of my dead flesh.'

When I met Blackie, he was in a wheelchair, with a urinary catheter, sentenced to forty-eight years. With a face sculpted like an African statue, he wore a permanently standoffish expression. His legs were paralysed and hypotrophic, his skin was scaly and he had such a deep sore in one buttock that two limes could have fitted in it. The wound exposed the anatomy of deep muscle bundles and part of his hip joint.

One of the guys in the infirmary dressed the wound on a daily basis. With tweezers, he'd poke around in it with a tuft of gauze soaked in nitrofurazone ointment mixed with sugar. He had to be quite forceful in order to stimulate healing. It didn't hurt as it had lost all sensitivity.

Blackie was respected by all, even the warders. Occasionally, when his wound was being dressed, I would be called over to inspect it. Apart from that, our relations for the most part didn't go beyond 'good afternoon' and 'goodnight'. I never saw him relaxed, laughing or joking with someone. His scowling face made him look as if he was always on the defensive.

One afternoon, I crossed paths with him in the gallery; there were just the two of us and his creaking wheelchair.

'Hey, how's the sore?'

'It's getting better. It's dry and not as deep.'

'It'll heal.'

'Thanks. God protect you.'

I think I saw the faintest of smiles and watched the anger drain from his expression. Not that he was the picture of peace, far from it; but for a fleeting moment he looked disarmed, with a twinkle in his coal-black eyes.

Mango

All letters were opened before they were delivered to the prisoners. Three people carried out the task. At a table, one inmate would cut the side of the envelope with a pair of scissors, a prison employee would empty out the contents and look for strange objects and another inmate would staple everything together. No one was curious to read them; besides, there wouldn't have been time, as there were thousands. Then the correspondence was separated by pavilion, to be distributed to the individual cells by the postmen.

One of the lessons I learned from Waldemar Gonçalves was to listen to the prisoners who delivered the post. 'To know how a prison's doing, it's imperative that you talk to them, Doctor.'

Mango, a postman in Pavilion Seven, liked to chat with me – and I with him. He was a tall, well-spoken man with a booming voice, who had fled his hometown in Northeastern Brazil because the brothers of a girl who claimed to have lost her virginity to him wanted to avenge their sister. Over time, Mango came to trust me so much that he would give me detailed descriptions of the movement of drugs in the prison, which helped me in my strategies for the AIDS-prevention campaigns. For example, he was the first to say: 'Doctor, you don't need to insist the guys stop slamming, because it's over now. You can search the whole prison and you won't find a single syringe to tell the tale. The thing now is crack. It's come to kick the cons up the ass.'

Mango swore he had ended up in the Casa de Detenção due to a legal error. Years earlier, when he was released from prison in Sorocaba without a penny to his name, a friend had lent him half a kilo of marijuana. He had sold it in the streets of Liberdade, the Asian district of São Paulo, including in Rua do Estudante, where he lived. It paid the bills and there was a little left over: 'To buy clothes for the baby that was about to be born, order a pizza on Sunday, and look after the wife, give her the pampering that every woman needs.'

Then along came Sonha, a neighbour with whom Mango did business.

'Sonha was caught with twelve bricks of weed stashed in her pressure cooker and, to get off the hook, she gave them my name. That was when the DEIC grabbed me.'

The police raided his house and found a kilo of marijuana. 'I had to hand everything over and part with a decent sum of money for them to let me off. They told me to lie low for a few days.' He went home from the police station depressed, once again without any money. 'My son had just been born and I was so hard-up I was lookin' up to beggars.'

At this delicate time, Genival, one of his customers, rang the doorbell.

'Hey, Mango, sell me a brick and I'll pay you tomorrow.'

'I'm not selling you nothing, 'cause I have to stop for a few days. Take this one here to smoke with the loonies over by the church and leave me out of it. I'm staying low-key at the request of the cops.'

Genival thanked him and left. After a few hours Mango went for a walk to think about life. As he turned a corner, he saw Murky Waters coming towards him.

'I was just goin' to your place to get a brick.'

'Too late, I gave the last one to Genival.'

Murky Waters didn't like the answer.

'The guy arrived from Alagoas just the other day, he barely knows his way around and he already thinks he's a dealer.'

Mango didn't know anything about Genival's past.

'You refuse me but you sell to that bastard who's got some serious shit to his name, a rape conviction and everything, and now he wants to come smoke with our gang!'

Murky Waters pulled a length of pipe out of his waist-band and clouted Mango across the head. He hit him with so much force that the metal rang in the air. Mango quickly ducked, but the pipe clipped his eyebrow. Blinded by rage and blood, he pulled out his knife and before his adversary had time to attack him again, he drove it into his chest. Murky Waters lost his balance and staggered backwards, but didn't drop the pipe. Mango reasoned: 'If I don't finish this madman off now, I'll never be able to walk the streets in peace again.'

It took another three good stabs, two in the stomach and one in the back as Murky Waters fell into the gutter, face down.

He abandoned him in a pool of blood, with frightened passers-by looking on, and ran home. He got his wife and newborn son, locked everything up and fled to his mother-in-law's house in the district of Vila Madalena.

'Things were going from bad to worse: the agreement with the police had cleaned me out, then I had to liquidate Waters, plus the baby had all kinds of needs and, to top it all, we were staying with the mother-in-law, who was always on her daughter's case about the life I was leading.'

So as not to depend on the mother-in-law, he decided to steal a tape deck with a guy whose nickname was Big Mouth. The tape deck was in a florist's van, next to the Cardeal Arcoverde Cemetery. They had barely opened the door, which was his friend's speciality, when the alarm went off. Big Mouth ran, while Mango tried to pull out the tape deck, but he didn't have any experience in this kind of theft.

'The alarm was honking non-stop and I was fumbling

with the tape deck that wouldn't come out. Then people started shouting "Catch the thief!" and I was surrounded. I had to jump into the cemetery. Do you know where I fell?'

He really was having a run of bad luck.

'Right into an open grave. The cemetery was huge, and I had to go and jump right into a grave! It was a deep hole, Doctor. When the cops pulled me out I couldn't put any weight on my leg.'

Down at the police station, in pain, Mango gave a false name. Two days later, he was identified and transferred to the Presídio do Hipódromo, where he found a vindictive enemy. He was still down on his luck.

'Murky Waters' brother, who went by the name Cross Eyes, was doing time there. I discovered that Waters hadn't died, although he had been left with a huge scar in the middle of his belly. Cross Eyes and I had words, but there they've got guards to put an end to misunderstandings and all we did was shout, "I'm gonna get you on the outside." "It's gonna be you or me!" "You can bet on that!"'

Mango got out first, got back into the marijuana trade, returned to Rua do Estudante with his wife and son and bought a revolver. One night, he ran into his enemy in the district of Baixada do Glicério.

'Cross Eyes and me, face to face, about ten metres away, like from here to that wall there at the back of the gallery. I jumped behind a parked car and fired at him six times. And he fired six times too.'

Their twelve stray bullets broke the windows of the vehicles parked nearby. When they realised they were both out of ammunition, the confrontation became hands-on. The fight started at the top of a block and rolled downhill. It ended amid a crowd of onlookers, with the two of them exhausted and covered in blood. They were arrested by a passing police officer.

They were taken to the local police station, each charged with the unlawful possession of a weapon and released on bail.

'After a month, a friend of mine, Butterball, who did hold-ups with me, did one with Cross Eyes. When they were divvying up the takings, Cross Eyes made off with a bigger cut. When Butterball realised he'd been scammed, he went and put three bullets in him; two in the head, just to be sure. I never saw Murky Waters again.'

Because of the circumstances of his last arrest, Mango was accused of Cross Eyes' murder. Without a lawyer or a convincing alibi, he was sentenced to nine years in jail. He couldn't believe his bad luck.

'After all the marijuana I've sold, the hold-ups, burgling shops, and I get locked up precisely for a crime I didn't commit. Justice is blind, Doctor.'

Mango was one of the prisoners who escaped through the tunnel in Pavilion Seven. Two years later he wound up back in the Casa de Detenção. Late one afternoon he came to me about a private matter. We talked in the doctors' room; the sun was shining through the window and projected a barred shadow on his face. He handed me an envelope with flowery writing on it. In the letter, his wife said she was tired of suffering because of him and had decided to take her mother's advice. She had moved to the state of Minas Gerais with their two children, the youngest of which had been born after his escape, and was never coming back.

He sobbed as I read out the letter. When I finished, I sat there quietly waiting for him to calm down. The tears finally stopped rolling and he dried his eyes, stood, thanked me and left before I could say a single comforting word.

Old Jeremias

Jeremias had a misunderstanding with a warder and was given thirty days in Solitary Confinement. I went to visit him with Waldemar Gonçalves. Through the window of the dark cell, I could barely make out the old black man's features and kinky white hair. When he was released from Solitary, he came to thank me for the visit. He was thin and his eyes were sad. He transmitted, however, a strength of character that reminded me of my father.

'For someone who just spent a month in seclusion, you don't look bad,' I said.

'After so many years inside, Doctor, the mind learns to control the body.'

That was how our friendship began. He taught me a lot about life in prison as well as on the outside.

Jeremias had fled the drought in the state of Bahia in the 1940s and had climbed off the coach at Estação da Luz as a newlywed; his bride with a handkerchief on her head, freezing cold, and Jeremias carrying the couple's belongings in a cardboard suitcase.

They had eighteen children, who had given them thirty-two grandchildren and six great-grandchildren. Jeremias was determined and had managed to provide a decent life for his family; his daughters had all had church weddings, the boys had never set foot in a police station and his very Catholic wife visited him every weekend, although she never condoned his errant ways. 'At home, if she discovered a single grain of birdseed that I hadn't earned with the sweat off my back, she'd go off and report it to the police. It took a lot to stop her and the children had to intervene. That's why, Doctor, you can't tell your wife everythin', no matter how much you love her. Marriage ain't a confessional.'

Jeremias was one of those men who had buried his past. I never had the courage to ask him about his life in crime; nor did he ever give me such an opportunity. Only once he told me he had been arrested in the city of Santos as he was getting ten marijuana cigarettes from the basement of his grocery shop to give to two dock workers. He mentioned it in passing and then changed the subject.

He had a faint Northeastern accent and his speech was punctuated by suspenseful moments of silence and colourful expressions. It was a pleasure to listen to him. If he hadn't been illiterate, Jeremias could have written a prison-survival manual. 'Seen from the past, the Casa is a child's playground now. When two or three men die, everyone gets scared. I tell 'em: you should have seen it twenty years ago.'

In those days, forty or fifty men would die in disputes in Eight and Nine alone. Then they would cross over to the other pavilions and kill even more. 'When the dealers got busted 'cause someone had grassed, a convoy of twenty or thirty guys'd go out into the gallery with knives, stabbin' everythin' in sight; whether it was them or whether it wasn't. Even fags got killed. We had a barrel of gunpowder on our hands there!'

The bodies would be taken to the room where cleaning supplies were stored on the ground floor of Five; the emergency morgue. 'Death reunited everyone there. Piled up on top of one another, until the man with the black book'd come and hang a card around the dead man's neck with his info on it. Things've happened in here that we don't like to remember!'

Experienced and respected, he was never fazed by skirmishes in the galleries, arguments in cells, or even the fights on Rua Dez. For him, it was the peaceful moments that were dangerous. 'When you see the prison in silence, hardly a soul in the galleries, too much obedience, somethin's about to happen. Someone's diggin' a tunnel, two or three are gonna die; it's all about to explode. Everyone knows, but no one can say anythin'. You have to have eyes in the back of your head in this place!'

Jeremias said that he had learned from the older prisoners not to stand about chatting or hang around with other inmates so as not to get involved in other people's problems. For him, solitude was a survival strategy. 'I might die of a disease, but not murdered in the cooler. When I've finished talkin' to you, I go straight to my cell and shut the door. I don't trust anyone and I don't have a single friend. I don't want jailbirds for friends! Lots of guys know me, I've been here so many years. I just say, "Hi, hi," and keep walkin'. Inside, you have to keep to yourself, and God. It's like walkin' on eggshells!'

In spite of all the rapes in the days before intimate visits were allowed, he says there was a lot of respect. The prison administration still owned the cells in those days. 'They didn't care if it was already full. They'd keep shovin' in another three or four, here and there. You had to ask permission to enter, take your shoes off, 'cause they used to spread blankets on the floor, and ask who'd been there the longest. The oldest'd tell you to read the rules on a piece of paper stuck to the door, and you had to obey them. These days it's all very mysterious!'

The codes were more rigid. Once, an inmate from Pavilion Eight became romantically involved with a homosexual. One Sunday, his wife paid him a surprise visit, found him with his lover and made a scandal. 'She scratched the fag's face up, and he got pissed off and shouted, "Get the hell out of here. You don't need to come back, 'cause it's me who bankrolls him now!"'

The other inmates were perplexed.

'What? It's all back to front: now fags are bankrollin' cons?'

It didn't take long for everything to come to a head.

'The next day, when they went to see exactly what was going on, they discovered it was the fag who was doin' the con. Everyone'd thought that he was the fag's husband, and there he was gettin' it up the ass. It was fatal: they killed him and the fag too. There's no pity or mercy in this place!'

I once asked him if anything good had ever happened to him in jail. He answered that the feeling of walking out into the street, free again, with his wife waiting at the door was indescribable. 'It's a happiness that can't be contained in your chest. You want to laugh, but that's not it; you feel like cryin', but you're ashamed.'

As for the bad things, he told me, 'There's two things inside which are the most awful: a guy steals, kills and runs amuck on the outside, and when he gets here he has to be a fag. The other one is endin' your days in a puddle of blood in the gallery.'

At the start of one year, Jeremias was transferred and I never saw him again. Time went by. One morning, I arrived at the Sírio-Libanês Hospital to find a young man waiting for me. It was his son. His father had been released and was going to turn seventy that Sunday. Because he had spoken of our friendship to the family, they wanted to give him a surprise and take me to see him on his birthday.

That Sunday, I got off the metro at the last station on the line, Itaquera, where I met his son and we caught a bus that took another forty minutes to reach its final stop. From there, it was almost half an hour on foot along dirt roads until we reached a little house with a porch overflowing with children and grandchildren. Jeremias was in the garden with two boys, who were holding up a trellis covered with chayote so he could fix the fence, next to a flowerbed of dahlias. When he saw me, his eyes filled with emotion. I wanted to give him a hug, but was too shy.

Veronique, the Japanese

The first time I treated the inmates of Yellow, as I mentioned earlier, an Assembly of God pastor asked me to examine a transvestite with a painful rear end.

She insisted I call her Veronique. Despite her protests, the inmates all called her 'the Japanese', because of the slanted eyes she had inherited from her native Indian ancestors. Ever since she was little she had played with dolls and dressed up in her mother's clothes. As a child, her first sexual arousal had been because of a man, as often happens with boys who later discover they are gay.

She began taking female hormones at the age of eleven and, at thirteen, debuted in a motel with an older man who only hired minors. A year later, tired of being slapped around by her brother, she and a friend ran away from their hometown of Corumbá, in the state of Mato Grosso, to Porto Velho, in Rondônia. From there, they made their way to São Paulo, where they rented a room and started working as streetwalkers on a busy avenue.

Veronique found herself a black market silicone injector, who gave her some passion fruit juice to calm her nerves and injected a litre of industrial silicone into her buttocks. With time, this silicone, purchased at a hardware store, infiltrated her muscular fibres and provoked chronic inflammation, which caused her to suffer in Yellow. The backs of her thighs were swollen, red and so painful that she could barely walk. I had her admitted to the infirmary.

She was so extroverted that she became the star attraction there. She comforted the suffering, joked and sang in the gallery, and everyone laughed at her saucy ways. 'The cons need us in this place, Doctor. It's too many men locked up together, without somethin' feminine to give 'em support. I listen, I give advice, I'm affectionate with 'em, and later they thank me with a packet of cigarettes, a sweet, some jewellery.'

Two men had left a mark on her heart: a jealous drug dealer in jail and a Frenchman on the outside, who had initially thought she was a woman. She was married to the dealer for one year; to the Frenchman, eight months. He gave her a gold bracelet, clothes, money and a pearl necklace, which she hocked. 'There was also a hairy Arab, father of three, who fell in love and wanted to put three bullets in me when he found out I was havin' an affair with a police sergeant.'

Veronique was always squabbling with the other

transvestites in Five but once she had calmed down, she would forgive her companions.

There's a lot of competition between us, because everyone wants to be better than the next. If one says she's goin' to Italy, her friend who doesn't have a pot to piss in says she's been invited to do catwalk work in Japan. If one buys a chicken, the friend who doesn't have a pot to piss in will even sell her body to show that she's chic and eats chicken too. They want to make themselves out to be better in everythin'. That's what causes the knock-down, drag-out fights and the hair pullin'. Then they calm down and make up, 'cause we don't hold grudges like them criminals, who'll kill their friends. Deep down, we're united because we need each other to survive.

Rumour had it that years ago in Pavilion Five, late at night, the entire gallery heard a threat from Veronique. 'It's Christmas time. Veronique here would like gifts from certain cons so that she won't tell anyone about the shameful things they ask her to do to them. Verô is very upset. They've got twenty-four hours to calm her down, if they don't want to sully their reputations!'

The next day, a snoop was astounded by the quantity of expensive presents scattered across her bed.

It was true, discretion wasn't her greatest virtue, and many of her problems stemmed from the fact that she didn't possess this quality, which was fundamental in prison.

Once, security director Jesus was consulting with inmates in his office in Pavilion Six when Veronique walked in, all effeminate, and said, 'Help, Jesus, things are gettin' ugly.' She crossed the room as she spoke and left through a side door. Immediately behind her came an inmate holding a knife to a warder's neck, threatening Jesus: 'If you make a move, he's dead. I want a transfer to Avaré!'

Days later, Jesus humorously referred to the incident. 'She did warn me, grassing at the speed of light like that, but there wasn't enough time to do anything.'

In one of the many misunderstandings she got herself into in Five, her cell companions kicked her out. She gathered up her belongings in a huff and said: 'I'm glad to be leavin', 'cause you bitches are so common. Without Verô here to bring you treats, you'll have to wallow in the prison food the way it is. I'm classy and popular and I've got invites to live in any pavilion. You lot are gonna rot on the fourth floor of Five, you east zone scum!'

She did indeed spend the night in an inmate's cell in Seven. The fellow was a gentleman and gave her his bed while he slept at her feet, on the ground. Big mistake! The next day, the cleaners saw the scene through the window in the cell door and took the matter to the head cleaner, who expelled the gentleman from the pavilion: 'Have you ever heard anythin' so absurd? A respectable criminal puttin' a faggot in his bed and sleepin' on the ground! Is everythin' back to front now?'

Veronique's boldest play, however, was duping the director of correctional services, a man who had started his career decades earlier opening and closing the door to Pavilion Nine. A rumour was going around that there was a revolver in Eight. Talk about firearms in the prison was always taken seriously, because if it was true, everyone's lives were at risk. The director of correctional services locked the pavilion and had it searched cell by cell. They found nothing. He put his network of informers to work and waited, impatiently.

The next day, Veronique showed up in his office, mysteriously, like a cat.

'Lopes, I know a certain con who'll give you the owner of the shooter in exchange for a transfer to the Penitentiary. Except that he'll only talk once he's been transferred; he's afraid he'll die if he opens his mouth first.'

Once the director had accepted the proposal, Veronique came back with the alleged informer, a wavy-haired guy with a mole on the tip of his chin. She walked over to his desk, while the guy waited warily at the door.

'Lopes, tell the guy here that if he gives you what you want, you'll give him his transfer to the Penitentiary.'

'It's true, you can trust me; Veronique's already spoken to me.'

'See, scaredy cat, didn't I tell you?'

Lopes kept his promise. On the Tuesday he transferred the fellow and told his colleagues at the State Penitentiary to pass on the information as soon as he'd talked. Wednesday and Thursday passed without a phone call. On the Friday, the director of correctional services woke up irritated and went straight to the Penitentiary to see what was happening.

'What's going on? Are you trying to pull a fast one on me? I transfer you and get nothing in return?'

'What do you mean nothin', Lopes? I sent your 200 *reais* through Veronique.'

Lopes later told me that a lifetime wasn't enough to fully know a prison. At the time, however, he was angry, took the false grasser back to the Casa de Detenção and, to pre-empt any attempts at revenge, transferred Veronique to Yellow, where I went to see her that night, crying from the pain in her inflamed thighs.

Black Guy

When I got to the consulting room, Arnaldo wasn't there. Without him, consulting was complicated because of the bureaucracy with medical records and the release of medications. I enquired about him.

'He's resolving a little issue in the infirmary and he'll be right back,' I was told.

Arnaldo was taking a while so I decided to go look for him. I found him in the corridor arguing with a group of patients. The conversation was tense; they were accusing him of not delivering the medication that they had been prescribed. A prisoner with burns on his body turned to me.

'Sorry, Doctor, we're sortin' somethin' out with our friend here who's fucked up.'

To calm everyone down I said that Arnaldo had been working in the infirmary for three months and that I didn't have any complaints about him. A frail fellow, one of the most worked-up, answered:

'And that's why he's gettin' the opportunity to defend

himself. Because there's already guys sayin' that when he goes to deliver the medicine down at the back of the gallery tomorrow, he won't be comin' back.'

At this moment, a dark-skinned fellow came walking through the gallery and stopped a metre from the group. Everyone fell silent as he approached.

'I don't believe you're debatin' a problem like this in front of the doctor. Where do you think we are?'

His interference put an end to the argument. One by one, the group dispersed.

When I had finished consulting I called for the fellow who had put an end to the fight. 'Black Guy at your service,' he said. I asked him to intervene to avoid any violence against Arnaldo. He told me I could rest assured the situation had already been resolved.

After that, he would always show up to chat. He'd tell me about things that had happened in the prison and how he was worried about his family, especially his oldest boy, a reckless teenager who didn't obey his mother.

Black Guy's past was similar to that of many other inmates: a childhood spent in the unpaved streets of a poor district on the outskirts of the city, lots of siblings and the wrong company. In the 1970s, his father was sentenced to nine years in the Casa de Detenção, and when he got out he wasn't the same. 'He was disturbed in the head.'

Black Guy wound up in prison after events starting with a hold-up in a jeweller's in downtown São Paulo.

'The three of us arranged to meet on the corner near the shop. At nine o'clock, I left the *favela* and went to get a car with my shooter. Marlon, my neighbour, stopped by Big Brush's place.' It all went quickly. The shop assistants handed over everything that glittered, plus the money from the safe. They left without running, turned the corner, got into the stolen car and took off. They abandoned the car before they got to the *favela* and entered on foot.

In his shack, they had barely begun dividing up the takings, when Black Guy had an unpleasant surprise. 'So there I am, head down, and I glance out the corner of my eye and what do you know, Big Brush's hand is on his shooter! But he was a bit nervous, lookin' from side to side, so I took advantage of his distraction and took him out. It was a matter of survival. If I hadn't, I'd have been the one coppin' it.' He fired three times. Big Brush didn't have time to react; he stayed where he had fallen. Black Guy immediately pointed his gun at Marlon's chest. 'He might have been plottin' with Big Brush or taken the liberty to disagree with my actions.' It was neither; Marlon just sat there, frozen, with startled eyes.

'Why did you just sit there while I blasted him?' asked Black Guy.

''Cause he'd already called me and told me he was gonna take you out so we could split your part.'

His answer left Black Guy perplexed.

'Jeez, you knew he was gonna waste me and keep

all the takings, considerin' we're all in on this together and if one gets busted the others do too! You could've avoided this shit and talked him out of such an ugly idea.'

Black Guy says he only escaped with his life because he was systematic. 'When it's time to divvy up I don't sleep on the job. It's eye for eye, tooth for tooth, 'cause partners are partners and money's the Devil's curse.'

Marlon's excuse was that Big Brush had a number of homicides to his name and might have killed him if he had said something. Black Guy didn't accept his justification.

'Jeez, man, so you were scared, whatever; but you don't kill your friends. If you'd've said somethin', no one would've died, 'cause we would've talked it out. This business of shootin' friends isn't my thing.'

'Sorry, my friend, I guess I was a bit weak on that point,' replied Marlon.

'Then let's let it go. Plottin' to double-cross someone's the ugliest thing. A guy who acts like that is a Judas, the person who spat in Jesus's face!'

They dumped the body in a brook and the incident was kept a secret. 'In the *favela*, people have eyes but they don't see, ears are deaf and no one talks.'

A few days later, the body showed up in the Rio Tietê. 'All swollen, Doctor, ugly, decomposin'.'

Black Guy attended the burial. 'We'd grown up together. If I hadn't gone it would've looked like I was to blame for what had happened.'

To deflect any suspicion, he spent the entire wake next to the body. Leaning against the coffin, memories came back to him like in a film.

'Jeez, man, you really ballsed things up. That's not nice, wantin' to hog everythin' for yourself! You shouldn't have done that! 'Specially 'cause we grew up together, flyin' kites and pinchin' guavas from the old lady's house. See what happens when you get selfish? You end up with nothin'. The only thing you'll be takin' with you from this earth are those white rosary beads wrapped around your hand.'

A few months later, Marlon robbed a two-storey house in Pinheiros. He was unlucky: it belonged to a police detective. He was caught and the police hung him upside down to get him to give them the location of the things he'd stolen, which by this time had been sold. 'At a drug den in the *favela* of Mimosa, to a guy known as Good Hair.'

To escape the *pau-de-arara* without informing on Good Hair, who belonged to a heavily armed gang, Marlon decided to give them the name of the person who had killed Big Brush.

Black Guy wound up at the DEIC, where he found his informant friend.

'Marlon, did you give 'em my name for the job too?'

'No, not the job.'

'Shit, man, but did you have to go and give me up for the homicide? It would've been better if you'd given me up for one of the jobs.'

'I gave you up for the homicide 'cause Big Brush's brothers were thinkin' it was me who killed him. After all, we left his place together that day. I come back and he shows up deceased.'

Once again Black Guy was magnanimous.

'Jeez, my friend, that makes me sad! I could involve you in the homicide, but that's not how I do things. Since you gave me up, I'll back you up: that I killed him myself, threw him in the river and you're clean.'

Truth be told, his benevolence also served less altruistic interests; if he'd told the police everything, he'd also be tried for car theft and holding up the jeweller's. Besides which, getting Marlon off could be advantageous in the future. 'I've got a copy of everythin', showin' that he gave me up but I didn't grass on him. If he ever crosses paths with me in prison and tries to take advantage of me, it'll be my turn to say: now you're the one who's gonna get it, 'cause you owe me!'

Nevertheless, Black Guy claimed he wasn't in the habit of getting even like that, because of his principles. 'I don't operate that way, so as not to destroy the con's reputation, in which case he'd be beaten, robbed and kicked out. It's not my way. I prefer to have eyes but not see, have a mouth and keep it shut.'

The judge didn't believe his story that he'd killed his accomplice in self-defence. He also found him guilty of hiding a body and, as an aggravating circumstance, he deemed the fact that Black Guy had gone to the funeral and positioned himself thoughtfully in front of the coffin to be a cold-blooded act. He got nineteen years and six months.

One afternoon, as I was crossing the pavilion court-yard, I saw him having a serious conversation with a young fellow, whose skin was lighter than his. It was his oldest son, who had just arrived in the Casa, sentenced to three years and two months for armed robbery.

Eye for an Eye

Cigar walked in with his finger buried in a cooked onion. His left hand was supporting his right hand, the fingers of which were bent, with the exception of his index finger, which was knuckle-deep in the steaming-hot onion.

He sat down in front of me, with an expression of pain, and unsheathed the hurt finger. It was very swollen; just beneath the start of his fingernail there were two deep symmetrical cuts, in the middle of a pseudoaneurysm[1].

'Rat bite?'

'Yeah, Doctor. It hit the bone.'

The prison was infested with various breeds of rats. In the dark, they scampered through the galleries, corridors and the insides of cells. In the general kitchen, after dinner had been distributed, the cleaners would have barely finished mopping the pot-holed

---

[1] A haematoma that forms as the result of a leaking hole in an artery.

floor when the army of rodents would invade the territory and raid the pantry. When the new day dawned, they would hide in the drains until night fell again. They were invincible.

'It happened half an hour ago.'

'A rat bite during the day?'

'I was workin', Doctor, clearin' out that drain that gets clogged up in Two.'

Cigar had removed the iron cover of the drain in front of Pavilion Two. The hole was filled to brimming with gunk and old food floating in it. He climbed down into the filthy water, knee-deep, and started emptying it out with a bucket. When the thick drain-pipe emerged Cigar stuck his hand down the side to remove a plastic bag that was in the way. At that moment he felt a stabbing pain. 'It started as a fine, stinging pain in me fingertip, and spread like an electric shock down me arm. It was horrible; it even gave me a bitter taste in me mouth.'

He pulled his hand back in reflex and the rat came with it, hanging from his fingertip, biting hard. It was black, enormous. 'I even thought it might be one of those little dogs that posh ladies like.'

In his desperation, he swung his arm through the air and hit the rat against the cement, but its grip was so strong that it didn't let go. Tormented by the pain, with the rat dangling from his bone, Cigar lifted his arm as high as he could and slammed the animal onto the ground with all his strength.

'Then the wretched fucker, excuse the language, finally let go. It lay there writhin' with its paws in the air.'

'Did it die?'

'It didn't, Doctor. It was the Devil himself!'

That was when Cigar, blind with rage, grabbed his enemy with both hands, held its mouth shut so he wouldn't get bitten again and took his revenge.

'I sank my teeth into the miserable thing's mind. I bit hard, until he stopped thrashin'. Then I brushed my teeth, and that was that.'

Head Over Heels

Cigar had a white smile and perfect teeth, a rarity in the prison. He was a villain through and through, however, in the way he walked, talked and looked. An incorrigible thief, this was his second time in prison, with a sixteen-year sentence.

Two years after his run-in with the rat, he convinced Squint, a cross-eyed thief interned in the infirmary with scabies all over his body, to sell his own mattress to buy crack. Then he tricked his friend, smoked the rocks of crack on his own and, when an infirmary employee found out about the sale, Cigar kicked up such a big stink that Squint not only took the blame for everything, but also got thirty days in Solitary.

Two weeks later, Cigar appeared in the consulting room with a ceremonious air, accompanied by a big-nosed, Fellini-esque inmate.

'Doctor, do you think you could have a look at my friend here? He's got a pesky itch.'

It was the unsuspecting buyer of Squint's infested mattress.

After that, I didn't see Cigar for a while. One day, he returned with a bad cough, fever, laboured breathing and sunken eyes: pulmonary tuberculosis with fluid on the right lung.

With his mother dead, Cigar hadn't had any visitors since he'd arrived in the prison, for the second time, four years earlier. In the first few months, he still read the newspaper and asked for news from the outside, but he soon came to the conclusion that satisfying his curiosity only brought him more suffering and he alienated himself from events on the other side of the wall, as do many men without families who are serving long sentences.

He didn't miss his relatives, with the exception of his oldest son. 'I don't want to see the little one, 'cause he's fine with his grandmother, Rosirene's mother. Now, the big one, I don't know, because he lives with Rosane, my other wife, and she smokes crack.'

After serving ten years the first time he was in the Casa, Cigar was set free. When he got out, he discovered that Rosane, the mother of his first son, had just been sent to prison. One Sunday, he went to visit her in the Tremembé penitentiary. He took his son to see his mother along with five grams of cocaine, as a present. On the bus home, with his firstborn on his lap, he was approached by a classy-looking lady.

'Listen, dear, I'm in the business too, you know. I

came to visit my sister and saw you giving your wife some stuff. That was your wife, wasn't it? Look, I'm a dealer. Is there any chance you could fix me up with about ten grams? You can trust me because I'm in the business too!'

Cigar felt he could trust her. On the Tuesday, he caught two buses to get to Jardim Míriam. 'I took a bit of snow. I didn't know that part of town; it was really hard to find her place.'

In the woman's bedroom, Cigar handed over the drugs and sat down to talk to Machado, an elderly man who lived with her.

That was when temptation walked through the back door, smiling, wearing a strappy dress: Rosirene.

'A mulatta with delicate lips, a perky little nose, a samba-school ass and there I was doin' cold-turkey, just out after ten years inside. I thought to myself, I need to bed that chick no matter what! I don't know if it's ever happened to you, Doctor; it was love at first sight! I was head over heels!' He was so taken with her that he had a word on the side with Machado.

'Tell me about that girl there.'

'That girl there . . . yours if you want her.'

'Then tell that girl there that I'm gonna take her to Santos tomorrow.'

He returned the next day, but he didn't need to take her as far as Santos. 'We went straight to the Hotel Flor da Lapa, where we partied and spent money like there was no tomorrow. Then, I thought

OK, so I've tasted the fruit, and now that's it. Except she didn't leave.'

Since they couldn't afford the Flor da Lapa every night, they rented a room in a slum tenement near the old bus station, so they could live together, madly in love. 'Although I sometimes had to smack her around a bit, 'cause the lady had a lot of cheek.'

One night, Cigar went to bed completely stoned and woke up to shouting.

'Hey, wake up, your place is on fire!'

It was the neighbours.

'There was smoke everywhere. I raced out of the room at a million miles an hour.'

Rosirene had thrown all of his belongings, clothes, flip-flops, shoes, onto the double bed and set it on fire. The neighbours were threatening to call the police and he wasn't sure whether he should put out the fire or try to calm the neighbours first. If the police got there, they'd arrest him on the spot, as he had only just been released from prison. The firebug was watching everything on the other side of the street, laughing cynically. 'She torched everythin', even my good trousers! It took a lot of convincin' to get the neighbours to let it go. The cops wouldn't have listened to me.'

When the fire was out, Cigar went out barefoot to get some air. Rosirene followed him. He stopped at a campfire someone had made.

'I was fuming; I wanted to break her bones.' He sat down. She followed suit, though she wisely sat on the opposite side of the fire, in front of him. After a while, Cigar got up slowly with his unlit cigarette in the corner of his mouth, picked up a cinder as if he was going to light it and walked towards Rosirene. 'I poked her about thirty times with the cinder. There were sparks flyin' everywhere. It looked like we were in hell!'

Once avenged, he holed up in a bar and had a few drinks to wind down. Later, when he got home, he found the room in silence. 'The first thing I see is her asleep on the burnt bed! For fuck's sake, "Get the hell out of here," I shouted. "No," she said. And we were going, "Get out now," "No," "Out," "No," so she ended up not going and we went back to bein' all lovey-dovey.'

They lived together for two years. He forgot his son and wife in jail because of her. They got along so well that they'd wake up smoking crack, brush their teeth with the same toothbrush, have lunch at a bar and eat off the same plate.

'I stole and she hustled.' According to him, it didn't work: even when he'd steal enough money for them to spend a few days without any worries, he'd go out in the morning and when he'd come back at the end of the day, where was Rosirene? 'She'd be down at the Estação da Luz hustling. They get addicted, you know, and don't want to give it up. I couldn't do a thing. Wanna bit? She's your girl. The only thing I'd say was, "Just don't fuck a friend of mine or I'll break your neck."'

Fate caused them to part when he was in a bad way

from smoking too much crack and she went back to live with her mother, with their baby boy who had been born.

One night, they ran into one another in downtown São Paulo and Rosirene confessed that she was going out with a friend of his, Mato Grosso, and that they had plans to move to the town of Ponta Porã together. 'Well there you go, she was fucking a friend of mine and the two of them were makin' plans together!'

Later, he recognised that he had lost her because there is no harmony immune to crack. Even so, he was determined to settle things with violence. 'When I get out,' he told me, 'I'm going to kill Mato Grosso. Not her, 'cause he's the one in the wrong. He knows me and knows she's mine; he has no business puttin' the moves on her and takin' her away. He's the one crossin' me, not her.'

The decision to spare Rosirene's life, however, was the fruit of more recent considerations, because when he first arrived in the prison he had wanted to lure her to a deserted place, chop off her feet with an axe and tell her:

'I'm not gonna kill you 'cause we've got a son, and I don't want him to come tell me that I killed his mother. Later, he's gonna see you with no feet, and he's gonna ask why and you're gonna tell him, "I had sex with another guy." And then he'll know his dad was right.'

His intention was to do something so nasty that Rosirene would never forget it. After all, he had left

Rosane, whom he still liked at the time, because of her; in fact, the first time he had been locked up, he had thought he'd go crazy if Rosane left him. He had even made threats.

'If you don't visit me, I'll poke your eyes out.'

She smiled and reassured him.

'Who said I'm the sort of woman who abandons her man inside?'

She kept her promise. She visited him every week-end for almost ten years with bags of supplies and the boy. Until she was sent to prison herself. He was the one who betrayed her, because of Rosirene. 'I was an ungrateful dog. I left Rosane locked up in Tremembé.'

His punishment came swiftly when Rosane got out of jail before the date expected.

One night, he was sleeping peacefully in a little hotel with Rosirene, certain that his first wife was still behind bars, when Rosane, recently released, headed down-town to confront him. She enquired about the ingrate's whereabouts in a bar.

'He's asleep with his wife in Copa 70.'

'Really, his wife? The dog!'

When she entered the room she started breaking everything; she threw the TV on the ground and flew at Rosirene, who was twice her size. Cigar quickly pulled on his clothes and made himself scarce. He sat in a bar waiting for the dust to settle. Half an hour later, the Portuguese hotel owner appeared.

'Go see what that girl did. She beat up your wife,

stuck a pin in her bum, which drew blood, tore up her clothes and set fire to them!'

Cigar had fevers and night sweats; he was thin and his lungs had been compromised. He laughed, and his memories seemed to make him happy. In spite of his eternal gratitude to Rosane, he couldn't stop thinking about Rosirene. 'Doctor, if I die inside, I won't have any peace. I have to see that woman again. Then I'm gonna kill Mato Grosso, but the first thing I have to do is see Rosirene, just one more time. She's beautiful, Doctor! Jesus . . . that mulatta cast a spell on me.'

Not-a-Hope

Not-a-Hope said he wasn't a thief. A short, thin mulatto with a broad smile, the youngest of his siblings, he turned nineteen without ever having held a job. His parents did their best to give him what he wanted, within their possibilities. 'They really pampered me.'

One day, he had a fight with his family and ran away. 'Just to spite them.'

After two days, going hungry, in the very district where he lived, he stopped at a campfire where a few friends were keeping warm. 'They weren't thieves either, but they were thinkin' about takin' the revolver from the watchman at the quarry.' Not-a-Hope went with them, not out of any conviction, but because he didn't have anywhere else to go. Just so he wouldn't have to stay there alone at the campfire.

They all entered the quarry except for Not-a-Hope, who kept watch outside. When he noticed the trespassers, the watchman panicked and started shouting. One of them fired and hit the poor man in the head. They grabbed his radio, jacket and revolver, and fled.

The crime resulted in a trial for armed robbery that ruined his life. He was sentenced to twelve years and eight months. 'We were so naïve, Doctor, that we stole where everyone knew us. We grew up there. Not a hope.'

Behind bars, he learned the tricks of the trade, and was released in 1987. 'I started robbing properly.' He held up businesses, bakeries and mugged people in the streets. He specialised in the 'Adam's apple', a method in which he'd get a passer-by in a headlock, while his cohorts would relieve the victim of his belongings. He says he never killed anyone. He'd approach them saying 'This is a stick-up' and, if his victims didn't believe it, he'd thump them over the head with the butt of his gun to intimidate them. He never mugged women on their own, for fear of winding up in prison with a reputation as a rapist.

'I came back to the Casa in August of '91, 'cause of the Adam's apple and about fifty to a hundred robberies around the place. I landed another nineteen years, 'cause the judge didn't want to know about attenuatin' circumstances. Not a hope.'

He had already served five years of this sentence. Since he had arrived, no one had brought him even a packet of cigarettes. He got by with the help of his acquaintances. He sold watches and clothes for fellow inmates who were in debt; the owner of the item would ask for five, and he'd resell it for seven or eight. Everything he earned ended up in his crack pipe. 'One of my virtues is that I only smoke what I can pay cash for! You'll never hear that Not-a-Hope bought a crumb of crack on credit. I can walk through the galleries with my head high, not owin' nothing to any con. In here, with me, it's all about respect!'

After his mother died, he ceased to exist for his family. 'To society, I'm the scum of the earth, rejected like a mangy dog. If the guys here inside don't treat me with respect, why would anyone else? I'm nothing in this world. I've lost my identity as a human being. Not a hope.'

I treated him for a serious case of tuberculosis installed in his lymphatic system, causing swollen lymph glands in his neck and armpits. He was gaunt and almost died. After a month, having recovered from his fever and regained his appetite, he was discharged from the infirmary. I stressed the importance of keeping up the treatment and that it was imperative that he lay off the crack for a while.

In the pavilion, he did exactly the opposite and came back worse than ever. He was wasting away; the disease had spread to his lungs and the slightest effort caused him to huff and puff. The bacteria had become aggressive and resistant to medication. Within a matter of days he was weak, his breathing laboured, and he would lie in bed all day long. Nevertheless, he always smiled when I went to examine him.

One afternoon, I went to see him before heading for the consulting room. The cell was filled with a beautiful orangey light, caused by the sun reflecting off the naked woman on the wall. In a coma, curled up on the trundle bed, skin and bones, he looked like a child. There were breadcrumbs around his dry mouth and a column of ants was scurrying back and forth across Not-a-Hope's contorted face to retrieve them.

Valdomiro

Valdomiro, or Valdo, was a mulatto with a wrink-led face and tips of grey in his tight curls. In his prisoner's eyes, there was sometimes a light that brightened up his entire face. His seventy years of age and stories alongside legendary criminals such as Meneghetti, Quinzinho, Seven Fingers, Red Light and Little Promise made Valdo a man respected through-out the prison.

He had done time in a number of prisons. In one, after four months in Solitary in complete darkness, broken only when the window in the cell door was opened to pass plates of food through, which he had to swallow quickly before the cockroaches could get to it, Valdo pretended to have lost his mind. To convince the warders that he had gone insane, he tore up money and ate his own excrement. 'I had to make a mess to get out of that place. In those days, Solitary taught you the limits of a human being.'

Valdo was born on a sloping dirt road, the grandson

of a racist grandmother who discriminated against his black-skinned mother. 'My dad was weak-minded and kept bad company. He took off and left me on my own, with my mother and two little sisters.'

His mother took her three children and went to live with her mother, who gave them a warm welcome. 'My granny on my mother's side, who had her own brothel, took us in with open arms.' This grandmother's home, in São Paulo's red-light district, was a small three-storey building, where twelve women worked. Behind it was their house. 'With the money that granny made with her little massage parlour, we bought a travelling fair and started to move around.'

Valdo was a strapping lad of sixteen by this time. He looked after the target-shooting stand and was shacked up with Betina, one of his grandmother's former employees.

One day, as fate would have it, the fair burned down and the family moved into a small house owned by the grandmother, near the Guarapiranga Reservoir, on the outskirts of São Paulo.

Valdo got a job as a septic tank cleaner, built a little house of his own and led the life of a worker until events changed the course of things. His wife was the cause of everything, according to him. 'She was really jealous, of my dogs even. I love dogs and couldn't even treat them properly 'cause she'd get all irate, sayin' I paid more attention to them than to her. How absurd, Doctor, a human being tryin' to compete with an animal.'

His wife's temperament brought him strife. If he so much as said 'hi' to a female neighbour, from then on she'd call her a whore, and every time he was late home he'd hear about it for the next four hours at least. She created problems with the husbands and sisters of the women she insulted. He would try to calm her down, but it was an inglorious task.

'There was nothing to be done, Doctor. When a woman gets jealous, she's the Devil in a skirt. At night, you wanna go to bed 'cause you have to work early and she won't stop pesterin' you. You wanna have a drink after work, then you suck on some mint to disguise it, but when you get home she sniffs your breath and that's it! She automatically assumes you were with another woman, 'cause all men are worthless. And nothing'll convince her otherwise!'

One day, a beautiful mulatta moved in nearby. 'Gorgeous, Doctor, with legs shaped by God himself and swayin' hips to stop the traffic.' In the street, whenever he saw her coming, Valdo would discreetly lower his head. 'So as not to provoke the wildcat at home.'

And also to avoid provoking the ire of her husband, who was notorious for his own jealousy and had got into many a scrap over his wife.

One sunny Sunday, Valdo was at the front gate trying out the first pair of sunglasses he had ever owned when the mulatta went past, hips swaying. He was so distracted that he didn't notice Betina at the window behind him shaking out the dust rag.

'The troublemaker took it into her head that I was eyein' up the mulatta. She slipped out the door, sweetly, as if she was going to give me a hug, and wham! She grabbed my tackle. The cheek!'

In an instant, Betina assessed the hardness at hand and concluded that Valdo was a shameless lowlife and not worth the beans with which she filled his lunchbox.

The screaming brought the neighbours out of their houses. Valdo wished he could disappear. In the end, convinced that it was impossible to calm her down, he went to a bar, burning with shame. 'The slander followed me to the corner without lettin' up, carryin' on in that shrill voice of hers.'

In the bar he found Joca, who bought him a drink for his nerves and invited him to a game of snooker. Experienced with the cue and women, Joca was giving Valdo advice when the mulatta's husband appeared. He wasn't happy.

'What did you do to Cida?'

'I've never even looked at your wife, my friend. I apologise in any case, but what happened isn't cause for offence. My wife is the jealous, possessive sort and always makes a scandal. The whole district knows what she's like.'

'Your own wife said in front of everyone that you

can't take your eyes off Cida when she goes past. I'll teach you to respect your neighbour's wife, you black layabout!'

He pulled out a knife used for gutting fish. Joca, a true friend, didn't care for the insult and pulled out his revolver.

'So what if he's black? You're not exactly white yourself. But he isn't a layabout, 'cause he's got a proper job with signed papers. If you take one more step forward, you're the one who's gonna die!'

The husband was either blind with jealousy or he really was brave. Even after taking a bullet he still tried to stab Valdo. The only reason he didn't succeed was because Valdo whacked him across the forehead with the billiards cue.

The husband died in hospital. Joca, who was wanted by the police, took off to the Northeast of Brazil. As for Valdo: 'I was stupid. Two days later I turned myself in at the police station, poor, without a lawyer, pleadin' self-defence.'

On visiting day, a month later in the Casa de Detenção, Valdo's name was called to go and receive a visitor at the entrance to the pavilion. Filled with fury, he said, on his way to the door he decided to strangle Betina, that possessive woman responsible for the misfortune that had befallen him.

At the gate, however, it wasn't Betina who was waiting for him.

'It was the mulatta who had sparked the whole

tragedy, in a red dress, with quiverin' eyes and sparklin' lips. She smiled such a white smile, Doctor, that I was spellbound. And on that blessed day our love began, which, by the grace of God, is still strong.'

The Prodigal Son

Valente didn't go out alone at night because he was afraid of thieves. The son of evangelical rural workers in the state of Paraná, he had moved to the outskirts of São Paulo to live with a cousin. He did well until he fell in with the wrong people, started snorting cocaine, lost his job and had a fight with his cousin. Six months later he started holding up bakers', butchers' and businesses on pay day, and killing people. 'Sometimes you talk to a guy, or you're gonna do a job with him, but you don't like him. You don't see eye to eye. For someone in crime, killin' him is like drinking a glass of water.'

One of his friends, Salviano, lived with a woman who had gone out with a police officer. One night, out of jealousy, Salviano invited Valente to help him kill the police officer. He said he accepted the invitation because he had nothing else to do. 'We waited at the bus stop. He was supposed to arrive at ten, but he showed up at eleven-thirty. We shot him eight times and got out of there.'

Another time, he was taking his girlfriend home when a guy going past said a swear word. Valente left the young lady and went after him. 'When I caught up with him, I said, "Hey, gutter mouth!"'

He shot him five times. Valente was a man of few words. 'Lots of people in crime even get into a debate with their victims; with me there was no chitchattin'.'

Following that, he killed two shop owners who tried to react as he was robbing them, a thief who talked about him behind his back to a neighbour, and another guy in a bar because of a spilled beer.

Number seven took place while dividing up $30,000 that he had stolen with two partners. They were counting out the money when one of them had the bad idea to go to the toilet. 'I pricked up my ears, 'cause thieves can get greedy.' When his partner came out of the toilet, his leather jacket was draped over his arm, partially covering his right hand. Valente didn't think twice. 'I grabbed my shooter from the table and shot him three times. It was a waste of bullets, as the first one got him right between the eyes.'

His other companion got a fright.

'Are you crazy? You killed him!'

'He was gonna shoot me.'

They went over to the body, lifted up the jacket and found that his hands were empty. His revolver was still tucked into his waistband. 'Oh well,' said his partner. 'It was his own fault: the table's full of money and he shows up like that, from behind, with his hand covered! Bad luck, he slipped up.'

After three years in crime, Valente decided to organise a gang to rob banks. He travelled to Rio de Janeiro and bought a machine gun in the *favela* of Rocinha. He didn't actually get to use it, because two of his partners were killed in a hold-up and another one moved to another city, leaving just him and Salviano, with whom he had killed the police officer.

Around that time, Salviano fell in love with a 16-year-old girl and left the police officer's ex-girlfriend. Her pride was hurt, so she went to the police and turned them in.

The police arrived while he was sleeping. He tried to reach his gun, but there wasn't enough time. He had never imagined he'd be arrested so easily.

I suffered ten days on the *pau-de-arara*, half an hour a day. There were days when they'd string me up twice. They wanted a lot out of me, even things I hadn't done. Because of the machine gun, they wanted me to confess to eight bank robberies, even though I hadn't even done one. I only confessed to what I'd done, except for four homicides that I left out.

At first I got eighteen years. Eight months later, with the next jury, I got 112. The total sentence came to 130 years and nine months.

It brought me down a bit. But I didn't change

my ways – I actually got worse. I went to Pavilion Nine. There, I wanted to show that I was a dangerous criminal. I'd go up to a guy and say, 'Are you a fighter? If so, show me your knife now!' Then, if he didn't want to fight, I'd say, 'Then you leave your TV and things and head on over to Five, 'cause that's your place.' I thought there was no fixing my life, that I was going to die inside, and it didn't matter if it was right then and there. If that had to be my fate, so be it.

One rainy day, he took shelter by the wall next to the chapel on the ground floor of Nine and overheard the pastor preaching.

'The Bible says in Isaiah Chapter 9, Verse 6, that Jesus Christ is the Counsellor, Mighty God, Everlasting Father and Prince of Peace. You who live the wrong life, God has a plan for you. Come today to Jesus, because tomorrow may be too late. It doesn't matter if you're a criminal, how many you've killed, Jesus Christ wants to forgive you for all of your sins, lead you out of darkness and work a miracle in your life.'

Valente entered the church and stood near the door. He felt that the Holy Ghost was speaking through the pastor.

'Who wants to accept Jesus? If you do, raise your hand!'

The veins in the preacher's neck pulsed and his eyes spat fire. Valente thought his appearance had been disfigured by the Holy Ghost. He felt a cold dagger plunge into his flesh. He raised his arm.

'Kneel down, brother!'

Valente obeyed and started to cry. 'I repented for my crimes, the whoring and the evil things I'd done. I sobbed like a baby in his mother's arms.'

When he got up, his mind was clear. He felt the Lord's pardon had come to rest on his forehead.

He continued living in Nine, but his fellow inmates found the change in him strange. 'There were some less acceptin' ones who threatened me: "OK, so you've been born again. Well now you're going to die, 'cause we don't like repented criminals."'

He would wander through the galleries of Nine holding the Old Testament, without evil in his heart, struggling to set his companions on the true path.

'Suddenly, I got all restless to get out of Nine. It had to be quick. It wasn't my place anymore.' He asked the brothers of the Assembly of God, in Five, to take him in and joined them on the fifth floor. He was a changed man. 'I had stopped using slang and bad words and there was no more perversity in my soul. I was in God's plans, it was Jesus simplifying my life, deciding that I should remain alive in His kingdom, because two days after I left, the riot squad stormed Nine, with dogs and machine guns.'

Condoms for Cons

Two days after Valente's restlessness took him out of Pavilion Nine, I gave the transvestites a talk on AIDS prevention at the back of the cinema. It was the first Friday in October of 1992.

At the end, I insisted on the danger of unprotected sex and asked if there were any questions. Next to me, a slender fellow known as Pérola Byington, with his legs crossed like a woman's and a limp wrist, biting his nails the whole time, spoke up.

'Doctor, you've been telling us how we can and can't get this virus for the last half hour. I'm sorry, but it's no news to us. Lots of our girlfriends have already died of it. What we need is condoms, not lessons! If there aren't any condoms for us to force the cons to use, what use is this talk, Doctor?'

Shortly after that I saw Dr Pedrosa, the director general of the prison, who, back then, used to walk through the entire prison unaccompanied, a habit that he later had to give up.

'How are you doing, Doctor? When you're done, stop by my office for a coffee.'

As we had coffee together, we talked about distributing condoms to the inmates, a measure that in those days evoked emotional reactions among legal authorities, such as that of a public prosecutor in a grey suit and navy-blue shoes who told me in a debate: 'If society can't deliver a litre of milk to children in the *favelas*, you'll never convince me to hand out condoms to louts in jail.'

The director and I came up with a strategy to present the problem personally to some influential people within the system. Then he showed me a twelve-metre cord, made of strips of blanket carefully rolled around wires, which gave it enough resistance to support the weight of a man trying to scale the wall. This led to other escape stories and before I knew it, it was already twelve-thirty in the afternoon.

'I need to head off to the hospital, it's getting late. And I've already taken up a lot of your time.'

'No you haven't. Today's Friday, the day when they wash everything for the weekend visits. The prison's a picture of calm.'

Approximately two hours later, there was a misunderstanding between two prisoners in Pavilion Nine.

The Uprising

That afternoon, in Nine, Furacão 2000 and Burgo Paulista were playing one another in the pavilion's internal football tournament. Upstairs, the prisoners were straightening up their cells. All calm, as the director had imagined.

While the game was in progress, unexpectedly, as all of the most serious events in prisons are, Beard had a fight with Coelho on Rua Dez on the second floor, one armed with a knife, the other with a piece of wood. A run-of-the-mill fight, if it hadn't been for its terrible consequences.

The reason for the conflict was never properly clarified, according to Baiano the Fornicator, a cocaine trafficker and part-owner of a pizza parlour who bragged that he had gone out with the most beautiful women in his part of town, and who had been an eyewitness to the fight. 'Some say it was over a debt of five packets of cigarettes. Others think it was about marijuana, but some guys who were close even said it was an argument about football. So many theories that the truth'll never be found.'

Coelho and Beard belonged to two rival factions from São Paulo's north and south zones respectively, which hadn't been seeing eye-to-eye in the pavilion for some time. When the fight was under way, their fellow faction members gathered around the two antagonists and exchanged death threats. Due to the disorder that broke out, the inmates who had been playing football headed back up to the second floor and the confrontation took on more serious proportions.

Old Jeremias said that at times of tension like that the outcome depended on a delicate balance. 'In jail fights, Doctor, if they pass a certain point, they get out of control, and then they only stop after a handful of men are dead.'

To keep a lid on things, the warders took the inmates still gathered on the pitch inside, a preventive measure that makes it easier to lock them up to avoid the worst, if necessary. But there was no way to force the excited inmates to enter their cells at that point. The clash was irreversible.

The tension rose so fast that when Majesty – a highly respected inmate and the pavilion sports president, one of the last to leave the pitch – arrived inside with the balls and goal net, he didn't even try to reason with the younger inmates as he usually did at such moments. 'It was like a fish market, Doctor. When it's like that, tryin' to make peace is useless. Everyone's blood boils and they all go crazy. I went upstairs, mindin' my own business, but I saw so many knives passin' me on the stairs that I had a feelin' it wasn't gonna end well.'

When the running and shouts of 'you're gonna die' began, even those who had nothing to do with it grew wary. Zelito, a tall, strong black man whom I later met in the infirmary, blinded in both eyes by tear gas, took his knife out of its hiding place. 'I had nothin' to do with that spat, but I hadn't seen so many blades and clubs in one place in my life. I'd better get mine out too, I thought to myself. In the middle of that fight it was possible that somethin' might come my way.'

Majesty, who had escaped a 1985 rebellion with his life, convinced his cellmate to retire to their cell. 'Let's mind our own business, until whoever has to die is dead.'

The running and shouting caused the tumult to spread to the other floors. Prisons are like pressure cookers: when they explode, there's no containing them.

Adelmiro, a thickset inmate of Portuguese descent, crossed paths with a warder who, against regulations, was bringing him correspondence without it passing through censorship and whispered discretely, so as not to be called a traitor by his fellow inmates, 'Get out, 'cause things're gettin' ugly, boss.'

The warder got the message and quickly headed down to the inner courtyard, where about ten of his colleagues were, impotent in the face of a tumult that size. Behind him came a band of inmates in ninja-style hoods who started to vandalise Incarceration in the hope of destroying their own criminal records.

The warders on duty said that this was when the first casualty in the north zone group occurred and that after that there were others on both sides, in retaliation. Later, the military police confirmed that they had found dead bodies when they stormed the pavilion. In the prisoners' version, no one died in the settling of accounts.

Another point of divergence was when the warders left the mutinying pavilion. Some said the tiny team on duty, so as not to risk being taken hostage, abandoned the pavilion and locked the door from the outside. The warders involved said that the military police, who had been alerted by the guards on the wall, were already in the prison grounds and gave orders for them to leave.

At any rate, without the warders there, the pavilion fell into the rebels' hands. In Nine of all places, mostly inhabited by younger inmates who were in prison for the first time. Men without prison experience, like Nardão, a novice thief who joined in the confusion because, by coincidence, he had just shot up cocaine in his cell when the commotion broke out. 'The prison fell into our power. I say "our" because, on that occasion, everyone was involved. We started protestin' for improvements, 'cause the atmosphere wasn't exactly the best, lots of men wanted transfers, there were guys with expired sentences waitin' for open-regime, visitors coming in dribs and drabs, and it just escalated.'

It was true: the warders had been saying for some time that the atmosphere in Nine left something to be desired, but what could they do? In a pavilion like that, with 2000 men packed in like sardines at the time, tense phases occurred periodically. How to divine when it was all going to blow up?

With the exception of some more sensible inmates, who locked themselves in their cells, the prisoners started up a hellish shouting, running and breaking things, out of control, armed with knives, sticks and iron pipes, infecting the masses with their excitement, like a stampede.

At that moment, Santão, the guy missing his right ear who set up the equipment in the talks at the cinema, whose eighteen-year sentence would be over in February of the following year, looked through his cell window and saw the riot squad lined up outside the external door of the pavilion, with ninja-masks covering their faces, shields, machine guns and dogs.

On the floors of the pavilion, as agitated as ants before a storm, the inmates were burning and destroying whatever was within reach. Some used old grudges as an excuse to pillage other inmates' cells, provoking retaliation on the part of their victims.

Later, the mob's irrationality would have disastrous consequences, according to C'mon Now – a cleaner with such a long neck that he looked as if he had stepped out of a Modigliani painting and the typical Italianised accent of the district of Mooca, who had been caught in a truck full of firewood transporting marijuana from the Northeastern state of Pernambuco to a warehouse in São Paulo. 'C'mon now, let's face it, we really did go crazy. Some idiots got their hands on some cans of oil from the cleanin' supplies room and tipped 'em down the stairs so the cops'd slip. I say idiots 'cause they really were boneheads. Their trap worked against us.'

Meanwhile, military police officials, accompanied by legal authorities, took command of the prison. The director tried to convince them to let him talk to the prisoners. He actually got as far as the door to the court-yard outside Nine, but before he could enter, the riot squad in tactical formation behind him burst through the door and stormed the pavilion. From that moment on, according to Dr Pedrosa, the only ones who can say what went on in there are the riot squad, the prisoners and God.

I only talked to the prisoners. Their version of what happened is relayed in the following chapters.

The Attack

Locked in his cell, Majesty, since a child a fanatical Corinthians supporter like his uncle who used to take him to watch training sessions at São Jorge Park, heard the riot squad announce from the ground floor:

'Everyone in their cells 'cause we're coming in.'

According to the inmates themselves, they obeyed, because that was what happened in the prison. 'We might all be uneducated thieves and criminals, but we're not stupid. No one likes to die. When the riot squad comes, we all run to our cells, 'cause they've got boots, dogs and they're armed to the teeth. There's no way we can take them on in the gallery with knives and pieces of wood.'

On the third floor, when he heard the order to get out of the gallery, Dadá – a thief who had survived six bullets from a hit man hired by local shop owners; the only member of a family of born-again Christians who had strayed from the path and who had received a letter from his mother the day before asking him to please read Psalm 91 – got the wrong impression. 'It was ominous. There was a bunch of men in masks, with only their eyes showin', machine guns, dogs barking and a helicopter flyin' lower and lower, with a gun stickin' out of it. They stormed the ground floor firing, but I was stupid and thought they were blanks.'

Dadá ran to his cell, where he found another thirteen men trying to hide from the troops, like himself. He found a corner behind a low wall next to the sink and squatted down.

He didn't have to wait long in this uncomfortable position. The riot squad was quick to arrive at the third floor. From the yelling that ensued he realised that the bullets weren't harmless, as he had first imagined.

'Didn't you ask to die, fuckers? Didn't you call me? It's just the sound of a machine gun.'

The guys who hesitated to hide were the first to fall. All you could hear were shots and cries of 'Please, God, no!' We kept quiet in our cell. I was like an ostrich – I didn't dare raise my head to look over the sink.'

Death ran through the gallery and arrived at the door to his cell.

A uniform opened the window in the door, stuck his machine gun through and shouted, 'Surprise, the Devil's here to carry you lot off to hell!' He sprayed bullets here and there. It filled the cell with smoke and the smell of gunpowder. I only realised I was still alive when I felt somethin' warm drippin' down my back. It was blood. At the time I thought it was mine. I looked at my cell-mates: all smokin', filled with bullet holes, with blood comin' out of their mouths. Eleven were killed. The only ones to escape were me, with a graze wound on my neck, and one other guy who made it out unscathed, the lucky bastard.

On the second floor, Jacó – one of the cleaners of Nine, a short, quick-talking cocaine dealer who prided himself on the fact that he had only conducted business by phone, without ever touching the drugs – had a narrow escape.

'It was a major panic; everyone runnin' for their cells. They were comin' to kill all the cleaners. As soon as they appeared on the second floor, one of them shouted, "Let's get rid of the fucking cleaners!"' Because they didn't know the prison, however, the officers headed down the gallery in the opposite direction to the clean-ers' cells. Jacó was lucky, but not the postman, who was the first to die; precisely the man who had survived a famous episode in which the guards of a police lock-up in São Paulo had locked fifty men in a tiny cell, killing eighteen by asphyxia. After the postman came the others in the same wing.

In his cell, Majesty, whose premonition had been confirmed, sat on a little stool with his elbows on his knees and his grey head in his hands, staring at his feet. His cellmate was terrified, trembling in a corner of his bed. When their cell door was opened, Majesty just sat there, unmoving, with his head down. He could only see the officer's boot out of the corner of his eye and waited for the *coup de grâce* in the back of his neck.

'After ages, he asked if we were involved in the confusion. I said that I was no child, without taking my eyes off the ground, and that we were only involved in sports. He could see the balls strewn about the place. He was quiet, and I waited for him to fire. Then the boot turned back towards the gallery and I heard my cellmate start sobbin'. I just sat there like a statue.'

Majesty's neighbours weren't as lucky. Among them, the centre forward of Furacão 2000, who had been radiant moments before the rebellion after kicking five goals (past Marcão, the Burgo Paulista goalkeeper, who also met his death), and who was due to be released the following Tuesday.

On the fifth floor, in a cell with nine people in it, seven were killed, including two brothers from Rio, who had been caught a week earlier after hijacking a car on the Castelo Branco motorway so they could get back to Rio in time to attend their cousin's wedding. 'One died sitting on his bed and the other as he jumped up in fright.'

In this cell, Minimum Wage, a thief arrested for holding up two police officers, survived thanks to his low stature. As bullets flew, he curled up in a corner and pulled the enormous dead body of another cellmate over his own.

The Attack

It was already after three o'clock in the afternoon when the riot squad stormed Pavilion Nine. The attack was carried out with military precision: it was quick and lethal. Its violence didn't give anyone the opportunity to defend themselves. Although it affected everyone, the heaviest casualties were on the third and fifth floors.

Approximately thirty minutes after the order had been given to go in, cries of, 'Stop, for the love of God!' 'Don't kill us!' 'Enough, it's over! It's over!' were heard in the smoke-filled galleries.

One by one, the machine guns silenced.

The Aftermath

When the shooting stopped, a deathly silence fell over the galleries.

Behind his little wall, all Dadá could think about was how upset his mother was going to be over his death and regretted not having read Psalm 91. A few minutes later, he heard footsteps.

'Whoever's still alive, get up, strip and come out naked!'

He and his cellmate stood up.

'I tried to revive a guy I knew from the outside, but his eyes were already rollin' back. I went out into the gallery. It was lined on both sides with uniforms shoutin', "Run, run!" I got clubbed across the back and kicked in the legs.'

When he got to the cage, before the stairs, an officer released a black German shepherd, which jumped at the wounded inmate's throat. Dadá dodged the animal and made it to the stairs, but a kick came out of nowhere and he lost his balance on the greasy steps, fell and hit his head. The German shepherd went for him. 'The fall knocked me out. It was probably a good thing, because at the time I didn't even feel the dog bitin' my legs and nuts.'

He was woken by an officer's baton.

'Get up, fucker, hands on your head!'

Like Dadá, the other survivors took off their clothes and ran through the corridor of baton-wielding officers and down the stairs, slipping in the oil and blood, with the dogs at their heels.

Jacó, the dealer who did business over the phone, said there was no room for altruism. 'I came out of the cell and a dog came after me. When it had almost caught up with me, I ducked behind a fat guy. Unfortunately for him, poor thing, the dog latched onto his arm and wouldn't let go even when he swung it around in the air. I couldn't help the fellow, because it was each man for himself and God for whoever He thought deserved to make it out.'

Majesty kept his nerves under control and his head in his hands, until he heard the order to vacate. 'I raced out to avoid the beatin'. I was in such a hurry that I forgot to take off my clothes.' He charged down the stairs in Bermuda shorts and the Corinthians shirt from which he couldn't be parted. When he got to the inner courtyard, there was an officer with a machine gun pointed at the men leaving the stairs. The officer was standing with his legs on either side of a dead man who had blood running out of his mouth. It was Santão, who used to help us in the cinema.

Despite his many years of prison experience, Majesty got a shock when he saw his friend's body. 'When I saw Santão lying there like a trophy under the uniform with the tommy, I stopped rationalisin'.'

Seeing him in clothes, the officer cocked his gun.

'Hey, airhead, why're you still dressed?'

When he heard the gun cock, Majesty and everyone around him threw themselves to the ground, on top of one another. He said he'd never taken off his clothes so quickly. 'I fell face-down to the ground and got up naked.'

The officers lined up the prisoners in the inner courtyard of the pavilion and ordered them to sit with their arms crossed under their thighs and their heads between their knees. Anyone who looked up to see what was going on was beaten with batons and bitten by the dogs.

They sat there in the courtyard for hours, naked, in silence, with the agitated officers and dogs around them.

Sitting there quietly, only concerned with staying alive, Chico Heliópolis, a thief from the *favela* of the same name, lost the gold chain and saint pendant that he had been given by his godmother at his first communion. 'The uniform squatted down next to me and said, "See what it's like when you do this to others, scum?" and snatched the chain off my neck. Me of all people, who only robbed businesses, banks and mansions and never dirtied my hands with petty stuff.'

At around ten o'clock at night, the riot squad took up

position on the stairs and in the galleries and started taking in the prisoners. They escorted up the fifty or sixty in the first row. Minutes later, there was more shooting, shouting and barking.

In the courtyard, the men tried to discreetly scoot back to the last rows.

Stutter, an illegal lottery operator and marijuana dealer who worked in the warders' kitchen, described the walk back: 'The stairs were covered with blood, with bodies strewn everywhere. You couldn't stop, the queue had to keep movin' – the uniforms ordered everyone to run and threatened, "If anyone flicks blood on me, they're dead!" You had to run barefoot in that bloodbath, without lifting your feet so as not to get the uniforms dirty, 'cause they were just lookin' for an excuse to kill.'

The riot squad's aversion to the blood on the ground cost a number of clumsy inmates their lives, said Isaías, a thief who had lost the movement in his left arm from a crack overdose and who years later died of tuberculosis in the infirmary. 'It was all so crazy and fast, and they made us shout, "Long live the squad! Long live the squad!" There was an older man who stepped sideways to avoid a corpse that was in his way, but he stepped in a puddle of blood, which splattered up onto a uniform's trousers. The uniform didn't think twice: he stopped all movement on the stairs and pow, pow, put two bullets in him, in front of everyone.' Having shot the man, he pulled the body aside and shouted at an inmate in glasses who was behind him on the stairs. '"You there, carry this cadaver downstairs!" At that moment, the guy's mind must have gone into melt-down, 'cause he started sobbin' and said he didn't dare. "Really? You don't, do you?" He shot him at point-blank then turned to the queue and shouted, "Don't stop! Don't stop!"'

The men were randomly assigned to cells. They would put as many as possible in each one, lock them and fill up the next, until they were all locked up.

The bodies had to be carried down to the ground floor by the prisoners themselves. Jacó was one of the carriers. 'They came up to me and four others and said, "You there, go get the cadavers from the gallery on the second floor and take them to the school, downstairs!" We'd pick 'em up by the arms and legs and take 'em down. All in a rush, with the uniforms houndin' us.'

By this time, although that day's events had already numbed his fear of dying, Jacó was worried about the fact that he was barefoot, with his feet grazed from playing football. 'So much HIV inside, if I get out alive, I'm gonna end up gettin' AIDS. That was when a uniform ordered us to pile the bodies up properly in the school, 'cause it was all a big mess of arms and legs and their heads were all over the place. As he was speakin', someone in the pile moved. He went to beat him in the face with the butt of his machine gun and I took advantage of his distraction and lay down in a corner, among the stiffs.'

He stayed there unmoving in the space between bodies, almost holding his breath, until the other four had brought in the last cadaver. The officer turned to them.

'"Done?" he asked. They said they were. Takatakataka, he gunned 'em down. They fell on top of the men we'd been carryin'.'

While his fear of AIDS was saving Jacó's life, a military police official was ordering Dadá to take the bodies down from the third floor. 'In the cage on the third floor there were about thirty bodies piled up. The pile was almost two metres high. We took them down to the Forensic Institute car that was parked at the entrance. They were already stiff, with holes in their chests.'

When Dadá and his companions had finished, the lieutenant called him over.

'Tell me, scum, you're in for killin' some of our boys, aren't you?'

'Not me, sir. I'm in for aidin' and abettin' fraud.'

'I don't believe you. You killed police officers!'

'I've never killed anyone, sir. I've got a light sentence, just three years. I'm in for fraud.'

'Well, before I regret it, head on up with that line there. Get out of my presence. You're lucky 'cause you look like my oldest boy!'

Later Dadá thanked God for his physical similarity to the lieutenant's firstborn. 'I was convinced his son had saved my life, after seeing the other carriers disappear forever.'

With the prisoners locked away, the police and

Institute of Forensic Medicine cars carted away the dead until late at night. The atmosphere in the cells was tragic, said Dadá. 'We couldn't sleep in the cell. First, 'cause we were all perturbed, and second, 'cause there was a strong smell of death. The floor was awash with blood. It was only the next day that we cleaned everythin', and I found myself a Bible.'

In the holy book, Dadá finally read Psalm 91, recommended by his mother only two days earlier, and said he cried like a baby when it said: 'A thousand will fall at your side, and ten thousand on your right, but it will not come near you; no plague will come near your tent.'

On 2 October 1992, 111 men died in Pavilion Nine, according to the official version. The inmates claim there were more than two hundred and fifty deaths, counting those who left wounded and never returned. There is no reference to the wounded in the official records. No military police officers were killed.

Afterword

Brazilian society turns a blind eye to what goes on in prisons. When most believe that the aim of imprisonment is merely to punish those who have committed crimes, why would there be any interest in providing better living conditions on the inside?

Our jails are built to punish criminals and keep them off the streets, not to rehabilitate them for life in society. Humanitarian concerns regarding their fate will only gain strength the day that inmates from more influential families end up in the same cells as those from the poorest families.

Carandiru is an illustrative case. The complex of buildings that housed over 7000 men and almost 1000 employees, located on one of São Paulo's busiest avenues, had the same importance to the city as a barnacle stuck to a ship's hull.

Until the massacre in 1992, when 111 inmates were recorded as killed, the prison had only appeared in the national news after an attempted armed escape in 1982.

Except for this episode, press coverage was restricted to the crime pages of tabloid newspapers, and even then only when there were rebellions or when fugitives inexplicably escaped through the front door or crawled through tunnels dug with cinematographic guile.

It is hard to believe that a prison complex of such dimensions remained in silent anonymity for half a century, in spite of the daily coming and going of delivery trucks to meet the needs of a population larger than that of many towns, not to mention the thousands of women and children who formed kilometric queues for weekend visits.

The only explanation for this phenomenon is in the social invisibility that is characteristic of the excluded.

Every day dozens of detainees would arrive and dozens would be released, many of whom were responsible for the kidnappings, hold-ups and murders that rob Brazil's streets of their tranquillity. Considered the dregs of society, from parts of town through which members of the middle and upper classes would never venture, they face two kinds of prejudice: first, because they live outside of the law; second, because they are poor.

If we believe they are all the same: perverse, merciless villains, regardless of the nature of their offences, why would we care what happens to them? Let them rot like caged animals until death carries them off to the depths of hell. Isn't giving them free food and shelter already an unbearable burden that the civilised world obliges us to carry?

Keeping prisoners behind bars and jails out of the press was what law-abiding citizens expected of the men in charge of running the prison system.

Then the massacre of 1992 took place. Overnight, Carandiru became the most famous prison in the world.

It was never the same again. Inmates making unreasonable demands and attacking warders became routine. In the days following the tragedy, when Waldemar Gonçalves, the director of sports, was leaving the pavilion after work, he was approached by Barra, a drug dealer both respected and feared by his fellow inmates.

'I'll see you to the gate. The atmosphere's weird. I wouldn't want anything to happen to you; you don't deserve it.'

He wasn't the only one to be escorted out by a prisoner, an inversion of roles that would have been unimaginable just a few weeks earlier.

Aware that the state had emerged from the episode the worse for wear and that further armed repression would be politically impossible, the more experienced inmates formed coalitions in order to seize power: that abstract space that men never leave unoccupied.

As Charles Darwin predicted over a century and a half ago, the strongest prevailed in the fratricidal competition that arose between these different groups of prisoners, and, in just a few short years, the leading faction came to impose its draconian laws on most of the prisons in the state of São Paulo, as well as the neglected streets of the state's poorest districts.

After many years without investments in the prisons, the two state governments prior to 1992 had built a number of more modern, well-equipped facilities in the city of São Paulo and the interior of the state. This effort, however, was overshadowed by the media's interest in the Casa de Detenção, an antiquated, problematic institution that denigrated the image of the state's penitentiary system.

After much debate, the government decided to deactivate and destroy it, as a result of its bad press. Contrary to what had happened in previous eras, now everything that happened there made headlines.

On the day the building was brought down I got together with a group of former warders in the cafeteria on the top floor of a neighbouring building, with a panoramic view of the prison. There was an air of beer-fuelled excitement, with everyone talking and telling stories. When the loudspeakers projected the state governor's distant voice into the air, the animated voices hushed. In the end, standing side by side on the balcony, we listened to the countdown that preceded the explosions.

In seconds, the pavilions swayed and buckled clumsily as if enormous hands had knocked their legs out from under them. An orange cloud of thick dust spewed from the entrails of the twisted metal and concrete monster and trailed away over the city.

In the emotional silence of the balcony, Waldemar Gonçalves murmured, 'It didn't have to have been like that.'

The implosion of Carandiru was a landmark in all of our lives, but especially those of the warders. The world in which they had lived collapsed the instant the walls came down. The violence, the petty corruption in exchange for small favours, the deaths they had witnessed without being able to prevent them, the cowardly attitudes, the value of one's word, the acts of heroism in defence of their colleagues and the prisoners, the good and evil that went hand-in-hand, all buried under the rubble of that big house, resuscitate like ghosts every time we see one another in the other prison where I continue my voluntary work or when we get together for drinks in the city.

Drauzio Varella, São Paulo, June 2012

Note On The Author

Drauzio Varella was born in São Paulo, in 1943. With a degree in medicine from the University of São Paulo, he worked at the Cancer Hospital for twenty years. He was a voluntary doctor at the Casa de Detenção in São Paulo (popularly known as Carandiru) for thirteen years.

Lockdown was originally published in Brazil as *Estação Carandiru* in 1999, and won two prestigious Jabuti Prizes – for the best work of non-fiction and the book of the year. Varella is also the author of *Macacos* (Publifolha, 2000), *Por um fio* (Companhia das Letras, 2004), *Borboletas da alma* (Companhia das Letras, 2006) and *O médico doente* (Companhia das Letras, 2007), as well as two children's books, published by Companhia das Letrinhas: *Nas ruas do Brás* (2000; which won the Novos Horizontes, Bologna Children's Book Fair and Rio de Janeiro Biennial Revelation awards) and *De braços para o alto* (2002).